Post-Compulsory Education
and the New Millennium

Higher Education Policy Series

Edited by Maurice Kogan

Higher education is now the subject of far reaching and rapid policy change. This series will be of value to those who have to manage that change, as well as to consumers and evaluators of higher education in the UK and elsewhere. It offers information and analysis of new developments in a concise and usable form. It also provides reflective accounts of the impacts of higher education policy. Higher education administrators, governors and policy makers will use it, as well as students and specialists in education policy.

Maurice Kogan is Professor of Government and Social Administration at Brunel University and Joint Director of the Centre for the Evaluation of Public Policy and Practice.

Part-Time Higher Education Policy, Practice and Experience
Tom Schuller, David Raffe, Brenda Morgan-Klein and Ian Clark
ISBN 1 85302 668 9 hb
ISBN 1 85302 669 7 pb
Higher Education Policy Series 47

Innovation and Adaptation in European Higher Education
The Changing Conditions of Advanced Teaching and Learning in Europe
Edited by Claudius Gellert
ISBN 1 85302 628 X pb
ISBN 1 85302 535 6 hb
Higher Education Policy Series 22

Higher Education in a Post-Binary Era
National Reforms and Institutional Responses
Edited by David Teather
ISBN 1 85302 425 2 pb
ISBN 1 85302 627 1 hb
Higher Education Policy Series 38

Changing Relationships between Higher Education and the State
Mary Henkel and Brenda Little
ISBN 1 85302 645 X pb
ISBN 1 85302 644 1 hb
Higher Education Policy Series 45

Experiential Learning
Norman Evans
ISBN 1 85302 736 7
Higher Education Policy Series 52

Higher Education Policy Series 54

Post-Compulsory Education and the New Millennium

Edited by David E. Gray and Colin Griffin

Jessica Kingsley Publishers
London and Philadelphia

First published in the United Kingdom in 2000 by
Jessica Kingsley Publishers Ltd,
116 Pentonville Road, London
N1 9JB, England
and
325 Chestnut Street,
Philadelphia, PA 19106,
USA.

www.jkp.com

© Copyright 2000 Jessica Kingsley Publishers

Library of Congress Cataloging in Publication Data
A CIP catalog record for this book is available from the Library of Congress

British Library Cataloguing in Publication Data
A CIP catalogue record for this book is available from the British Library

ISBN 1 85302 774 X

Printed and Bound in Great Britain by
Athenaeum Press, Gateshead, Tyne and Wear

Contents

Management and Funding

Initial Teacher Education

International Comparisons

Chapter 1

The Changing Framework of Post-16 Education

The Rhetoric of Reform

Colin Griffin and David Gray

Learning to succeed: success and failure in further education

The post-16 educational sector is facing a complete reshaping of its future. The contributors to this book address many of the most important issues facing further education today, and present a graphic picture of the kinds of problems which face the colleges as they move into the new millennium. Many of these contributions challenge the likelihood of policies succeeding which do not address the most fundamental issues of structure, funding, management and ethos which they identify.

Despite its traditional 'Cinderella' status, further education has become increasingly the object of political attention in reports such as those of Tomlinson (FEFC 1996) and Kennedy (FEFC 1997). The government acknowledges the importance of the sector in the achievement of a learning society, and particularly in the development of a skilled workforce for the competitive conditions of the global economy. And yet the public policy profile of both schools and higher education remains higher than that of further education. Making the education and training system more responsive to the needs of employers, and to the needs of workers for employability skills, is a crucial element in the restructuring of policy. The ongoing review of the qualifications and curriculum framework (Hodgson and Spours 1997) should put the sector at the heart of the government's project of reform. But despite the rhetoric of parity of esteem, it is hard to believe that the 'jewels in the crown' of the academic route from A-levels to university are yet being put on a level with training or work-based learning.

The current debate about the proper sites of education and training, whether these should be in classrooms, the workplace, or in the community, or at home by virtual technology, raises issues about post-16 provision which should be of central concern to the further education sector. The separate identity of further education itself, in view of its increasingly organic relations with work-based training, sixth form study and higher education, remains unclear. The rhetoric of lifelong learning makes these traditional divisions of organization, status and funding rather meaningless, and it is unclear how long they will continue in their present form. Today's policy rhetoric is of learning, and not of education and training, the distinction between which is increasingly problematic.

The Department for Education and Employment published its White Paper *Learning to Succeed: A New Framework for Post-16 Learning* in June 1999 (DfEE 1999). It contains proposals which would radically affect the funding and structure of further education in England, and is intended to implement the vision of the learning society described in the earlier Green Paper *The Learning Age* (DfEE 1998).

The National Learning and Skills Council, to be established in April 2000, will be an executive non-departmental public body responsible to the Secretary of State for Education and Employment. Its responsibilities will include strategic development, planning, funding, management and quality assurance for post-16 education and training, but excluding the higher education sector.

The new body will take over the funding of training from the TECs, the FE colleges from the FEFC, and adult and community learning from the local authorities, and will establish a single consistent and coherent system of funding for the whole of this sector. It will therefore be intended to meet the learning needs of individuals, communities, employers and everyone with an interest in education and training for employment.

The main funding functions of the Learning and Skills Council will be directed towards accredited qualifications, and the distinction between vocational and non-vocational qualifications (Schedule 2 and Non-schedule 2) will be abolished. This means that all kinds of learning are ultimately funded from the same source, although funding for learning in pursuit of recognized qualifications will receive priority.

Other remits of the Learning and Skills Council include the National Learning Targets, the University for Industry, and the adult information, advice and guidance services. The Council will also have responsibility for securing adult and community learning and for working with employers to support the kinds of learning required for employment. Funding for work-based learning will be transferred from the TECs to the employment service.

Membership of the Learning and Skills Council will comprise employers and other interested bodies such as trade unions and community and voluntary organizations, and it will be served by two advisory committees, one for young people and one for adult learning. These committees will have the responsibility for advising the Learning and Skills Committee in matters of provision, funding, participation and standards.

The National Learning and Skills Council will work through a number of Local Learning and Skills Councils, representing local learning needs and organized along the same boundaries as those of the Regional Development Agencies. Local Learning and Skills Councils have the responsibility of setting local priorities and targets to meet local needs, develop provision, widen access and promote equal opportunities. Their plans will be submitted for approval to the National Learning and Skills Council, and in consultation with the Regional Development Agencies. The responsibilities of the Local Learning and Skills Councils will be to develop a market of provision alongside other bodies responsible for education and training, such as Local Education Authorities and the national Local Learning Partnerships network. They will also take responsibility for standards and quality maintenance, the rationalization of the structure of the sector, developmental strategies, consumer-orientation assessment, and assessment. They will work closely with local businesses to ensure that provision is directed towards meeting learning needs for employment.

Local Learning and Skills Councils will be expected to identify local gaps in provision, such as skills shortages or provision for the socially excluded. This may involve local funding negotiation. Local Councils will also liaise and collaborate with Local Education Authorities. Thus, for example, they will establish priorities for 16–19 provision, which are intended to be taken into account by the LEAs in their own planning for this sector.

Thus the Local Learning and Skills Councils will relate to the whole range of interested bodies, such as the Regional Development

Agencies, the business sector, local authorities, and the proposed Local Learning Partnerships.

Local Learning Partnerships are intended to 'drive up' standards and the quality of provision, and bring greater coherence at the local level, making sure that it meets local learning needs. They are intended to function as a 'catalyst for collaborative action at the local level', thus ensuring co-ordination amongst the range and variety of provision. They also play a key role in identifying and achieving the National Learning Targets, which will continue as part of the remit of the National Learning and Skills Council itself. The Partnerships already consist of a core membership of colleges, TECs, local authorities and careers services. But they may also include employers, the voluntary and community sector, and schools and higher education. The Local Learning Partnerships are also envisaged as a forum for feedback to improve the quality of provision.

The main functions of Local Learning Partnerships will therefore be to advise Local Learning and Skills Councils on the planning of provision in their local area, and maximizing participation in learning on the part of young people. They will also be a way of ensuring that local businesses can influence provision, and for the development of the local economy.

It is proposed that there should be a new Support Service for Young People organized along the same divisions as the Local Learning and Skills Councils. This will be directed towards the needs of young people who are not in education, training or work, and is intended to provide a comprehensive system of advice, support and guidance for all young people between 13 and 19. This will have the effect of making more consistent and coherent the system which used to be divided between a number of providers, such as the Youth and Careers Services.

Another major proposal of the White Paper is to make OFSTED responsible for the inspection of provision for 16–19-year-olds in schools and colleges. In the case of post-19 provision, and work-based provision for all age groups, it is proposed to establish a new independent inspectorate, which would work with OFSTED on sixth form, tertiary and FE colleges. Adult and community education would also fall within the remit of the new inspectorate, as would inspection for the University for Industry. Joint inspection programmes for 16–19 provision are therefore proposed, and it is also proposed that all inspections should be based on a common framework, and a single reporting system put in place.

The Local Learning and Skills Councils will also promote quality of provision by undertaking research on long-term quality issues, advising the Secretary of State, providing guidance on staff training and development, and working with the National Training Organizations to improve work-based training. In particular, the government proposes to build on the work of the Further Education National Training Organization (FENTO) which will eventually lead to the development of a range of qualifications for all post-16 teaching and training staff.

Rhetoric and reality

The White Paper is, in part, a response to the perceived weaknesses within the existing post-16 system, such as in areas of participation, responsiveness, relevance for employment, coherence and consistency in funding and inspection, and so on. While acknowledging the significance of the further education sector in post-16 provision, however, its proposals would affect many of the issues and themes represented in this book, and it has to be said that some of these would remain unaddressed.

There is a strong emphasis upon partnership, standards and the need to combat social exclusion in education and training. However, with its very strong emphasis upon employability, this does not necessarily ensure a more inclusive society, even if, as it promises, the government *could* deliver full employment. The idea of a highly skilled, adaptable and flexible workforce is in tune with current thinking about the consequences of the global economy and the need for competitiveness, which is a common theme of worldwide lifelong learning policy (EC 1996; OECD 1996). This is also conveyed through the adoption of a *strategic* stance on the part of government, whereby it sees its function as providing the conditions in which individuals, communities and employers must ultimately bear the responsibility for education and training provision. At the same time, it is made clear that only learning for recognized qualifications will be directly funded. This rather limits the scope both of individual choice and for achieving some of the developmental aims envisaged, such as giving young people more of a personal stake in their own futures.

There is a strong rhetoric of responsibility, standards, partnership and participation, but the approach to change is strategic and incremental rather than in the direction of traditional, social democratic policy for redistribution.

The post-16 system of provision, with its sector divisions, remains relatively unchanged, except for the stress upon partnerships amongst stakeholders and the Learning and Skills Councils frameworks. Higher education, together with the division of academic and vocational routes, although 'broadened' and made more flexible, will essentially remain distinctive and hierarchic.

Another key theme is the way in which these strategies for education and training are tied into the government's general policies for the reform of the welfare state. They lay stress upon the individual responsibility of individuals and employers to identify and take steps to meet their own learning needs, within a framework of fiscal incentives as a reward. It is a vision limited therefore by the need to adopt strategic positions in response to global trends and the pace of communications technology. But it remains a vision *limited* by strategy and the kinds of target-setting which this imposes. It is also limited by the impossibility of quantifying the kind of 'learning culture for Britain' envisaged by the earlier Green Paper on *The Learning Age*. The vision of the White Paper is limited by its reliance on traditional measures, such as participation rates, skills levels, target achievements, inspection rates, and so on.

Evolutionary or incremental and employer-led change in post-16 education and training provision will not address the divisions of interest and status which exist within the system. There is no reason to suppose that the emphasis upon partnerships would shift these well-entrenched hierarchies, particularly since it is clear that employers will have the greatest degree of influence. There is also an emphasis upon driving up standards, often 'bottom up'. However, this acknowledgement of the hierarchical nature of the system of education and training does not extend to identifying who or what represents the 'top' or the 'bottom' in the driving up of standards. Given the frequently asserted primacy of employers' interests in the White Paper, it seems more likely that standards will be driven up 'top down' than from the education and training base. However, behind the rhetoric lies the assumption that employers' interests have been neglected, and therefore their interests represent a kind of 'bottom line' of employability. The apparently democratic rhetoric needs to be understood in these terms. 'Bottom up' will certainly not mean that standards are driven by the needs of individual learners as such.

The needs of learners tend to be addressed entirely in terms of their own needs for employability and employers' needs for a skilled, adaptable and flexible workforce. So the definition of learners' needs remains somewhat problematic. Adult learners' needs, for example, are not identified as distinctive, except that they may require more 'flexibility'.

Community, too, is a word often mentioned without it being really clear what it stands for except in organizational terms, or the voluntariness of civil society itself. It is distinguished only in its difference from personal learning or the business and employment sector: it tends almost to be a residual category. It could be a locality, defined for example by the scope of the Regional Development Agencies, or a whole range of social identities, in which the various 'partners' may have a range of vested interests.

The problems of the present system, in terms of its 'piecemeal' and incoherent structure, have arisen *because* of the wide range of learning needs it has traditionally addressed, which seems wider than the White Paper itself acknowledges. The narrow view of learning needs which this projects may be reproduced in any new system which is intended to replace it. In other words, the justifiable attempt to address bureaucracy and incoherence may gloss over real differences between learners' needs, and contradictions between the interests of the various partners themselves.

The new structure of Learning and Skills Councils will further erode the responsibility of LEAs for the provision of learning opportunities, and further remove education and training from local democratic control. Thus it will continue the policy of the previous government of relocating education and training into the sphere of private provision and the market economy. This in turn reinforces the sense in which current government strategies for education and training need to be seen in the context of welfare reform.

Despite the frequent assertion of the need for a more coherent and consistent system of provision, the proposals of the White Paper do not seem to herald a diminishing bureaucratic apparatus. It is not clear that the funding system, in particular, will be any simpler than it was in the past. The whole system will in reality be driven by National Learning (and other) Targets, and the role of Local Councils and Learning Partnerships will only be to mediate between these targets and local needs.

In terms of quality and standards, too, the approach would seem to be top-down rather than bottom-up, and there is little sense of the problematic nature of standards-driven concepts of quality. League tables and other such 'transparent' measures of quality have created as many problems as they solve, and the White Paper cannot be said to reflect the more complex measurement of quality which has emerged in recent years. In particular, conformist and externally imposed standards do not sit comfortably with adult learners' own perceptions of their learning needs and outcomes. The quality issue therefore represents another source of ambiguity in the 'bottom-up' rhetoric.

Strategies for the education and training of young people also need to be more directly addressed to the needs of individuals in a society in which there is not, as yet, full employment. The exclusion of young people which is being addressed seems to be exclusively constructed in terms of their employment, rather than their community identities or their individual learning needs; and, again, a much broader strategy would be needed to address this particular issue. The alternative needs to be related to a much broader discussion of community learning needs, rather than subordinated to the needs generated by employability.

As far as adult learners are concerned, it is again clear that adult learning needs are constructed in terms of employability, and the Learning and Skills Council will work with the University for Industry to co-ordinate training provision. The transfer of work-based learning from the TECs to the employment service will be linked to the benefit system, in accordance with the policy of incorporating education and training into social welfare reform. Individual responsibility for learning will also be reinforced by means of Individual Lifelong Learning Accounts, again closely tied into employment and employability. The stress on employment and work-related learning leaves little space for exploring the relations between learning, leisure and community, and adult learning for purposes such as these is not recognized as an integral element in the new post-16 system being envisaged.

The White Paper sets out government strategy for responding to the competitive nature of global economics and the need to reform the welfare state. The rhetoric is one of standards, partnership, participation, and 'bottom up'. The reality is the need to assimilate the education and training system to the political demands of the system, rather than the learning needs of individuals as such.

The scope of this book

The White Paper *Learning to Succeed* can be understood within the context of the evolving debate over post-16 provision. This is one sense in which the contributors to this book provide an invaluable source of knowledge and expert analysis on many of the themes that the White Paper purports to address (and many that it does not). Also of significance is the fact that many of these chapters trace the recent history of policy initiatives in the post-16 area. They show how intended outcomes have often been eroded or even distorted by the interaction between policy intention and resistance from various agents and stakeholders within the sector. It is worth reflecting, then, that this too may be the fate of some elements of the White Paper. If *Learning to Succeed* does not recognize that there are competing and conflicting interests within the system, can it hope to succeed itself?

As we have argued, one of the problems faced by vocational education and training in the past is that successive governments have actually shied away from developing a clear policy for the 16–19 age group. Several authors note that it was only in 1976 that any government interest developed, and this was around the rather restrictive notion of 'the world of work' and the 'schools to work' debate, initiated by Callaghan's Ruskin College speech (Chitty 1991; Ainley 1990). As we have seen, the White Paper reiterates these themes. Perhaps one reason for this lack of interest is that this sector is, as we shall see, one of bewildering complexity, offering, in principle, a wide range of educational opportunities, but, in practice, often assigning young people to an educational experience which is narrowly constraining. As Macfarlane comments:

> The 16–19 sector provides a microcosm of the tensions, inequalities, conflicting ideologies and confused aims and objectives present in the educational system as a whole. (Macfarlane 1993, p.xi)

Recurring themes of this book are the long struggle to promote vocationalism (and in doing so develop tighter linkages between education and the world of work), and the impact of 'the market' on the sector. As Chitty shows (Chapter 2) the attempts of Dearing (1996) to paper over the academic/vocational divide have not necessarily been successful and may, in fact, be preparing the way for even more divisive 'triple track' routes through the post-16 vocational and educational systems. The introduction of an Advanced Subsidiary qualification from September 2000, and the introduction of a six-module Advanced GNVQ, though welcome, keeps the basic structure unchanged. He sees the introduction of the market into the post-16 sector as disastrous in terms of the competition between colleges it has engendered and the restrictions it has imposed on genuine student choice.

Bailey and Ainley (Chapter 3) take this theme further by examining the evidence of a recent government Select Committee examining the sector five years after incorporation. What we find is a far from coherent view of the sector. The evidence given by, for example, college principals, the Further Education Funding Council and the Further Education Development Agency shows often sharp differences of opinion on key issues affecting colleges including funding, franchising, accountability, governance and credit frameworks. The key messages to emerge from the Committee are the need for more substantial funding for the sector and better national strategic leadership and local management of resources. As the authors comment, the reader is invited to compare the recommendations of the Select Committee with what actually emerged in the White Paper.

Another recurrent theme in the government's post-16 agenda is that of lifelong learning. Jarvis (Chapter 4) looks at this issue critically, arguing that what we are seeing emerge is not so much lifelong learning as vocational lifelong learning or what he terms *work*life learning. He relates this to the constant industrial changes that are taking place, both nationally and globally, and the pressure on so many people to update their skills and knowledge. Institutions of higher education have not proven sufficiently large to cope with this demand – hence the rise of a new phenomenon, the corporate university, and the growth of franchising of higher education programmes to further education colleges. A major trend is that, increasingly, much of this learning is work-related. It is also market driven. Governments will try to influence this, but will tend to do so by limiting their funding only to programmes that are work-related, marginalizing other forms of learning. In many ways, the White Paper confirms these concerns.

It can be argued that this focus on the world of work is itself limiting and confining. Hutchinson (Chapter 5), in examining the NVQ framework, concludes that its emphasis is on competence rather than capabilities, which creates significant limits on the autonomy of individuals and a sense of dependence and powerlessness. What is needed is a reconceptualization of work itself with a promotion of democratic values of fairness, justice and equality.

The theme of vocationalism is also addressed by Gleeson and Hodkinson (Chapter 6) who argue that GNVQs were a political solution of the former Conservative government to leave A-levels untouched while addressing the need for new vocational qualifications. Hence, as Chitty described in Chapter 2, we have tripartite provision: academic A-level; GNVQs, full-time vocational fast-track; NVQs, part-time and work-based. But Gleeson and Hodkinson go on to show that in all previous tripartite frameworks, it is the middle strand that has been squeezed. Making GNVQs more like A-levels (for example, similar grading procedures and size of programmes) may give them a new lease of life, but this remains to be seen. The authors recommend common certification for ages 14–19 as offering broader whilst still specialized provision. Readers are invited to compare these recommendations with the Qualifications and Curriculum Authority's plans for qualifications revision in the year 2000 (QCA 1999). These offer more flexibility (AS level and the encouragement to mix A-levels with GNVQs), but still within the framework of 16–19 provision.

Dyke (Chapter 7) locates the current debate about vocationalism and qualifications frameworks within a late-modern perspective which characterises the period as one of constant and rapid change, with people required to reflect on new information and reassess their taken-for-granted perspectives on the world. Education may be a valuable tool to enable people to navigate through this increasingly complex world, but only a broader, more flexible qualifications framework will provide this. Hence his recommendation for an overarching Advanced Level award made up of NVQ, GNVQ and A-level subjects. Clearly, however, while the Qualifications and Curriculum Authority have made some movement towards broadening the post-16 curriculum these plans fall far short of Dyke's concept (QCA 1999).

Initiatives such as *Learning to Succeed* may lead us to believe that new policies, and new assessment and the new qualification framework, will be implemented smoothly and without obstruction. Elliott (Chapter 8) shows, however, that there can be resistances and unanticipated outcomes to government legislation. He describes the changes in management in FE colleges after incorporation, with: new terms and working conditions for lecturers imposed by the College Employers' Forum; new quality assurance arrangements; the introduction of the Training and Development Lead Body assessor and verifier awards for lecturers; lecturer appraisal; and college performance indicators. Elliott's research shows that not all of these are seen in negative terms by lecturers, but their main criticism has been the way in which they have been introduced. The implications of the introduction of competition and business models into FE remains one of the major concerns of lecturers who see education as a means of producing not compliant individuals, but learners who can engage in critical thinking.

Bradley (Chapter 9) also makes clear that not all the new management changes have had the results that were anticipated. The new Further Education Funding Council's (FEFC) funding mechanism, for example, had the planned effect of largely eliminating Local Education Authority control from further education colleges, increased competitiveness in the sector with institutions responsive to student and employer needs, and increased class sizes and contact hours for lecturers. Unintended consequences have included: 'poaching' of students from rival colleges; artificial boosting of 'units of activity' by students taking peripheral subjects; and no account being taken of colleges in areas where poor socio-economic groups have low uptake of courses. The result has been severe financial strain for many colleges and threats of economic collapse and merger. As Bailey and Ainley note (Chapter 3), New Labour has made additional funds available to further education, but it remains to be seen whether these are sufficient to deliver ambitious targets.

For the sixth form sector, Robinson (Chapter 10) shows that the results of incorporation have been slightly different when compared to FE due, largely, to the different histories of the sectors. Interviews with a sample of sixth form principals found an emphasis on retaining an academic focus and standards, with new FEFC promoted courses as 'add-ons'. The principals show a resistance to FE styles of working such as use of part-time staff, recruitment of part-time students, evening work and GNVQs. Yet sixth form colleges face rising competition for students from schools as they develop their own sixth-forms and with FE colleges. Threats of closure and merger also stalk the sixth form sector, posing an interesting question of what ethos will emerge triumphant if FE and sixth form colleges merge.

In the higher education sector, Williams (Chapter 11) also discusses the impact of new funding arrangements. He argues that new management information systems have given governments the opportunity to steer the system from a distance. The result has been the creation of a quasi-market, coupled to forms of regulation in the form of quality assurance arrangements. Yet the market has brought less freedom of HE institutions rather than more, certainly in terms of their ability to make academic and financial decisions. So while universities have more flexibility to respond to the need for lifelong learning, and are more responsive to customer (student) demand, they are less attractive to the suppliers – the academic staff.

Elliott (Chapter 12) looks at the pressures faced by FE lecturers and shows that there have been a range of pressures on them to increase student participation and achievement rates, and to be more 'accountable', whilst at the same time suffering increasingly harsh management strategies and new contracts of employment. He speculates that it may be the intention of the government to introduce competence-based models of assessment (based upon the Further Education National Training Organization (FENTO) standards) into teacher training for the vocational education and training sector. He warns that pre-ordained performance criteria are inadequate for measuring higher order skills such as management or teaching which require judgement, intuition, behaviour under stress and the ability to weigh up ethical issues.

Lucas (Chapter 13), however, criticizes what he sees as the government's neglect of teacher training for further education. GNVQs have brought new challenges to teaching and ways of working including new forms of assessment, recording student achievement, and team working across subjects. He takes issue with what he perceives as the narrowness of the Training and Development Lead Body (TDLB) assessor's awards, and argues for the need for multi-skilled professional teachers and a qualifications framework for lecturers overseen by a strategic General Teaching Council for FE.

The contribution of Evans, Behrens and Kaluza (Chapter 14) allows us to examine a crucial element of the post-16 system, vocational training and apprenticeships, by comparing the systems in the UK and Germany. Indeed, these systems, the rigid German apprenticeship system and the UK's deregulated economy, provide alternative routes for future European development. The authors' research shows how the opening up of the former East Germany to market forces has shattered automatic, guaranteed trajectories into segments of the labour market. What they recommend is a European model of vocational education and training which allows people to gain recognition for combinations of education-based and work-based learning. Recent proposals by the QCA (1999), however, while broadening the post-16 curriculum, retain an academic rather than work-based focus.

Where does this leave *Learning to Succeed*? Can we achieve lifelong learning linked both to employment and leisure opportunities, or are we doomed to endure 'education without work' and a training in narrow, competence-based skills, many of which hardly measure up as skills at all. Social democracy at the end of 1945 offered a vision of education which held at least the *promise* of equality of opportunity for a very broad section of the population, even if, in practice, many of those promises were not fulfilled. Today's New Labour vision seems inexorably linked to the rhetoric of the market, and to notions of employability, efficiency (i.e. lower costs) and targets. If this is the language of business, it should come as no surprise, since most of the changes envisaged in the White Paper seem linked to the needs of employers. Yet there *are* alternatives. It is our hope that the contributors to this book light the way towards some of them.

References

Ainley, P. (1990) *Vocational Education and Training*. London: Cassell.

Chitty, C. (ed) (1991) *Post-16 Education: Studies in Access and Achievement*. London: Kogan Page.

Dearing, R. (1996) *Review of Qualifications for 16–19 Year Olds: Summary Report*. Middlesex: SCAA Publications.

Department for Education and Employment (DfEE) (1998) *The Learning Age: A Renaissance for a New Britain*. Green Paper CM 3790. London: The Stationery Office.

Department for Education and Employment (DfEE) (1999) *Learning to Succeed: A New Framework for Post-16 Learning*. White paper CM 4392. London: The Stationery Office.

European Commission (EC) (1996) *Teaching and Learning: Towards the Learning Society*. White Paper on Education and Training. Brussels: EC.

Further Education Funding Council (FEFC) (1996) *Inclusive Learning* (The Tomlinson Report). London: HMSO.

Further Education Funding Council (FEFC) (1997) *Learning Works: Widening Participation in Further Education* (The Kennedy Report). Coventry: FEFC.

Hodgson, A. and Spours, K. (eds) (1997) *Dearing and Beyond: 14–19 Qualifications, Frameworks and Systems*. London: Kogan Page.

Macfarlane, E. (1993) *Education 16–19 in Transition*. London: Routledge.

Organization for Economic Co-operation and Development (OECD) (1996) *Lifelong Learning for All*. Paris: OECD.

Qualifications and Curriculum Authority (1999) *Curriculum Guidance for 2000: Implementing the Changes to 16–19 Qualifications*. London: QCA.

PART I

Issues in Vocational Education and Training

Chapter 2

Vocational Education and Training into the New Millennium

Clyde Chitty

Introduction

The history of post-16 education and training in England and Wales since the end of the Second World War is one of makeshift and invariably short-lived initiatives and missed opportunities. When Sir Ron (now Lord) Dearing and his team began work in 1995 on the lengthy process of reviewing post-16 provision, they were faced with at least 16,000 qualifications for 16–19-year-olds – a stark reflection of decades of short-term solutions to intractable problems. So complex was the overall picture that even those charged with the task of providing advice for young students sometimes found it difficult to negotiate a clear path through the jungle. In the words of the ensuing report:

> What we have for 16–19-year-olds is the product of history. Initiatives have followed one another over time. Each has been designed for its own purpose, with limited concern to provide coherence and ready understanding on the part of students, parents and employers, or to provide a framework in which it is possible to combine elements from different pathways, or to move from one pathway to related study in another … It is all too easy for those professionally engaged in the central administration of qualifications to over-estimate the level of knowledge about the present maze of qualifications among parents and small-and-medium-sized employers. Even those engaged in education sometimes need help. (SCAA 1996, p.11)

How have we arrived at this sorry state of affairs? Why is it that this is an important area of curriculum provision where there is little evidence of coherent or long-term planning?

Developments since 1965

In the 35 years since a Labour administration published Circular 10/65, declaring the government's intention 'to end selection at eleven plus and to eliminate separatism in secondary education' (DES 1965, p.1), the drive for comprehensive education has transformed the early years of secondary education. Yet this tide of radicalism has barely reached the 16–19 sector where A-levels have continued both to dominate and distort the curriculum of most comprehensive and other schools.

For quite understandable reasons, the early pioneers for change failed to challenge a system that permitted the whole idea of 'standards' for 16–19-year-olds to depend upon a single course taken by a small minority. As I have argued elsewhere (Benn and Chitty 1996, p.349):

> Elite criticism of the comprehensive idea forced comprehensive schools to collude with the system because A-levels were one way in which they could establish their own academic credibility in a political world where this was continually being challenged. Thus comprehensive educators continued to support A-levels even when it was clear that the dominance of external exams for a minority was preventing the development of 16–19 education for the majority, comprehensive or otherwise.

It is true that several governments made weak attempts to reform the narrow scope of post-16 academic courses during the 30 years after 1965, most aiming to 'broaden' the range of subjects that 'academic' students could study after the age of 16. Some 'reforms' – like the N and F levels – were proposed as early as the late 1960s; they failed to gain acceptance. So, too, did a similar type of reform – Q and F – proposed in the late 1970s. Later, recommendations from committees that governments had set up – for example, the Macfarlane Report of 1980 and the Higginson Report of 1988 – were also ignored, though the proposals from all of them were far from radical. Apart from the introduction of the Advanced Supplementary in 1987, which could be seen as *strengthening* rather than *challenging* A-levels, no significant change or amendment has been made to the structure of the main academic qualification for the 16–19 age group since its introduction back in 1951.

International comparisons

While successive governments in this country were making feeble attempts at reform, other countries were developing late selection, high participation systems designed to get across the message that post-compulsory provision should not be an élite phenomenon. The 1970 Donnison Report shrewdly observed that 'the most striking feature of the British System, when compared with those of other countries, is the heavy loss of pupils at the minimum leaving age' (Maclure 1986, p.344). The post-Sputnik era of the 1960s and early 1970s was, after all, a period of massive expansion in 16–19 provision in most Western countries which were anxious not to fall behind the Soviet Union in technological achievement. These countries understood the importance of encouraging their young people to stay on in mainstream education until at least the age of 18 to obtain meaningful qualifications through a rich combination of academic, technical and vocational study within a common learning system.

Sweden developed 16–19 colleges with a choice of over 20 different lines of study organized around a common core; while France opted for half a dozen baccalaureate programmes within a system of common schools. The United States was able to boast a common high school offering an elective system of courses organized in a unified modular structure with common credit accumulation.

By 1981, still only 18 per cent of 16–18-year-olds were in school in the United Kingdom, whereas in Japan the figure was 58 per cent and in the United States 65. If one includes other non-school, full-time education and training, the figures are still equally depressing, as Table 2.1 shows (DES 1985).

Table 2.1 Participation in full-time education and training of 16–18-year-olds in seven countries, 1981

Country	%
United States	79
Netherlands	71
Japan	69
France	58
Italy	47
Germany	45
United Kingdom	32

Figures published five years later (DES 1990) show how little had changed in the course of the decade (Table 2.2).

Table 2.2 Participation in full-time education and training of 16–18-year-olds in five countries, 1986–88	
Country	%
United States (1986)	79
Japan (1988)	77
France (1986)	66
West Germany (1987)	47
United Kingdom (1988)	35

Writing in the *Times Educational Supplement* at the end of August 1990, Anne Corbett pointed out that Britain's poor comparative performance was directly related to her early selection, low participation system and an outdated attitude towards technical and vocational education:

> It is no surprise to see that the education systems which score well in international comparisons of achievement are those which defer selection, and in which technical education is linked as strongly to learning core skills as to vocational techniques. If Britain is to educate people to higher levels, it must surely ... get rid of the debilitating division between those selected to learn, those left to train and those for whom education and training ends at 16. (Corbett 1990)

Britain's lamentable failure to cater for youngsters' needs has also had the obvious effect of seriously limiting the proportion of older teenagers moving on to some form or other of higher education. Speaking in 1987, John Ashworth, the Vice Chancellor of Salford University, said: 'we are brilliant at educating a small, highly academic élite, but very poor at educating the majority of the population' (quoted in O'Connor 1987, p.2).

At the beginning of 1988, Andy Green was able to claim that Britain had 'the highest rate of early school leaving, the lowest rate of achievement in nationally recognized qualifications and the lowest rate of participation in higher education of almost any country in Europe, except Portugal and Spain' (Green 1988, p.24). At the end of the 1980s, Britain had around 15 per cent of the relevant age group in higher education – compared with 20 per cent in Germany who were studying at a university or polytechnic, the 30 per cent in the United States who went on to study at degree level and the 37 per cent in Japan who went on to college or university. In a speech at Lancaster University in January 1989, the then Education Secretary, Kenneth Baker, called for a doubling of the proportion of young people going into universities or polytechnics (to around 30 per cent) over the next 25 years. But he made it clear that the expansion he anticipated in higher education should be based on American models of private funding rather than on the Western European system of increased public finance (Chitty 1991, p.26).

The IPPR solution

Both major political parties have shown a marked reluctance to tackle the twin problems besetting curriculum provision for the post-16 age range: the academic/vocational divide and the continued dominance of A-levels. Yet this is not for want of a carefully argued strategy for getting us out of our present difficulties.

In July 1990, the Institute for Public Policy Research (IPPR) published *A British 'Baccalaureate'* as its Education and Training Paper No. 1 (IPPR 1990). Its subtitle – *Ending the Division Between Education and Training* – neatly summarized the IPPR's principal objective.

The Paper accepted that A-level courses could be criticized for being 'too narrow, specialized and old-fashioned'; it recognized that vocational training was, in general, regarded as being 'too job-specific, low level and ill co-ordinated'; and it criticized the labour market in Britain for encouraging early entry to work through inflated youth wages, age limits on entry into training schemes and poor recompense for those with qualifications. But these were all seen as symptoms of a deeper malaise: the separation of 'academic' students from 'the rest' through the different institutions, different curricula, different modes of study and, above all, different qualifications which catered for the two groups.

Far from seeking to *reform* the existing divided system, the Paper argued that only the *abolition* of the separation of academic from vocational studies could serve as the starting-point for change. It therefore proposed a new, unified system of education and training leading to a single Advanced Diploma – the 'British Bac' of the title. The system would be designed to encourage substantially greater full-time participation post-16, but would also guarantee education-led opportunities for those who did not choose to stay on full-time. The present qualifications system was seen as 'an educational obstacle course', designed to 'weed out' the majority of students; the new arrangements, on the other hand, would result in a 'late selection – high participation' system, appropriate to the needs of the twenty-first century.

At the institutional level, the IPPR Paper recommended a system of tertiary colleges as the most effective and efficient means of delivering a unitary, education-led post-16 provision. Since, however, it might not be 'feasible' to legislate for 'an immediate switch to tertiary college-based education post-16', the authors proposed that in some areas the existing 'mixed-economy' of institutions should remain. However, in order to generate positive change, even in the short term, it was suggested that this 'mixed-economy' should quickly develop into a framework of 'tertiary systems', as proposed by Spours and Young (1988), which would be planned by LEAs and united by common curricula and qualifications.

The recommendations of the IPPR Paper were totally ignored by the Conservative government led by John Major, which outlined a very different approach to the problem of post-16 provision in the White Paper *Education and Training for the 21st Century*, published in May 1991 (DES 1991). This described how sixth form and further education colleges would be severed from local authority control and financed by new funding councils. It argued for the development of new diplomas recording achievement in academic and vocational qualifications; and declared that schools would be permitted to admit part-time and adult students to their sixth forms. Crucially, it refused to contemplate any reform of A-levels and reiterated support for a divided post-16 structure, albeit with marginally greater flexibility for transfer and combination within different areas.

Whereas the IPPR Paper envisaged a unitary education-led post-16 system, the Conservative government was content to remove some of the existing barriers to equal status between 'the so-called academic and vocational routes'. Henceforth, academic and vocational qualifications were to be held in equal esteem. Yet it was not at all clear how this was meant to be achieved, particularly when education ministers insisted on referring to the A-level as the 'gold standard'. It was the 1992 Further and Higher Education Act which implemented many of the proposals in the 1991 White Paper and took FE colleges and tertiary and sixth-form colleges out of LEA control.

The 14–19 continuum

It is becoming increasingly difficult (and counter-productive) to discuss post-16 provision without reference to the needs of the 14–19 age group as a whole, though there was a short period in the late 1980s and early 1990s when the idea of a '14–19 continuum' appeared to suffer a serious setback.

The introduction of a national curriculum as one of the major provisions of the 1988 Education 'Reform' Act represented a 'defeat' for the thinking of a significant faction within the Conservative Party of the early 1980s often referred to as either the 'Industrial Trainers' or the 'Conservative Modernizers' (see Chitty 1993, pp.146–153). Led by David (now Lord) Young, and rejecting many of the key assumptions of the Far Right, this group had developed ideas and policies in the context of a 14–19 continuum and campaigned for the restructuring of the secondary-school curriculum – particularly at what is now called Key Stage Four – in preparation for academic and job opportunities available to youngsters post-16. The Modernizers' main achievement in the area of curriculum initiatives – during David Young's period as Chairperson of the Manpower Services Commission (1982–84) – had been the introduction of the Technical and Vocational Education Initiative (TVEI) in the autumn of 1983. This had started life as a collection of 14 pilot projects in a number of carefully selected schools; by 1986, it had grown to involve 65,000 students in 600 institutions working on four-year programmes designed to stimulate work-related education, make the school curriculum more 'relevant' to post-school life, and enable students to aim for nationally-recognized qualifications in a wide range of technical and vocational subject areas.

The Modernizers found little to attract them in the National Curriculum, which was seen as prescribing an educational diet to which large numbers of pupils – particularly older pupils – were simply not suited. Unlike the Cultural Right, the Modernizing tendency had no time for the grammar-school tradition and considered it to be largely responsible for Britain's long industrial decline. At the same time, it has to be emphasized that there was nothing remotely egalitarian in their approach: as they saw it, the secondary curriculum should be strictly differentiated in order to prepare pupils for the differing tasks they would be expected to perform in a capitalist economy. Their concept of educational 'opportunity' was succinctly summarized by Lord Young in September 1985:

My idea is that ... there is a world in which 15 per cent of our young go into higher education ... roughly the same proportion as now. Another 30 to 35 per cent will stay on after 16 doing the new TVEI, along with other courses, and ending up with a mixture of vocational and academic qualifications and skills. The remainder, about half, will go on to a two-year YTS. (Reported in *The Times* 4.9.85)

The reversal in the Modernizers' fortunes – characterized by the introduction of a backward-looking, subject-based 5–16 curriculum – proved to be short-lived. The last two years of compulsory schooling rapidly became the most problematic area of the government's hastily conceived curriculum project; and it soon became clear that there was little future for a framework that took no account of recent curriculum initiatives. There were practical problems involved in fitting so many subjects and cross-curricular themes into a finite amount of curriculum time. Many teachers complained that it would not be possible to teach all ten foundation subjects (and RE) to students of all abilities, without risking student resentment and indiscipline. And as general economic prospects worsened, it became fashionable once again to blame the school curriculum for rising levels of youth unemployment. Ideas associated with the Modernizing tendency, and with clear implications for the structure of post-16 provision, were to be debated all over again in the changed conditions of the 1990s.

The Dearing reviews

Realizing by the Spring of 1993 that the framework for the National Curriculum – and particularly Key Stage Four – could not survive in its existing form, the government of John Major asked Sir Ron Dearing, chairperson-designate of the new School Curriculum and Assessment Authority (SCAA) to be established in October 1993, to carry out a full-scale review of the National Curriculum and its assessment. The scope for slimming down the Curriculum was included as one of the four main issues that the Review should cover in Education Secretary John Patten's remit letter of 7 April 1993.

The recommendations of the 1993 Final Dearing Report (SCAA 1993) – and, indeed of Dearing's later review of post-16 qualifications (SCAA 1996) – can be seen as constituting a real link with the work and thinking of the Manpower Services Commission in the mid-1980s. Common to all these approaches is a belief that there are separate 'routes' or 'pathways' constituting the direction in which young people should be 'guided' according to preconceived and often simplistic notions of their ability, aptitude and future career prospects. What appears to be lacking is any sense of the now discredited HMI view that all students, regardless of ability, should have access to an 'entitlement curriculum' viewed as a broad synthesis of the vocational, the technical and the academic (see, for example, DES 1983).

The 1993 Final Dearing Report marked a significant departure from one of the main principles underpinning the National Curriculum of the 1988 Education Act in allowing up to 40 per cent of the 14–16 curriculum to be decided by individual schools. And it explicitly linked this greater 'flexibility' with the provision of 'greater scope for academic and vocational options'. It identified three broad pathways in post-16 education and training: the 'craft' or 'occupational' linked to NVQs (National Vocational Qualifications); the 'vocational' linked to GNVQs (General National Vocational Qualifications); and the 'academic' leading to 'A' and 'AS' levels. It was argued that the development of these three pathways raised the question of whether students aged 14 to 16 should be allowed to follow a well-devised vocational course as one element in a broadly-based curriculum. In the words of the Report: 'it will be a particular challenge to establish how a vocational pathway which maintains a broad educational component might be developed at Key Stage Four over the next few years as part of a 14 to 19 continuum' (SCAA 1993, p.47). The Report then went on to recommend that the School Curriculum and Assessment Authority (SCAA) should be asked to work 'closely and urgently' with the National Council for Vocational Qualifications (NCVQ) to identify whether various possibilities concerning GNVQs could now be developed.

The same three broad pathways appeared in the 1996 Dearing Report, along with the pious hope that some students would be able to build up a 'portfolio of achievement' that included qualifications from both the 'academic' and 'applied' pathways as they progressed through four levels: entry, foundation, intermediate and advanced. Yet, at the same time, the Report was anxious to stress the 'distinctive nature' of the various pathways, arguing that 'it would be wrong ... to seek to build up common elements if this were to undermine the distinctive purposes being served by an A-level or a GNVQ' (SCAA 1996, p.17). Moreover, it suggested that guidelines should be issued outlining the principles for determining the allocation of particular subject areas to particular 'tracks' – possibly in an attempt to avoid a situation where vocational options might appear to be invading territory designated as 'academic'. None of which could be said to be particularly encouraging from the point of view of removing the academic/vocational divide or of creating a truly unified post-16 system.

New Labour policy on post-16 qualifications

In *Aiming Higher*, published in March 1996, the Labour Party said that although its long-term objective was the creation of 'a coherent and integrated 14 to 19 plus curriculum', its first priority was to 'develop a high-standard, flexible post-16 curriculum' with broader A-levels within a single framework of qualifications, increased standards in GNVQs, an Advanced Diploma and greater study time (Labour Party 1996, p.17).

Two years later, the objectives and priorities seemed to have diminished in scope. A letter from Minister of State Baroness Blackstone to Sir William Stubbs, Chairperson of the Qualifications and Curriculum Authority (QCA), dated 3 April 1998, accepted that there was much wrong with the present system of post-16 provision and made a number of pertinent observations:

> Young people aged 16 to 19 in England typically follow a narrower programme of study at advanced level, and are taught for less time, than young people in most of our European competitors ... For the great majority of young people, this serves neither their own nor the country's best long-term interests. It is also difficult at present for young people to combine academic and vocational learning, and too many are still deterred by the relatively low status of vocational studies. The existing system has been criticised for being narrow, over-specialised and inflexible for many years. Its reform is long overdue. (DfEE 1998)

Yet the proposals emanating from the government as a result of the consultation exercise set in train by the publication of *Qualifying for Success* (DfEE 1997) amount to little more than well-intentioned tinkering and contribute little or nothing to the creation of a unified post-16 system – or even of a single framework of qualifications. One can welcome the introduction, from September 2000, of a reformulated Advanced Subsidiary (AS) qualification, for which schools and colleges have long campaigned and which will provide young people and adult learners with a worthwhile qualification half-way between GCSE and A-level. One can look forward to the availability – provisionally from September 2000 – of a new six-module Advanced GNVQ, equivalent to a single GCE A-level, with the possibility of a three-module qualification at a later date. But, despite these reforms, the basic structure remains unchallenged. As John Dunford, General Secretary of the SHA, has argued (Dunford 1998, p.5), 'the current proposals do not represent the watershed for which many of us had hoped.' Above all, he observes, they fail to remove the academic/vocational divide which has 'bedevilled English education for generations.'

The government is imprisoned within the mind-set of the outgoing administration and seems frightened to contemplate a system of post-16 qualifications that integrates 'academic' and 'vocational' knowledge. Indeed, New Labour's support for the academic/vocational divide could be said to be based on a cynical attempt to conceal a basic truth: if vocational education is all about preparing young people to occupy a particular position in the labour force of a class-divided capitalist society, then A-levels are as 'vocational' as GNVQs; they simply hide their 'vocationalism' beneath a thin veneer of 'objective' academic inquiry and the pursuit of 'liberal values'. There is a strong case for arguing that the obvious limitations of the academic/vocational 'pathways' approach can be remedied only by the introduction of a single system of qualifications which encourages students to accumulate accreditation over a given period of time. Members of the NATFHE and of the NUT have long campaigned for a common approach to assessment which is both criterion referenced and student-centred – and which not only accommodates a variety of learning needs but also allows flexibility and progression towards higher education.

At the same time, we need an organizational framework which would be compatible with the new curriculum and assessment arrangements. The operation of the free market, which is usually justified on the grounds of *facilitating* choice, actually *denies* choice to the 16–19 age range by pitting institutions against one another and making it financially suicidal for any school or college to encourage its students to take up subjects or courses – even a single A-level – elsewhere (see Benn and Chitty 1998, p.51). It also makes genuine curricular diversity almost impossible because it forces each college to maximize its student numbers by concentrating on the most profitable and marketable course and qualifications. What is clearly required is a structure of co-operation for post-16 provision, where either tertiary colleges are developed more widely or the sixth forms of schools are encouraged to co-operate with one another and with local further education colleges in some form of common system. New Labour has to accept that the market 'structure' has no legitimate place in a public education service which should be there to serve the whole community and all age ranges within a framework of democratic control and accountability.

References

Benn, C. and Chitty, C. (1996) *Thirty Years On: Is Comprehensive Education Alive and Well or Struggling to Survive?* London: David Fulton Publishers.

Benn, C. and Chitty, C. (1998) 'Post-16 provision: the next battleground for comprehensive education.' *Forum 40*, No. 2, 50–51.

Chitty, C. (1991) Introduction to C. Chitty (ed) *Post-16 Education: Studies in Access and Achievement.* London: Kogan Page. pp.9–30.

Chitty, C. (1993) 'Key Stage Four: the National Curriculum abandoned?' In C. Chitty (ed) *The National Curriculum: Is It Working?* Harlow: Longman. pp.146–153.

Corbett, A. (1990) 'Let's follow France bac to the future.' *Times Educational Supplement*, 31 August.

Department of Education and Science (DES) (1965) *The Organisation of Secondary Education.* Circular 10/65. London: DES.

Department of Education and Science (DES) (1983) *Curriculum 11–16: Towards a Statement of Entitlement: Circular Reappraisal in Action.* HMI Red Book Three. London: HMSO.

Department of Education and Science (DES) (1985) *Statistical Bulletin, 10/85.* London: DES.

Department of Education and Science (DES) (1990) *Statistical Bulletin, 1/90.* London: DES.

Department of Education and Science (DES) (1991) *Education and Training for the 21st Century.* Cmnd. 1536. London: HMSO.

Department for Education and Employment (DfEE) (1997) *Qualifying for Success: A Consultation Paper on the Future of Post-16 Qualifications.* London: DfEE.

Department for Education and Employment (DfEE) (1998) '*Qualifying for Success*: The Response to the Qualifications and Curriculum Authority's Advice.' Letter from Baroness Blackstone to Sir William Stubbs. London: DfEE.

Dunford, J. (1998) 'Half a step forward.' *Education Journal*, June, 5.

Green, A. (1988) 'Lessons in standards.' *Marxism Today*, January, 24–30.

Institute for Public Policy Research (IPPR) (1990) *A British 'Baccalaureate': Ending the Division Between Education and Training.* London: IPPR.

Labour Party (1996) *Aiming Higher.* London: Labour Party.

Maclure, S. (1986) *Educational Documents: England and Wales: 1816 to the Present Day.* London: Methuen.

O'Connor, M. (1987) 'Ruskin ten years on.' *Contributions 11.* York: Centre for the Study of Comprehensive Schools. pp.2–10.

School Curriculum and Assessment Authority (SCAA) (1993) *The National Curriculum and its Assessment: Final Report* (Dearing Report). Hayes: SCAA Publications.

School Curriculum and Assessment Authority (SCAA) (1996) *Review of Qualifications for 16–19 Year Olds* (Dearing Report). Hayes: SCAA Publications.

Spours, K. and Young, M. (1988) *Curriculum and Organisation: Issues in Post-16 Education.* London: Institute of Education Post-16 Education Centre, Working Paper No. 7.

Chapter 3

Further Education Under New Labour
Rhetoric and Reality

Bill Bailey and Patrick Ainley

The rhetoric

It is still too early to assess the likely overall impact on further education in England of the New Labour project. Nevertheless, there has been a great show of activity and a great flourish of rhetoric by the new government in which FE has featured prominently. However, despite repeatedly expressed concern for 'Lifelong Learning', the main focus of policy has as usual been upon 'Foundation Learning' in schools and to a lesser extent upon higher education, especially the universities. This chapter will review developments to the time of writing from the publication, shortly after the government came to office, of *Learning Works*, the Kennedy Report to the Further Education Funding Council (FEFC) on 'widening participation in further education' in June 1997. To do so, the chapter updates the authors' conclusion to their 1997 book *The Business of Learning, Staff and Student Experiences of Further Education in the 1990s* (Ainley and Bailey 1997).

The Kennedy Committee's Report was followed weeks later by Sir Ron Dearing's Report on higher education. Both these reports were initiated under the previous Conservative administration and, as it were, inherited by the new government. So too was the Tomlinson Report on learning difficulties and disabilities (FEFC 1996). Discussion of the future of FE was for a time eclipsed by the media attention given to Dearing's recommendations for HE. As expected, these expressed the bipartisan consensus on introducing fees for HE, to which the new government unexpectedly added the ending of maintenance grants for HE students. Professor Peter Scott (1997) described this as an attempt to reverse the previous Conservative 'go-stop' policy on HE expansion to one of 'stop-go', which was qualified by the addition of fees and removal of grants. It was unclear, however, how far government would act on other recommendations of Dearing's final report and over the summer of 1997 it appeared that it would take some time to digest its implications.

A new National Advisory Group for Continuing Education and Lifelong Learning (NAGCELL) was then announced. This, it seemed, was to add the expertise in continuing education of its joint chairs, Bob Fryer and Alan Tuckett, to the reports by Kennedy and Dearing to provide the basis for a White Paper covering the entire field of post-compulsory education from FE and HE to adult education. The NAGCELL reported in November under Professor Fryer's sole authorship (Fryer 1997) but the response in the form of the promised White Paper was repeatedly postponed and eventually rejected – reportedly, on the highest authority – on the grounds that it failed sufficiently to address the problem of standards and examinations in further education (*Times Education Supplement* 13.2.98). Instead of a White Paper, the Green Paper, *The Learning Age*, was issued in February 1998 (DfEE 1998a).

Funding, as everyone involved agreed, was the key to the future of further education as colleges continued to struggle for survival under a still converging funding regime. Yet for the first year and a half, the New Labour government adhered rigorously to its pre-election pledge to stay within the spending restrictions it had inherited from the previous Conservative administration. The government then initiated a Comprehensive Spending Review with the intention of announcing spending plans as targets for the second half of its first term of office. As this review took place, more student places were promised with a target of 700,000 extra by 2002, most of them part-time adults. The 'New Deal' for 18–25-year-olds did not, however, benefit the colleges as much as had been anticipated, even though New Deal was subsequently extended to over 25-year-olds.

The future of the Training and Enterprise Councils (TECs), administering New Deal in conjunction with the employment service of the DfEE, was seemingly guaranteed for the remainder of the government's first parliamentary term, although consultation on their future continued (DfEE 1998b) and they were later abolished (or, rather, absorbed into the Learning and Skills Councils announced in 1999). As the first consultation made clear, Regional Development Agencies which began operating from April 1999 would not yet integrate TEC functions along with those of LEAs and the higher and further education funding councils. In fact, it is not at all clear how RDAs will call independent colleges to account in 'regional partnerships' or 'local fora', though it is clearly in the direction of this 'new regionalism' that policy is moving. In a related development, the New Start Strategy introduced in September 1997 was intended to integrate school and college provision across TEC areas for 'disaffected' 14–17-year-olds, thus complementing New Deal for 18-plus (see Barnes *et al.* 1998).

Evidence on these and other issues affecting the work of FE colleges is contained in the Report of the Select Committee on Education and Employment published in May 1998 (House of Commons 1998). When the details of the Treasury's Comprehensive Spending Review were announced in autumn 1998, many of the recommendations of the Select Committee – notably, the centrality of the further education colleges in widening participation and improving achievement – appeared to have been endorsed by government policy. The report and the evidence from various stakeholders involved in the sector can be seen as forming the basis of a new consensus on many issues of importance facing the sector today. We draw upon that evidence and the Committee's conclusions to present a picture of the contemporary condition of the colleges and to examine whether current government policies provide a coherent and secure future for them.

The reality

The Education and Employment Committee of the House of Commons decided to take FE as the subject of its first inquiry after the election of the New Labour government in May 1997. The Committee's decision was to 'take stock' of the FE sector five years after incorporation, given that colleges had recently been the 'subject of some controversy' (House of Commons 1998, Vol.1, para.3). The oral and written evidence to the Committee covered the full range of issues affecting colleges, though the final report tends to focus on 'how FE is funded, planned and managed' (House of Commons 1998) with reference particularly to franchising, staffing and accountability and little attention to the curriculum.

Evidence was taken in public session from many individuals representing the sector – notably principals, the National Association of Teachers in Further and Higher Education, the Further Education Funding Council, the Further Education Development Agency, the

Association of Colleges and the Department for Education and Employment. Many other groups submitted written evidence, most of which is published in Volume Two of the Report. The Report's first volume contains the Committee's 60-page summary of the current state of FE, followed by 50 conclusions and recommendations. While there was considerable agreement, not all groups and individuals giving evidence put forward the same views and the proceedings show up strong differences in opinion among the witnesses. Examples of issues on which such differences occur are those of franchising, where its benefits and effects on the sector as a whole divide principals and others, the FEFC's convergence policy (see below), and the means of making college management and governance more accountable. So, for example, on funding there was broad agreement amongst many witnesses on the necessity for convergence of Average Levels of Funding (ALF) but acceptance too that the FEFC's methodology should be less complicated. There was also unanimity, on the straightforward need for an increase in the 'quantum' of finance for FE, since the methodology is but a sophisticated instrument for dividing up the total public money allocated to the FEFC. In the first five years of incorporation from 1993–98 there was a 29 per cent increase in student numbers and FTEs. In the same period there was an overall reduction of 27 per cent in the funding of full-time equivalent students (compared with a 13 per cent reduction in FTE funding in higher education). Many witnesses told the Committee that those 'efficiency savings' had gone as far as they could without damaging the quality of provision, or, as the Association of Colleges (AoC) put it in their written submission, 'without threatening the stability of the sector as a whole' (House of Commons 1998, Vol.2, p.420). The FEFC reported that more than half of all colleges were either 'financially vulnerable' or 'financially weak' – the number in the latter category having increased from six per cent to 27 per cent of all colleges since incorporation (Vol.2, p.195).

Baroness Kennedy stated in her evidence that the government 'should be putting more money into FE than it has in the past and that will probably mean less money for higher education' and that 'further education needs to move higher on the list' (Vol.2, Q.11–12). The Committee recorded that colleges were finding further efficiency savings in 1997/98 of between five and seven per cent while the universities in recent years had been required to achieve annual savings of one per cent (Vol.1, para.24). When asked directly by the Chair of the Committee, Margaret Hodge MP, whether the FE sector was underfunded, Baroness Blackstone answered that, in May 1997, the incoming government had 'inherited a situation which was frankly dire ... a financial crisis as a result of the end of the Demand-Led Element.' The Baroness would not commit the government to transferring resources to FE colleges from schools or universities, preferring to express her 'hope ... that we will be able to find more additional funds and not have to rob Peter to pay Paul' (Vol.2, Q.730–731).

On the principle of convergence – a common, national rate of funding – and on that of the level playing field – a common funding formula applied to all providers of post-16 education and training – there was general agreement amongst witnesses. But there was division between principals of London colleges and those from outside London on the question of whether a special case should be allowed for the London colleges to converge more slowly and to be granted higher ALFs because of additional costs in inner London. Against this, Edward McIntyre, Principal of Birmingham College of Food, Tourism and Creative Studies, advised the Committee that they should have convergence 'tomorrow' with a loan fund from which colleges in difficulties could borrow – even if this meant letting colleges in financial difficulties 'go to the wall' (Vol.2, Q.174–179, 194–197). In their conclusions the Committee did not agree that London colleges had been 'especially hard done by' compared with those in other regions (Vol.1, para.97).

On franchising also, there were divergent views expressed by principals, with the FE21 group of colleges particularly involved in franchising stressing the gains in access and participation (Vol.2, Appendix 37, Memorandum from the FE21 Group). Principals Patricia Morgan-Webb and David Eade (Clarendon College and Barnsley College respectively) justified the recent growth of 'outward collaborative provision' (as the FEFC refers to franchising) with local community and private training providers in terms of their increased training for UK plc through partnership with employers. Information supplied to the Committee showed that between 1994/95 and 1996/97 the number of funding units earned through franchised provision increased from three to 17 million. In the same three years the percentage of students enrolled on franchised schemes grew from five per cent to 19 per cent of total FE enrolments, although with the withdrawal of the Demand Led Element (DLE) early in 1997 there was a fall in numbers. Principal Rospigliosi of Plymouth criticized franchising on educational grounds; it left much to be desired as a learning experience – 'some NVQ guru going around ticking boxes' (Vol.2, Q.554) – and was a poor substitute for the day-release student's experience of college. He also put the view that the unplanned growth in franchised work had led to an unforeseen increase in FE spending which in turn led government to remove the DLE. This in turn had affected the financial positions of the whole sector and 'tended to destabilise the infrastructure' (Vol.2, Q.548 et seq.).

These and other points in favour of and against franchising were discussed in the Committee's proceedings and at considerable length in the final report (Vol.1, paras 101–136). A key question identified was whether in-house training funded by the franchising college would have been paid for by the employer, i.e. whether FEFC funds were being used to subsidize employers. Baroness Kennedy, for all her commitment to pioneering approaches to widening participation, was clear in her evidence that any 'diversion of money is just inappropriate at a time when there just is not enough money around for education anyway' (Vol.2, Q.47). This view was shared by Rospigliosi who objected to 'mainstream organic provision' being cut because of the capping of funds caused in turn by money being, as he regarded it, 'thrown away on franchising' (Vol.2, Q.559). The Committee, in attempting to reconcile conflicting views, acknowledged in its report the gains associated with franchising but recommended that the FEFC should continue to review and clarify the funding, quality and control regimes of franchised operations. Only in exceptional circumstances should franchising take place outside the area of the 'parent college' (Vol.1, paras 128–136).

On issues to do with the organization and planning of further education, witnesses commented on the relative absence of guidance or strategy for the sector as a whole. Professor David Melville for the FEFC told the Committee that the Secretary of State's annual letter of guidance to the FEFC 'has been nothing but a shadow' compared with the guidance to other sectors (Vol.2, Q.105). In the competitive market-driven system introduced in 1992/93, the assumption was that national needs would be met by the combined efforts of corporate colleges; overall control of the college sector was limited to decisions about the quantum of funding and the approval of qualifications through Schedule Two of the 1992 Further and Higher Education Act. This had placed the FEFC, as its first Chief Executive, Sir William Stubbs, had observed on a number of occasions, in the position of a funding not a planning body (e.g. Ainley and Bailey

1997, p.17) with no responsibility or authority to provide a strategic plan for the sector as a whole. The Committee's final report reflected an end to this phase and an assumption that the FEFC would have to be more representative of the sector as a whole without going so far as to rescue heavily indebted colleges like Wirrall and Bilston. As noted by Keith Scribbins in the *Times Higher Educational Supplement* (13.2.98): 'The FEFC seems prepared to take the lead in rationalising provision. As a consequence it is moving from a monitoring to a planning body.'

Like Professor Melville, NATFHE witnesses recognized that change in this direction was necessary and was already taking place. As Paul Mackney, the new General Secretary, put it: 'We can see a value, if you like, in a mixed economy of planning and healthy rivalry and competition between colleges, but it is targeting of resources on which we want to put the emphasis' (Vol.2, Q.654–655). Given agreement on the general principle of clearer guidelines for national and local 'planning' of FE expressed by these and other witnesses, some general ideas for its implementation emerged from the evidence. However, it must be recalled that there are large areas of further education for which the FEFC has no responsibility: LEA-run adult education and youth work; school sixth forms; and training provided by TECs and employers. Thus, the 1992 Act represented and achieved only an incomplete attempt to rationalize the FE sector. Those speaking for the FEFC, NATFHE, the AoC and the Local Government Association, among others, developed the view that the FEFC's regional committees could be used as the basis of an authority/forum to co-ordinate all post-16 education and training in their regions. This would require the strengthening of the regional committees by the addition of representatives from local communities and employers and would enable the committees to deliver the FEFC's overall responsibility to ensure 'adequate and sufficient provision' – in the words of the 1992 Further and Higher Education Act.

Given that some FE colleges had been the focus of 'some controversy', it was to be expected that the Committee would take evidence on issues of governance and accountability. Many of those appearing before the Committee were questioned on the accountability of governors and the competence of senior managers. Others referred to this in written evidence; for example, Unison drew attention to the effect on the whole sector of 'tales of sleaze, corruption and incompetence at the most senior levels' (Vol.2, Appendix 35, paras 2–3). Their view that there had been some failure of corporate or management accountability was shared by Baroness Blackstone (Vol.2, Q.756), the FEFC (Q.109) and FEDA (Q.382). Members of the Committee visited Stoke-on-Trent, where the former principal and chair of governors had worked closely together but failed to inform the whole governing body of their actions. This had led to excessively high claims for funding from the FEFC, which in turn had to be repaid at the cost of cuts in jobs and courses. When questioning the Chief Executive of FEDA, (then) Stephen Crowne, Margaret Hodge referred to this case and said that everybody they had asked about the scandal – governors, inspectors, etc. – had said there was nothing they could do; the constant answer was 'Not me guv' (Vol.2, Q.385). The buck-passing eventually ended in the Committee's sessions when Baroness Blackstone indicated that the government would welcome a more interventionist approach on the part of the FEFC in the case of college mismanagement and added that the DfEE should act if the FEFC failed to do so.

Another prominent issue of governance raised in evidence was the lack of accountability of governing bodies. Consequently, there is an opacity about their proceedings and scope for breaking the rules with little risk of early discovery (Stoke-on-Trent College evidence in Report, Vol.2, Q.220). In the government's consultative paper *The Learning Age*, this issue is referred to as 'concerns about the style of working and remoteness of governing bodies' and 'a controversial management style which is unacceptable for publicly funded bodies' (para.5.5). The NATFHE delegation recommended codes of practice in the appointment of governors with staff and student represent-atives alongside those from LEAs in open meetings and these – together with safeguards for whistle-blowing – feature prominently in the Committee's final report and recommendations (Vol.2, para.169).

Curriculum issues were not part of the Committee's terms of reference, yet, given the centrality of qualifications to the aims of FE students and to the funding system, it was to be expected that these would be discussed in evidence. Nor is it surprising that, given the extent of agreement on the issue, the need for the development of a unit-based credit framework was generally accepted though not extended to the endorsement of modular A-levels. A unit-based credit framework was also recommended by the Kennedy Report (p.86) and was developed to the Committee in evidence from FEDA, AoC and NATFHE. The justification for this was often made in terms of efficiency – for example, gains in cost-effectiveness resulting from increases in class sizes as a consequence of fewer rationalized units, many of which would be common to a number of programmes and qualifications. But witnesses also saw it as a necessary condition for the implementation of the government's widening participation agenda.

Geoff Stanton's argument to the Committee for a unitized curriculum offer was based on a chemical analogy: just as it is possible to create thousands of substances out of 92 naturally occurring elements, so it should be possible to have the 20,000 qualifications currently available to FE but without the need for 200,000 programme units or modules. This reduction in the numbers of units, the use of 'common' units or modules across different programmes and qualifications, would be more comprehensible and efficient, but because of the shift from 'whole rigid qualifications', it would, Stanton said, enable students to keep their options open and the colleges 'to match the needs of adult learners and the new target groups in particular' (Vol.2, Q.405).

The Committee was under no misapprehension about the difficulties – political, conceptual and practical – which a move to a unit-based credit accumulation system would involve. These were shown in two pieces of evidence: first, one of the Committee's advisors, Professor Alan Smithers, criticized the New Zealand national qualifications framework and by extension proposals for a unified framework of qualifications in this country as a 'basic mistake' (Vol.1, para. 191). Second, Baroness Blackstone evaded a direct question from Valerie Davey MP about the government's decision to retain A-levels and the extent to which this was 'compatible with aspirations in "The Learning Age" for both small steps and breadth.' The Baroness's answer to this was that the government was committed to 'some broadening while retaining the rigour of A-levels' and that 'increasingly adults will come back into the system by other routes than A-levels'. 'A-levels,' she continued, 'are very effective and suitable qualifications' (Vol.2, Q.790).

Staffing issues were raised by a number of witnesses. Roger Ward CBE, then AoC Chief Executive, referred in his evidence to the 'very dramatic steps' which were taken when 'we [then the Colleges' Employers' Forum] were modernising the further education sector post-incorporation' (Vol.2, Q.341). A NATFHE spokesperson told the Committee that: 'all of us recognised that something had to change in the employment relationship and when I talk with principals now they often say, "We wanted Roger Ward to break the back of the Silver Book [1973 national agreement on lecturers' pay and conditions] but we wanted something put in its place. We did not want the chaos we have now'" (Vol.2, Q.659). The AoC in its supplementary written evidence informed the Committee that the Association was convinced of the need for 'a national framework for pay and conditions whilst at the same time allowing colleges to take account of their local needs' (Vol.2, Appendix 74, para.5). This new accord between employer and union – both sides in the process of putting their houses in order – is perhaps another sign of a possible new era for FE, although NATFHE members later carried a ballot for further strike action. The Committee conceded, however, that teaching and support staff had been the 'major factor in the major achievements made since incorporation' (paras 172 and 175).

Evidence was also received from principals and NATFHE on the loss through early retirement and voluntary redundancy of staff at all levels, often experienced teachers who had helped their colleges to achieve high grades at inspections for quality (e.g. Vol.2, Q.197). In many cases they had been replaced by part-time and agency staff, the vast majority as hourly paid teachers. NATFHE's estimate in written evidence was that 42 per cent of staff employed for more than 15 hours per week were working on temporary contracts in 1994/95 compared with 15–17 per cent pre-incorporation (Vol.2, Appendix 53, para.43). The dependence on peripheral, part-time staff who cannot play a full part in curriculum development and tutorial systems was a matter of concern to NATFHE and the FEFC's Chief Inspector reported that teachers' employment status was an aspect to be reported on at inspections from September 1997.

Other aspects of the employment of part-time staff brought to the Committee's attention included the use of staffing agencies. The Committee found it 'inappropriate' that one agency should be regarded as a monopoly supplier and were 'unclear' why the Colleges' Employers' Forum had found it 'necessary or appropriate' to endorse a single supplier (Vol.1, para.184). Baroness Blackstone also registered her concern about the employment rights of agency staff and their entitlement to staff development. She told the Committee that, if the DTI's review of employment agencies then in progress did not examine fully the use of staff agencies in the FE sector, the DfEE would address the issue (Vol.2, Q.789).

Conclusion

In its summary and recommendations the Select Committee provides an assessment of the FE sector five years after incorporation and a framework for policy development in the light of New Labour's education agenda. The achievements are identified and applauded: increased participation and achievement by students; significant movement towards a national system, and average level, of funding; 'efficiency gains' higher than those expected and achieved in schools and universities. The available FEFC data on these aspects and on the quality of management and of students' learning demonstrate the overall improvement in the college sector. The Committee also identified issues requiring attention if the colleges are to play their part in enabling more young people and adults to gain qualifications and skills for their own and society's future. Chief among these concerns are the financial situation of many colleges and the accepted view that quality and stability in the sector cannot be assumed if levels of funding are driven further down and the long-running industrial dispute is not resolved with agreement on a new framework for conditions of service (Vol.1, para.175). While the majority of colleges had adapted well to their new status and responsibilities and, as the Nolan Committee concluded, there was no 'deep-seated trend' toward inappropriate management, the Committee took seriously examples of what Nolan had called alleged and actual 'failure of management accountability' (House of Commons 1996, para.48). This led to recommendations directed at achieving greater transparency in the selection and conduct of governors and senior managers and at strengthening the part played by the FEFC in ensuring the probity of the sector (House of Commons 1998, Vol.1, paras 164 and 166).

These conclusions are rooted in the view that the FE sector has a pivotal part to play in fulfilling the government's educational mission in creating opportunities for all and improving the skills and qualifications of the existing and potential workforce. In an important part of their analysis the Committee concluded from the evidence presented to them that the sector has suffered 'from a lack of leadership and national strategic direction' and that there has been 'a significant hole in Government policy in respect of further education', especially in comparison with schools and higher education where it is absolutely clear what government requires and is prepared to pay for (Vol.1, para.18). This led the Committee to recommend that the stage had been reached when government must identify and explain priorities and so clarify criteria for the allocation of public money to further education (Vol.1, para.18). Aware of the DfEE's emphases in the Green Paper *The Learning Age* (continued growth, raising standards, and expenditure directed at the unqualified and those on low incomes), the Committee's own suggestions for key areas are 16–19 provision, adult learning, widening participation, employment-related training and basic skills (Vol.1, para.87).

While it is impossible to assess in detail how far these and other recommendations have influenced decision-making in the government, it does appear that they closely match the priorities of David Blunkett and his team. In his speech to the AoC Conference in November 1998, the Secretary of State announced an extra £725 million for further education colleges from the Comprehensive Spending Review over the next two years (£255 million in 1999/2000, £470 million in 2000/01) 'to improve standards, widen participation and modernise equipment and buildings' (DfEE Press Notice 549/98, 26 November 1998, from which information in this section is taken). The detailed allocation of these amounts included:

- Standards Fund   1999/2000   £35 million
                                2000/01   £80 million

  (to raise levels of achievement and management and teacher training, etc.)
- Widening Participation   1999/2000   £180 million
                                2000/01   £335 million

  (to fund 700,000 additional students by 2001/02)
- Capital Projects   1999/2000   £40 million
                                2000/01   £55 million
                                2001/02   £100 million

  (for computers and other projects, including disabled access).

These allocations would enable the FEFC to require an average 'efficiency squeeze' of no more than one per cent during the year 1999/2000 (comparable to that expected of the HE sector) and to revise the convergence target for college ALFs to £17.00 per unit instead of £16.20, with more flexibility for high ALF colleges to converge by 2001/02 (FEFC 1998). In the same speech Blunkett also announced that the government would be providing £69 million in 1999/2000 and £114 million in 2000/01 to assist with transport, child care and other support costs for students in FE colleges and school sixth forms. These sums would extend access funds for these students and would fund 12 pilot schemes for Education Maintenance Allowances which would be targeted at students from low-income families. Finally, the Secretary of State announced the setting up in each area of new 'local partnership forums' to undertake the planning of provision through 'a co-operative framework'.

Much of David Blunkett's announcement reinforced and confirmed the areas of agreement and the priorities identified by the Select Committee. The 'biggest increase ever' in funding for further education, in his words, increases the quantum for financing the sector in the next few years. The FEFC's role with regard to standards in FE, and its responsibility to intervene in colleges deemed to be failing, are strengthened – similar to concurrent statements that the DfEE will act promptly in cases of failing schools and LEAs. This 'boost for standards' is set in the context of increased participation among adults and 16–19s to acquire qualifications in colleges.

There were, of course, some significant omissions in Blunkett's statement. There was no requirement upon the FEFC to simplify its funding methodology; instead, the Council appeared to have won agreement to its view that fairness, even if achieved through complexity, is more important than simplicity (Gravatt 1998, p.12). While the need for co-operation in planning was recognized in the promised local partnership forums, the composition and scope of these remained unclear; nor was their relationship to the Regional Development Agencies specified. Finally, there was no mention of movement towards a level funded playing-field for provision for 16–19-year-olds in school sixth forms and the FE sector.

The reality of the committed additional funding for further education will be dependent on the colleges being able to deliver on Mr Blunkett's 'new standards agenda for further education' and 'major progress' towards the extra 700,000 students by 2001/02. It is clear that the Treasury is not willing to pay colleges more for what they are already providing; and the sector as a whole must still continue to find an annual one per cent efficiency saving. Furthermore, the additional money is conditional upon the colleges' ability to achieve the biggest ever expansion of student numbers in its history: a 17 per cent increase in two to three years.

It appears that the 'hole' in government policy – the failure historically to state in detail the provision for which the public is paying in further education – was substantially addressed in Mr Blunkett's statement. As Margaret Hodge commented during the evidence to her Committee of David Melville, Chief Executive of the FEFC, further education 'is a sector whose time has come' (Vol.2, Q.53). The continued higher profile of further education colleges will, however, depend upon their success in meeting New Labour's rigorous agenda of standards and targets.

Note: Since the authors completed this chapter, the government has announced another review of all post-16 non-higher education and training for publication as a White Paper on 1 July 1999. While it was not possible to comment on its recommendations at the time of writing, they may usefully be compared with the Select Committee findings outlined above.

References

Ainley, P. and Bailey, B. (1997) *The Business of Learning, Staff and Student Experiences of Further Education in the 1990s*. London: Cassell.

Barnes, T., Momen, A., Ryan, C. and Watson, J. (1998) 'New start under Labour? A case study of the new settlement of education and training.' *Education and Social Justice 1*, 1, 22–28.

Dearing, R. (1993) *The National Curriculum and its Assessment*. London: School Curriculum and Assessment Authority.

Dearing, R. (1996) *Review of Qualifications for 16–19 Year Olds*. London: School Curriculum and Assessment Authority.

Dearing, R. (1997) *Higher Education in the Learning Society. Summary Report*. London: HMSO.

DfEE (1998a) *The Learning Age. A Renaissance for a New Britain*. Cmnd. 3790. London: HMSO.

DfEE (1998b) *TECs: Meeting the Challenge of the Millennium. Consultation Paper*. London: DfEE.

DfEE Press Notice 3549/98, 26 November 1998.

Fryer, R. (1997) *Learning for the Twenty-First Century. First report of the National Advisory Group for Continuing Education and Lifelong Learning*. London: NAGCELL.

Further Education Funding Council (1996) *Inclusive Learning: The Report of the Learning Difficulties and Disability Committee*. Coventry: FEFC.

Further Education Funding Council (1997) *Learning Works, Widening Participation in Further Education*. Coventry: FEFC.

Further Education Funding Council (1998) *Council News*, No. 50. Coventry: FEFC.

Gravatt, J. (1998) *That's the Way the Money Goes: Further Education Funding in England in the Next 12 Months*. London: Further Education Development Agency.

House of Commons (1996) *Second Report of the Committee on Standards in Public Life*. Cmnd. 3270–1. London: HMSO.

House of Commons (1998) *House of Commons Select Committee on Education and Employment, Sixth Report 'Further Education'* (two volumes). London: HMSO.

Scott, P. (1997) 'The Dearing Report.' *Parliamentary Monitor 5*, 8, 3–4.

Times Higher Education Supplement (1998) 'Merger is the price on Further Education's new money.' 13 February, 18.

Chapter 4

Lifelong Learning
An Agenda for a Late-modern Future

Peter Jarvis

The world is full of reports about learning! Indeed, it is full of reports about lifelong learning. Without any evidence, I would hazard a guess and say that there have been more reports about learning in this decade than there were about continuing education in the last. What has been surprisingly by-passed in this transition has been the concept of lifelong education – but this may be because things are changing at such a rapid rate that education hardly had time to go through that phase of change before the one after the next was reached! This shift, however, reflects wider social changes – changes that indicate that modernity as we know it is undergoing massive transformation and late modernity, or post-modernity, is already upon us.

Bauman (e.g. 1992) has argued that the fall of the Berlin Wall has demonstrated beyond all question that the centralizing, bureaucratic tendency of modernity has been ineffective and unable to achieve its desired ends of creating a better society for all. Modern rationality was inefficient in the modern world since it sought to respond to the perceived needs of the people, rather than responding to their newly generated ones in a world which is changing rapidly all the time and continuing to generate more and more wants/needs. These can perhaps only be met in the market place of late modern society – but it is a market place. A similar argument can be made out for centralized educational systems and their need to change and function in the market place of choice and learning. Education is a product of modernity having many of the problems of modernity associated with it, and so it must be decentralized. But learning, as it is now conceptualized, is a product of late modernity – of the market place, where individuals can choose what to consume/learn and when to learn it – and so it has now come to the centre of the educational debate at this time.

Perhaps it is significant to note that one aspect of this market argument was actually first conducted in the American adult education literature in the late 1970s and early 1980s – but in a different language, one of education and not social science. William Griffith (1980) argued that there was a need to co-ordinate adult education provision for the sake of efficiency whereas Knowles (1980), in the same volume, suggested that unco-ordinated systems are more adaptable to the rapidly changing circumstances of American history. He thought that lifelong education would provide the conceptual framework for the continuing development of adult education. While his analysis was more accurate than Griffith's, he was not completely right since American education, especially higher education, was not as flexible as he thought that it needed to be – a point that Eurich (1985) was to demonstrate with her study of the corporate classroom.

Now it is not education offering lifelong education which is at the centre of the educational agenda – it is a lifelong learning market, with a multitude of providers, offering learning opportunities and with the educational institution fast losing its earlier near-monopoly of the provision of learning. However, the learning market is not a free market; but few markets actually are! A variety of government reports in recent years have indicated that people's learning cannot be left entirely to their own inclination – it has to be directed, and perhaps regulated, by a government which focuses on the perceived needs of the nation in the current global market. Governments have their own agenda – but so do the providers and the learners! Consequently, this chapter has three main sections: the first looks at national and international agendas; the second at the future for providers and provision; and the third briefly examines the learners'/consumers' demands and needs in this lifelong learning market.

Governments' agendas

This is not the place to review all the official reports that have been published on education pointing in the direction of lifelong learning in the past decade, or indeed of all the reports by commercial and industrial bodies calling for more emphasis to be placed on lifelong learning – that would constitute a book in itself. Nevertheless, there are similar themes running through them all as a result of the significance of the global market – competitiveness, competencies, widening participation, and the need for workers to keep on learning so that countries can maintain their place in the economic world and their people their standard of living. In addition, most of them make some reference to the need for people to learn so that they can grow and develop and participate more in the democratic processes of their society. For instance, in the introduction to the OECD report (1996, p.13), the following occurs:

> Success in realising lifelong learning – from early childhood education to active learning retirement – will be an important factor in promoting employment, economic development, democracy and social cohesion in the years ahead.

In the European Union White Paper (1995, p.18), a similar claim was made:

> The crucial problem of employment in a permanently changing economy compels the education and training system to change. The design of appropriate education and training strategies to address work and employment issues is, therefore, a crucial preoccupation.

In the European perspectives (Collomb and Seidal 1998, p.8), we read the following:

> For Europe to be competitive, working adults need Lifelong Learning: a continual replenishment of their education. Adult Education and Lifelong Learning are essential ingredients in today's integrated Europe.

Even in the rather more utopian Delors Report (1996, p.70), we see that the significance of the economic institution in society is recognized:

> Under the pressure of technological progress and modernization, the demand of education for economic purposes has been constantly on the rise in most countries ...

Perhaps it is only in Germany where this relationship has not been fully recognized and developed by theorists. Dohman (1996, p.96) makes the point that:

> The fact that Germany's education policy has remained relatively unaffected by international efforts to realize lifelong learning ... appears to be due to the German's tendency to over-rate their educational system, their desire to preserve it and their somewhat apprehensive-skeptical attitude toward unsupervised learning.

While the German position might be one of over-valuing its education system, the apprehensiveness toward unsupervised learning comes out in a number of different reports – for the learning market must be influenced. Indeed, in the British government's policy, there is certainly more than a sense of focusing the learners on what they should learn, in what they should gain qualifications, and for what they will receive maximum funding. This has become clear in nearly all the reports that have been published in the UK during this period, but the recognition that the market is global means that governments cannot regulate it entirely, only seek to influence it.

In the Kennedy Report (1997) into further education, for instance, the relationship between learning for work and learning for life is clearly established but, significantly, the Report questioned whether the learning market is the most efficient distributive mechanism, and it suggested a middle way between bureaucratic centralization and the market:

> We have no desire to return to the centralised and bureaucratic planning approaches of the past. We would wish to see local strategy emerging, developing and being sustained by partnership approaches, involving all the key stakeholders, which recognise both the independence and inter-dependence of partners. (Kennedy 1997, p.39)

The Report recognized that funding is a most important lever for change and, perhaps, for creating some partnership agreements. Nevertheless, the power of funding lies only in as much as neither the providers nor consumers could afford to operate without it and, second, that there is no competition between partners to gain student enrolments, etc. While partnerships are to be applauded, there is also, however, a sense in which the funding of partnership arrangements seeks to re-create monopoly-type situations. This is clearly illustrated in Kennedy's emphasis on data-gathering etc. in order to provide relevant education. Kennedy, therefore, seeks to offer a rather modern answer to a late modern problem. But the generation of partnership arrangements reflects the fact that the barriers between educational and other providers are being lowered, and this diversity itself reflects a late modern situation.

The Report also implicitly recognizes that if there is insufficient funding, then the forces of the market are regenerated. At the present time, it seems that in the United Kingdom, further education hovers uneasily between partnership and entrepreneurial situations in its endeavour to provide learning opportunities for a larger group of students.

However, the government's agenda for lifelong learning is clearly recognized – it will only fund those educational courses that might be classified as vocational, are listed under Schedule 2 and lead to a qualification, while non-Schedule 2 courses are only funded by Local Education Authorities in a discretionary manner; and since such funding has been drastically reduced, many of these are now offered at near the market rate. Significantly, the government is also funding the establishment of the University for Industry, the name itself demonstrating the government's agenda. Kennedy clearly does not entirely approve of this division and actually warns against it. The government recognized this and in its response to the Kennedy Report, *Further Education for the New Millennium* (DfEE 1998b, p.10), it notes the importance of local authority adult education and the arrangements being made for courses outside of Schedule 2.

Amongst the other reports to appear was *The Learning Age*:

> Learning is the key to prosperity – for each of us as individuals, as well as for the nation as a whole. Investment in human capital will be the foundation of success in the knowledge-based global economy of the twenty-first century.

> David Blunkett, Secretary of State for Education and Employment, *The Learning Age* (DfEE 1998a, p.7)

The Learning Age is the government's Green Paper on lifelong learning, and it reflects the same priorities. In this Paper, the government proposes amongst other things: the establishment of Individual Learning Accounts towards funding individual education; starting the University of Industry in which advanced technology will be used to make learning materials available to all potential learners, with a national guidance service provided free through a centralized telephone system; companies are to continue to be encouraged to become Investors in People to plan for the future development of their workforce; the establishment of a national Skills Task Force to increase the support given to people to acquire basic skills. Clearly the government is seeking imaginative and innovative ways of widening the educational system in order to respond to the needs of the workforce of contemporary society.

But even in this document, so clearly focused on working life, there is reference to life beyond work:

> As well as securing our economic future, learning has a wider contribution. It helps make ours a civilised society, develops the spiritual side of our lives and promotes active citizenship. Learning enables people to play a full part in their community, it

strengthens the family, the neighbourhood and consequently the nation. It helps us fulfil our potential and opens doors to a love of music, art and literature.

The Learning Age (DfEE 1998a, p.7)

While the rhetoric of support for individual life development is strong in all the reports, the reality is that the government's agenda is that it must, and will, support vocational lifelong learning – or worklife learning.

Since the government has been tremendously active in fostering the learning society in the United Kingdom, it would be possible to analyse other reports, such as that of the Dearing Committee. However, at the time when this chapter was being finalized the second report of the Fryer Committee, *Creating Learning Cultures* (DfEE 1999), was published in which there was a wider orientation with the recognition that lifelong learning should be part of everyday life with pointers to such non-work dimensions of living as health (DfEE 1999, p.11).

It is not at all surprising that the concentration of government strategy should be on learning and the workforce since, however altruistic government may be, there is only a limited amount of funding available, and commercial institutions which are active players in the knowledge society need to see that they have government's support since they need highly skilled and qualified workers. Reich (1991), for instance, suggested that in the United States about 30 per cent of the workforce will be symbolic analysts (knowledge workers), 30 per cent will work in the in-person service industries and a further 30 per cent will be routine production workers. With the tremendous increase in the speed of knowledge change, so that its period of usefulness to the work situation is shortening all the time, all the symbolic analysts and many of the others need a worklife of continuing learning to keep abreast with essential knowledge, and all the others will require recurrent retraining in order to undertake their changing forms of work. Nearly all the reports, consequently, focus on the issues of extending provision and access to education – since such a large proportion of the workforce needs this continual updating. Participation needs to be extended in order to ensure that society does not lose some of its human talent in the competitive global market. This emphasis will continue, and the idea of 'lifelong learning for all' will continue to dominate the educational scene.

Besides funding, the other control mechanism available is academic qualifications. As the nature of knowledge is changing and more acceptable knowledge is practical and pragmatic (Lyotard 1984), the nature and validity of both the educational offering made and the qualifications available will necessarily change. Such qualifications must recognize the practical competency of the knowledge holders and their relevance to contemporary situations. Consequently, we are beginning to see national qualifications frameworks emerging in different countries around the world, e.g. United Kingdom, South Africa, Hong Kong. Once these are in place, among the questions that occur is, for how long will the educational institutions retain their monopoly of awarding qualifications?

The educational system is neither large enough nor flexible enough to respond to all the demands generated by these new social conditions and so there needs to be other providers – whether they will be partners or competitors is still perhaps an open question, although the likelihood is that in the medium term there will be a great deal of competition both between educational and other providers and also among educational providers themselves. There will also be other commercial arrangements, such as an increasing amount of franchising, which will enable lower level educational institutions to offer high level courses provided by universities and other institutions of higher education.

The government's vocational education agenda will be implemented whatever else the outcome, even though the government's role might change from being the only educational provider to being seen to be one provider for, and a supporter of, the main players in the market – the business and commercial institutions. But even non-vocational education is also increasingly being offered in the learning market by private providers – for those who can afford the purchase price – but there will be a considerable number who will be excluded from the provision of all forms of education, for the market always creates losers as well as winners. As this learning market gradually lowers its dependency on government funding, a new agenda for government might emerge, one with greater cultural and welfare orientation of offering even more help and education for the socially excluded, and then some of the other rhetoric in the reports might stand more chance of becoming reality.

The providers and provision

In this second section, we will look firstly at the providers, then at the provisions they offer in the learning market and, finally, we will look very briefly at the methods of delivery of the learning materials.

Providers

There are a variety of providers in the lifelong learning market, not all of which are from an educational tradition. This is perhaps not surprising when a large proportion of the workforce are working with knowledge (Reich noted about 30% for the USA and there is no reason to suppose that the UK figure will differ greatly), and government's priority in education is toward the creation of a highly educated workforce able to compete in the global market. The educational institutions alone are unable to provide all the learning opportunities that are necessary – for instance, there are new occupations and professions that have traditionally not been studied within the higher education system but which are working with very sophisticated knowledge demands.

The universities have not traditionally researched into some of these new professions and are, consequently, incapable of generating all the knowledge necessary for them – and so they cannot teach what they do not have. A typical example of that is Management Consultancy. With no centre for the study of management consultancy in an institution of higher education, it became necessary for the industry to create its own – so that in 1996 the Management Consultancy Business School was founded. But other large commercial organizations working with sophisticated knowledge are in the forefront of the development of their own essential knowledge (Eurich 1985), so that in the United Kingdom British Aerospace Virtual University has recently been founded, and throughout the Western world other commercial organizations – from Body Shop to Disney – are also establishing their own academic institutions. Some of these are designed specifically for their own workers, but the British Aerospace Virtual University does not see itself as only a provider for its own workforce. It sees the potential for partnership with other educational providers. In the same way, the Management Consultancy Business School entered an association with the University of Surrey in order to get its masters degree programme validated. Both of these commercial providers can offer learning opportunities which do not need the educational institutions' support, but which at present see advantages of partnership arrangements for some aspects of their work – such as award-bearing courses.

These are not the only partnership arrangements that are appearing. Increasingly, different occupational groups are seeking higher level qualifications for their education and training and the institutions of higher education are finding it advantageous to enter franchise arrangements with lower level institutions, so that further education colleges are enabled to offer undergraduate and postgraduate degrees. Franchising is also occurring between different countries, as universities in the UK, and USA and Australia, are seeking to get their courses offered by overseas colleges and universities. Clearly franchising arrangements are advantageous to the award-granting institution, but problems occur with the quality of the provision and recent reports, including specific reports on colleges of higher education, indicate that the award-granting institutions will have to implement more effective quality control mechanisms than exist at present, and this might mean that they will need to employ quality inspectors, or moderators, as well as external examiners. The academic award is now the benchmark of academic quality and the accrediting bodies are having to place much more emphasis on quality control than ever before. The awards are the symbol being sold (Baudrillard 1988) and the awarding body the guarantor that the commodity being sold is of value.

Such franchising arrangements could prove to be a prelude to mergers, and even takeovers, between institutions of different levels and the creation of larger educational institutions not only offering lifelong learning, but offering it at a wide variety of levels to a wider market in different parts of the world. Significantly, it is not only the smaller players which are involved in mergers in the international commercial market and neither will it be, I suspect, in the international learning market.

Provision

It is perhaps commonplace to argue now that the provision for lifelong learning is market-orientated and that its main driving force is the demands of industrial and commercial institutions. As the shape of these institutions changes in different countries, so do the demands that they make for education and training – these demands create the agenda for the future of most of the educational organizations.

Employees in both the service and knowledge-based industries are needing to continue their education beyond schooling and university, in order to keep abreast with the changes that are occurring. Clearly, this has already happened in the West, and it is possible to see the demands that these workforces make upon the university system. As we pointed out above, Reich predicted that about one-third of the workforce would be symbolic analysts, working with knowledge – a knowledge that is rapidly changing. Traditionally, however, universities have not admitted such a high proportion of the population at either undergraduate or postgraduate level, but as societies are adapting to the demands of the industrial institutions so more higher education places are being created, so that in some Western countries approximately one-third of all young people leaving school have opportunity for higher education. Naturally, in countries where the demands for knowledge-based workers is less, there are fewer pressures on universities to increase the number of places available – but as more knowledge-based occupations locate in countries other than Western cultural countries, the greater will be the demand for more places to be created in their universities for young people to gain qualifications before they enter the new workforce. Consequently, but very significantly, undergraduate education is becoming part of the initial education system.

Once these young people have graduated and got employment, however, their education must continue so that they can keep abreast with all the innovations being created by advanced technology. Universities are, therefore, beginning to adapt to the demands for continuing professional education for these workers. There are facilities for them to study part-time for higher degrees, many of which are work-based and modular in structure. For instance, Campbell (1984) records that since 1974 there have been more adults in universities in Canada than undergraduates. This is true of most North American and UK universities. These are not only symbolic analysts, but in-person service workers as well, and they are studying for taught masters and taught doctorate degrees – part-time, and even at a distance. These courses have to be relevant to the workplace and are often work-based. A greater proportion of university teaching is becoming postgraduate and vocationally orientated. The significance of this is simply that the role of the universities is changing rapidly in response to the changing world of production and they are becoming institutions of lifelong learning. This is another trend in adult learning: universities and colleges are beginning to place a great deal more emphasis on higher degrees orientated to the work situation which can be studied part-time and even at a distance.

It is increasingly being recognized, however, that the knowledge necessary for many of these professionals is actually only being generated in the work situation, so that two other major developments are accompanying these changes. Providers are running courses teaching workers how to learn, and reflect, in the workplace – learning to learn courses – so that they can make their practices more efficient. Once this occurs, the obvious next step is recognizing that these practitioners are also researchers – practitioner researchers (Jarvis 1999) – which means that knowledge-based workers are increasingly studying for PhDs part-time; their research is work-based and they are often funded by their employers. The idea that the doctorate was a route into university employment is changing – the definition of research is something else that is changing on the lifelong learning agenda.

The other major change is that institutions are now accrediting work-based learning. A number of universities, including the University of Surrey, are not only orientating their traditional courses towards the workplace, they are actually going into it and seeking to facilitate learning within it, and accrediting the learning that occurs.

There is, however, a second driving force in the learning market – demographics. People are living longer and wanting to continue learning after their retirement from work. Hence we have seen, first in America and then elsewhere in the world, post-retirement education emerge. By the early 1960s, institutions for retired professionals began in America and in the 1970s the universities of the third age. In America and in parts of Europe many of these institutions have become attached to traditional higher educational institutions, such as universities, but in the UK and parts of Australia and New Zealand the universities of the third age are non-governmental organizations. From the above discussion, however, it will be clear that the growth of these organizations, and the learning opportunities that they offer, lie outside much of the agenda for lifelong learning discussed above. Not only is it non-vocational, it is not offered nor pursued for qualification or award, although there are some older learners who do seek qualifications and do seek admission to the traditional educational institutions – some even wishing to undertake research at doctoral level. Learning and ageing will become an increasingly important item on the lifelong learning agenda as the population ages and the significance of learning for mental health is more widely recognized.

As the traditional liberal adult education changes as it struggles for funding, so the universities of the third age, and similar seniors' education groups, emerge. Here we see a potential development for liberal adult education – outside the government's present agenda and also, perhaps, outside the agendas of some of the providers of education, but clearly a new form of provision for a new and potentially very large group of consumers in the market of lifelong learning.

Mode of provision

Schumpeter (1976) actually argued many years ago that one of the strengths of the market is that it has necessarily to be innovative, something that may be seen to be true of the way that education has changed both in what it offered and how it offered it – from traditional face-to-face teaching in a 'real-time' situation to the utilization of a variety of methods, in a realignment of time and space. In order to compete in the global learning market, there has been a phenomenal expansion of all forms of provision of learning opportunities worldwide – an expansion not only made possible by the advance of information technology but also because of the globalization of the English language. There are, for instance, probably more people using English every day in their work situation, but for whom it is their second language, than there are first language speakers of English in the world. Universities and colleges are both able to attract people to come to their own institutions from, and also sell their learning materials in, different parts of the world – but with this growth comes the problems of quality and regulation.

Now some of the providers of learning materials for the global market are using Fordist methods of production – mega-universities catering for a mass market (Peters 1984). Even so, the standardizing tendencies of a mass market means that niche markets emerge, and so providers are also seeking out niche markets and utilizing appropriate modes of provision. Obviously this includes traditional face-to-face teaching, all forms of self-directed learning using whatever technology is appropriate, and any combination of techniques that makes the learning efficient for the learners.

The learning market is, then, characterized by a wide variety of providers and a similar diversity of provision – but what, then, of the learners themselves?

Learners and consumers

Throughout this chapter there has been some emphasis upon the fact that much of the learning is work-related throughout the whole period of the working life. Yet it is common to hear people say that many individuals will have two or three different careers throughout their lives. People changing careers in middle or later life, therefore, constitute a major group needing to continue their learning, so that initial preparation in new occupations for those who are changing, e.g. in consultancy for those who have been in management all their lives, becomes another growth area for lifelong learning. Potential learners will search the learning market for all forms of relevant learning opportunities; many, but by no means all, of which will be work-based during the working life. The National Learning Survey (DfEE 1997) found that:

> ... after excluding those still in full-time education, 74% of the re-spondents had taken part in a learning activity in the three years prior to the survey. These learning activities tended to be predom-inantly work-related – while 67% had done some recent learning to help with future or current work, only 30% had started a learn-ing episode for reasons unrelated to work. About one on four respondents (23%) had done both types of learning in the three year reference period. (DfEE 1997, p.49)

In this UK survey, a similar picture emerged when respondents were asked about the likelihood of their undertaking any form of learning in the near future. The learners' agenda is also work-related. Of those who had undertaken non-work-related taught learning, the majority were women (67%) but the age spread was much more even. Nevertheless, 41 per cent were between 50 years and 69 years of age. Regrettably, the National Learning Survey did not seek to discover the learning habits of those over the age of 70 years old – which perhaps indicates that their learning is not regarded as quite so important by the government.

Clearly, therefore, the learning agenda for those surveyed is primarily work-related, but the significance of the older consumer of learning materials was not highlighted in this survey. Theirs is a hidden agenda, but clearly not predominantly work-related. But they are consumers in this market, as the success of the universities of the third age movement illustrates. However, because their learning is often uncertificated it is not necessarily regarded as 'real' learning.

Conclusion

Lifelong learning has emerged and become increasingly significant in late modern society. The use of the terms 'learning' and 'learning materials' demonstrates that this is a market phenomenon in which there are many providers all seeking to sell their commodities to those who want or need to learn. That it is a market means that it will continue to be innovative, offering new products through a variety of different media. Governments clearly seek to influence the market through devising strategies which will be funding-based but, since there are now no monopoly providers in a global situation, they can do so only through what they will fund and the awards that they will recognize. There is, however, a danger in this situation since it is possible that only learning that is recognized by some form of award becomes defined as 'real' learning, while all the other human learning that helps make people what they are will be neglected and regarded as unreal – and even unnecessary – and lifelong learning will become equated with worklife learning.

References

Baudrillard, J. (1988) 'The system of objects.' In M. Poster (ed) *Jean Baudrillard: Selected Writings*. Cambridge: Polity. pp.10–28.

Bauman, Z. (1992) *Intimations of Postmodernity*. London: Routledge.

Campbell, D. (1984) *The New Majority: Adult Learners in the University*. Edmonton: University of Alberta Press.

Collomb, B. and Seidel, H. (1998) Foreword. In L. Otala *European Approaches to Lifelong Learning*. Geneva: European University-Industry Forum.

Delors, J. (Chair) (1996) *Learning the Treasure Within*. Paris: UNESCO.

Department for Education and Employment (DfEE) (1997) *National Learning Survey*. Research Report No. 49. London: Department for Education and Employment.

Department for Education and Employment (DfEE) (1998a) *The Learning Age*. London: Department for Education and Employment.

Department for Education and Employment (DfEE) (1998b) *Further Education for the New Millennium*. London: Department for Education and Employment.

Dohman, G. (1996) *Lifelong Learning: Guidelines for a Modern Education Policy*. Bonn: Federal Ministry of Education, Science, Research and Technology.

Eurich, N. (1985) *Corporate Classroom*. Princeton: Carnegie Foundation for the Advancement of Teaching.

European Union (1995) *Teaching and Learning: Towards the Learning Society.* Brussels: European Union.

Fryer, R. (Chair) (1999) *Creating Learning Cultures*. London: Department for Education and Employment.

Griffith, W. (1980) 'Coordination of personnel, programs and services.' In J.M. Peters and Associates *Building an Effective Adult Education Enterprise*. San Francisco: Jossey-Bass. pp.78–114.

Jarvis, P. (1999) *The Practitioner Researcher: Developing Theory from Practice*. San Francisco: Jossey Bass.

Kennedy, H. (Chair) (1997) *Learning Works: Widening Participation in Further Education*. Coventry: Further Education Funding Council.

Knowles, M. (1980) 'The growth and development of adult education.' In J.M. Peters and Associates *Building an Effective Adult Education Enterprise*. San Francisco: Jossey-Bass. pp.12–40.

Lyotard, J.F. (1984) The Post-Modern Condition: A Report of Knowledge. Manchester: University of Manchester Press.

Organization for Economic Cooperation and Development (1996) *Lifelong Learning for All*. Paris: OECD.

Peters, O. (1984) 'Distance teaching and industrial production: a comparative interpretation in outline.' In D. Seward, D. Keegan and B. Holmberg (eds) *Distance Education: International Perspectives*. London: Routledge. pp.68–94.

Reich, R. (1991) *The Work of Nations*. London: Simon Schuster.

Schumpeter, J. (1976) *Capitalism, Socialism and Democracy*. London: George Allen and Unwin.

PART II

The New Qualifications

Chapter 5

Vocational Training, Career Guidance, Work and Citizenship
Education in Democracy

Barry Hutchinson

Introduction

In the current (free) market (forces) led policy context, where maximizing profit and creating differential pay awards are major concerns, it may seem a little pointless, even daft, to raise the question of the relationship between vocational education and vocational training. Even more peculiar would be to ask, what, if any, is the relationship between careers guidance and a career? However, when the claims made for the introduction and development of the National Vocational Qualifications (NVQ) framework, and its associated careers guidance service, are compared with what has happened in their construction and with what is actually happening in their delivery, there would seem to be good grounds for asking them. The NVQ framework has been designed to 'facilitate access to relevant training and vocational education throughout working life for every member of the workforce, at every level from entry level to top management' (DOE 1988). While wishing to affirm the need to raise the status and the quality of vocational education and training in the United Kingdom, the experience of engaging in one attempt to do so, in the European Social Fund supported MENYU project (Meeting the Employment Needs of the Young Unemployed), gives rise to some serious issues which should be of concern to those who were instrumental in devising the framework and to those presently involved in operationalizing it. These issues concern both the shape and the direction which the framework is taking as it expands. One question to be asked is whether it is becoming what its producers intended, a relevant, work-related, system of qualifications for improving both the skill level of the nation's workforce and hence the country's economic performance. Another is whether this question is itself the appropriate one to pursue: Wellington (1993) asked whether such a project, 'based solely on competence and outcomes [could] be broad enough for the future.'

Regularly in *The NVQ Monitor* (e.g. Winter 1995), it is explained that: 'The primary purposes of the NVQ framework are to create a coherent classification for qualifications and to facilitate transfer and progression, both within areas of competence and between them.' Within this framework the qualifications are claimed to be 'based on employer-led occupational standards of competence derived from functional analysis of jobs and their related activities and skills' (Taubman 1994). Even if, as Field (1995) points out, many employers are not actually involved in identifying and drawing up the competence statements, there remains concern over the adequacy of basing vocational qualifications on the analysis of current work tasks alone. The apparently self-evident argument that using these in work-based training will indeed produce the more highly skilled, mobile and flexible workers, ones who will 'need to train and retrain throughout their working lives to keep pace with ever changing work requirements and occupational structures' (Taubman 1994), which it is claimed the economy needs, is upon closer inspection seriously flawed in at least three ways. First, the implicit view which is held of work itself is highly circumscribed and is curtailed to an instrumental role. Second, the picture which is drawn of the person as worker, especially at NVQ levels 1 and 2, resembles more that of a circus animal than that of a human being. This is of concern since it is at these lower levels that most NVQ awards are made (Field 1995). It would seem that little regard has been given to those human qualities and values which would enable workers as persons to achieve even some of the limited aspirations set for them. And third, little attention is given to a consideration of larger social values such as the relationship between vocational training and citizenship: should training promote the values espoused by a democratic state? It is in these three areas, the nature of work, of personhood and of citizenship, that education and training interrelate.

Competence and autonomy

In a recent Northern Ireland Curriculum Council document (NICC 1994) the claim is made that employers require workers who are not just technically competent but who can also think and act creatively and take responsibility. An earlier study by the European Centre for the Development of Vocational Training (d'Iribarne 1987) had argued similarly that workers needed new intellectual skills far beyond any technological competence. One early argument over the definition of competence used by the National Council for Vocational Qualifications was concerned with whether competence could be described in terms of the task requirements of specific jobs and occupations or whether it could best be defined in terms of personal qualities and capacities (Ashworth and Saxton 1990). The first approach, involving close analysis of tasks and functions in work situations, was that adopted by Manpower Services and NCVQ. The second, involving the identification of the personal characteristics required to be able to conduct one's work consistent with the values inherent to good practice, has been developed by McBer and Company and Dreyfus (see Elliott 1991). Two bones of contention between these views were concerned with the degree of specification, and hence prediction, with which competence could be defined, and the extent to which knowledge and understanding could be directly applied and observed in practice. However, while most protagonists accept that competence development and assessment are valuable, beyond that not a great deal else is agreed (Hyland 1993). One example of the difficulties involved can be seen in the recent attempt to encourage enterprise competencies. Watts (1993) describes how enterprise can mean having enterprising skills which 'can be used in all sorts of contexts, not only in employment, the community, politics, and in all sorts of ways.' Or, on the other hand, it can mean 'working in "enterprises" and having the skills you need for employment.' The first meaning is acceptable to 'progressives', the second to employers who reject the first because 'enterprising people rock boats, they ask too many questions, they don't fit in, they're not always good team members' (Watts 1993). This example picks out the central issue as to whether competence, in whichever way it is defined, is to be regarded as including the ability to think and to think critically, for oneself, to be autonomous. Put another way, is the definition of competence to focus solely on the acquisition of specific job skills, or is it, as the Crowther Report (1959) argued some time ago, to be 'concerned with the development of human personality and with teaching the individual to see himself in due proportion to the world in which he (sic) has been set.' Wellington (1993) quotes the Central Policy Review Staff report: 'resourcefulness, an enquiring mind, and enthusiasm are at least as appropriate for the jobs that will be available over the next twenty years as the rather dour and old fashioned views of obedience and discipline which were emphasised by some employers.' It is also clear that whichever definitions are settled for, they will have their distinct practical implications and consequences.

One recent attempt at trying to reconcile these different views in regard to competence was provided by Eraut and Cole (1993), who distinguished between performance and capability in the conduct of 'professional' affairs. According to Eraut and Cole, performance refers to behavioural skills which can be observed and assessed in relation to workplace outcomes. Capability on the other hand, refers to:

(a)   underpinning knowledge and understanding of concepts, theories, facts and procedures;

(b)   the personal skills and qualities required for a professional approach to the conduct of one's work;

(c)   the cognitive processes which constitute professional thinking.

They give as examples of key concepts and theories in teaching, 'subject studies' and 'learning processes'. Examples of facts and data are 'school policies' and 'teaching resources', and examples of procedures are 'lesson planning' and 'testing pupils'. They point out that personal qualities can refer to commitment or adherence to a code of practice, or to competence in interpersonal situations, or to special or exceptional personal expertise which goes beyond the minimum required. They give examples of these, in teaching, as 'ability to make sound professional judgements', 'professional integrity', 'empathy with clients', 'creativity/imaginative responses to clients', and 'self-evaluation'. Cognitive processes include 'the ability to analyse problems and situations, assess clients' needs appropriately and to discuss and evaluate alternative practices', as well as 'reflection on professional practices and values' (Eraut and Cole 1993).

Eraut and Cole make little reference to questions of power and control, arguably a major issue in competence-based learning, presumably because they are dealing with professionals, i.e. NVQ levels 4 and 5, whom they assume already exercise critical autonomy in the making of judgements and decisions in the interests of their clients. Two questions arise then: first, is the learner-trainee at NVQ levels 1 and 2, in order to develop the ability to take responsibility, to have initiative, to think for him/herself, to analyse, to be creative and so on, to be or not to be provided with the opportunity and support to exercise and to develop critical autonomy in the effort to acquire NVQs? Second, is critical autonomy to be exercised in the interest of the individual worker as private consumer or in the interests of the person as citizen?

What d'Iribarne also recognizes is that the workers' exercise of these abilities, as well as the exercise of their technical skills, is intimately related to 'their value system'. What he is hinting at, and what needs to be unravelled and given greater recognition, is that competence involves not just technical skill and theoretical understanding, it also involves other personal qualities, such as critical autonomy. It might be noted too that personal qualities, as Wellington (1993) revealed, which are 'sought in graduates are also required of non-graduate recruits.' He did point out that this:

> should not be seen, however, as implying that the two groups are interchangeable. There is strong evidence to show that employers recruit people from certain segments or strata of educational achievement. Personal qualities will be important within these strata but will not enable them to rise from one stratum to another.

This is rather too easy a claim, however, since it is likely that the qualities that employers report that they need are involved in actually working towards and gaining qualifications as well as in the gaining of employment. This consideration in turn raises questions over the social context in which these skills, understandings and qualities are to be developed. Elliott (1991) argues that definitions of competence (and hence of the criteria and the means to assess competencies) based on a science of management 'conceived as a production process', which atomize competence into discrete abilities, which refer to 'concrete tangible and measurable phenomena', and which are 'viewed as unchanging rather than culturally and socially relative' will reduce and limit the learner's autonomy and will create a passive citizenry. This is because such definitions render learners and workers subject to greater 'managerial control over their performance' (Elliott 1991). Wellington (1993), in pointing to the emergence of 'the biddable curriculum' and the growth of 'the contract culture', noted how the language of social justice has been replaced by the language of producers and consumers. More specifically he made the claim that: 'Autonomy has been replaced by accountability in the space of a decade.' If, as he claims, employers are more concerned with motivation, awareness, the ability to learn and co-operative working, trainability in other words, the question may then fairly be asked: which way is competence and its development to turn? Should it for example exclude, as it currently does, an ethical dimension at NVQ levels 1 and 2?

The MENYU Project

The MENYU Project took a particular perspective on competence development, one which was more aligned with the personal qualities than the job requirements approach. Something more of how it worked out its position is presented in the following section: the starting point, using the action research process, was to examine what the needs of the young unemployed were and then to develop training strategies that would enable them to develop their competencies in a manner which took account of their needs. It was assumed that existing employer-based definitions of their needs, and the common-sense view that their greatest need was for a job, served to pre-empt rather than to encourage any further consideration of their other real and important needs. It was not assumed that the young people themselves would find it easy to define these other needs since they may have had few opportunities to consider them. So ways of identifying these needs had to be constructed.

The view of the project was that even if it is possible to some extent to describe competencies and needs in performance terms, there arises another question: if competencies can be externally determined (by jobs, by employers, by courses and programmes of work-based training), are there any internal needs/competencies, personal qualities, which also 'need' to be addressed? If a competence or skill is definable in observable performance, what does it 'look' like from the inside, from the perspective of the performer? For instance, do skill application and improvement include processes such as self-assessment, self-development, self-fulfilment? If at the craft level, never mind beyond it, care, attention and judgement are to be exercised, then the inner side of competence, the personal, needs to be recognized and respected. Respect for the person is not something that has been heard much of in the competence debate; perhaps the time has come to give it some attention. Clearly this is a controversial and complex area in the sense that people will disagree as to what it means to be a person/worker, and whether in fact the question needs to be addressed at all! Would many employers see it as part of their responsibility to address the personal agency needs of their employees? Whether they do or not, it is the case that those engaged in vocational education and training ought to, since it is generally regarded that developing personal agency is part of what it means to be pursuing a vocation.

As Coffey (1989) argued, a vocation was synonymous with 'a way of living ... for which one held a special fitness', and vocational education 'would not be limited merely to the transmission of skills enabling a young person to engage in a particular paid occupation or cluster of occupations but would rather be aimed at integrating the individual as fully as possible in the whole range of adult occupations.' He warned of the dangers involved in reducing vocational education to training in a narrow range of skills and competencies as part of an uncritical response to 'manpower demand for labour'. 'Such a passive view of the function of education,' he claimed, 'would have no place for the educational purpose of acting as a change agency in the society it serves and of being unable consequently to work for adaptations of the economic system.' As vocational education has become synonymous with training in a narrow range of skills, so it seems has careers guidance become synonymous with job placement. But more of that in a moment.

In MENYU we began the focus on trainees' needs through discussion with the trainers. In what follows I shall focus primarily on three of them: Florence, Moira and Jeannie. Need as they perceived it was instrumental: trainees needed to get qualifications in order to get a job. Getting the qualifications required learning to do what the examiners (or assessors as they are called in the NVQ system) would be looking for: helping them to learn to do what was specified in the NVQ manuals was the trainers' task. When asked about what other personal needs trainees might have, after some thought, words like self-respect and confidence, but not many more, were suggested. However, even these too were construed as being instrumentally related to being able to do what was required: for example, the two trainers who helped their trainees learn job search skills (the ability to find a job advertisement, to make an enquiry, to write a letter of application or complete an application form, to be able to write a curriculum vitae, to be able to present oneself well at interview) saw confidence as a requirement of being able to sell yourself to a potential employer. Confidence and respect were not seen as part of what it might mean to be a person, a citizen, only as part of what it meant to be a worker-as-employee.

When the trainers began to interview some of their trainees, what became clear was the extent to which they had predefined their trainees' needs. Awareness of this arose from the realization of the extent to which they had interpreted what they heard their trainees say to be or not to be in accord with their own preconceptions. At the technical level, the early interviews revealed the trainers to be more or less asking their trainees to agree with their (the trainers') views. There was one exception: Florence, a Foundation Trainer (i.e. she provided training in basic literacy and numerical skills plus job search skills), was surprised at the extent to which one of her trainees, Claire, had parroted her advice on what to say in an interview. Virtually word for word, Claire had repeated Florence's advice on how to respond to particular questions she might be asked in a job interview. Seeing a video recording of this occurrence helped Florence crystallize what was for her a major concern: her trainees were too dependent on her. Prior to the video recording of the interview with Claire, Florence had noted how her trainees, who spend 12 weeks with her before going on work placement as part of their Training Plan, continually came back to her when they had placement problems, and did not go as they should have, to the work placement officers. In one sense, this was understandable: they had come to know Florence better in the 12 week programme than they did the placement officers who had only one or two short interviews and meetings with them. But in another sense, what this returning revealed to Florence was just how dependent on her they had all become. In the programme, she had told them how to do things; when problems arose after they had left her, they went to her to find out what they should do. Two of the other trainers on the project had been irritated by similar happenings. Moira, who trained lone mothers and other young unemployed women up to NVQ level II in a Child Care and Education award, was constantly annoyed by the lack of initiative her trainees showed. One of her biggest frustrations was caused by them not looking out for job opportunities and by not responding to those which she informed them of. What she ended up doing was not just sending for the relevant application forms, but also virtually filling them in for her trainees. Furthermore, when she videotaped herself holding a training session, she was surprised at how much and how often she found herself having to tell her trainees what to do and how to do it. In the first recorded session, which dealt primarily with 'lesson planning' (child care assistants prepare for and organize young infants' activities in much the same way as do primary school teachers – they have activities, which have particular purposes, which require certain material resources and which proceed through a specific sequence), Moira (who was a Montessori trained teacher) watched with amazement as she reprimanded and scolded and dictated to her trainees, all with no little good humour it may be said, in the methods of lesson planning. She began to realize that her trainees' lack of initiative might be related to her training practices as well as to their own view of themselves and to their expectations of and responses to training.

So too with Jeannie, manager and trainer in an East Belfast Job Club. Jeannie was quite clear in her own mind that her major task, besides helping her members acquire job search skills, was to match them to suitable job vacancies. This meant that each morning she would read the lists of job vacancies supplied to her and would then let anyone in her job club, whom she thought suitable or whom she thought would be interested, know of them. This meant she spent a lot of time telephoning members each morning; it also meant that she had to get to know well as many of them as she could when they first came to her. This, because of the numbers involved, was extremely difficult and she recognized that she could only get to know well a limited number of them. What, however, began to disturb her, were the number of instances in which a member, who had belatedly found out about a job opportunity which she had not informed them of, expressed disappointment to her. Her constant explanation was that she either, 'did not think it suited you', or that she 'did not think you would be interested in it.' To both, the equally consistent reply was that, 'I did', or, 'I would have been.' While all three of the trainers explained that they tried explicitly to provide a 'comfort zone', a deliberate attempt to create an ethos or a climate of acceptance or respite, Jeannie also believed that she should establish a 'friendly relationship' with her members. This, she was clear about, was to enable her to get to know them better so that she could match them with a job opportunity. What she came to realize was that by trying to do this she too was inadvertently making her trainees dependent on her.

Surprisingly this view of trainees (variously referred to as clients or members, depending on the particular context) was perfectly replicated by the NVQ view of what was expected of trainees to achieve. Level One qualifications prepare young people to be competent 'in the performance of a range of varied work activities, most of which may be routine and predictable.' At Level Two, first mention is made of work tasks which require 'some individual responsibility or autonomy.' At higher levels, this feature increases so that at Level Five, 'Very substantial personal autonomy and often significant responsibility for the work of others …' is required (NVQ 1995). What is remarkable therefore in the issues identified by the MENYU trainers whose work was coming under the NVQ rubric, was the high profile they gave to the degree of dependency which their trainees were placing on them. According to NVQ, this was to be expected and indeed respected: since all of the competencies were employment-defined it is clear that the hierarchy of the workplace, in terms of the need for and the opportunity to exercise responsibility and autonomy, was to be replicated in the vocational training and qualification system.

Similarly with regard to the careers advice they were receiving, particularly for those involved in Foundation Training programmes. The development of action plans in these preparatory programmes reflected the same kinds of careers guidance practices which had been instrumental in directing them onto the foundation programme in the first place and from it onto a work placement where the NVQ qualifications were to be gained. A straightforward matching process, between individual personality traits, interests and aptitudes on the one hand, and training/work opportunities on the other, was the form the guidance took. This practice, as Hodkinson and Sparkes (1997) explained, is underpinned by an 'implicit assumption of free will and rational action.' This they argue is based on the notion that making career choice 'is a simple, technically rational process, where (young) people assess their own abilities and interests, evaluate the range of opportunities which are available to them and then make a choice which matches ability to opportunity.' This view of making career choices is, they argue, inadequate in explaining the evidence they had of how young people actually made career choices. This process could be better understood through the concept they called 'careership'. Careership comprises of three interrelated aspects: 'pragmatically rational decision making, choices as interactions with a field, and choices within a life course consisting of interlinked routines and turning points.' One important difference between the matching and the careership models is that in the former the self-contained individual does not have to think: at all. This is because matching, as a cerebral process, simply means fitting together pieces of information (about aptitudes and qualifications and job opportunities for example) rather like fitting together pieces of a jig-saw. As with the jig-saw where the young people are not the designers (Schostak 1993) of the pictures, so with their career choices – all they have to do is match the pieces of information together and the decision will be made for them. With the introduction of computer programs to complete this task, the educational features of careers guidance are further reduced.

Here then were clashes, in regard to democratic values, relationships and practice, not just between vocational education and vocational training, but between education and training on the one hand, and between careers guidance and the structure of the workplace on the other. It seems that up to Level 2 NVQ, and that includes foundation training and prevocational personal development, little value is to be placed on, nor much attention given to, developing the capacity of young people to 'think for themselves: to deliberate, judge and choose on the basis of their own rational reflections' (Carr 1995). That is, the very basis of the liberal democratic view of preparation for living in a democracy was being excluded for those taking pre- and levels one and two NVQs.

Competence and work

Carr (1993) reminds us that work activities can be usefully distinguished into those which are purely instrumental to the production of things and those which are 'informed and directed by those values, principles and standards of excellence intrinsic to the activity and constitutive of good workmanship.' It is through these that 'people express themselves and their human identity and give meaning to their lives.' He also reminds us that: 'the language of the new vocationalism is not neutral: to accept and employ its vocabulary is already to express an allegiance to a particular conception of education, a particular view of society and a particular understanding of the relationship between the two.' Furthermore he points out that, in the process of responding to social needs, 'the dominance of any specific educational discourse reflects the success of some social or political group in persuading or coercing others to interpret and respond to those needs in a particular way.' For example, 'flexibility' is a cornerstone of the vocabulary used to describe the image of the new worker. Whether it has come to totally replace or incorporate its preceding cousin, 'enterprise', or not, what is likely is that it will similarly carry as many different meanings as did its predecessor. Wellington (1993) pointed out that enterprise could, on the one hand, refer to personal qualities such as, 'displaying initiative, making decisions, displaying drive and determination, and influencing others … risk-taking, flexibility, problem-solving, leadership and hard work,' that is, as Watts (1993) put it, 'encouraging people to be creative, in control of their own lives.' On the other hand it could refer to either activities – mini-enterprises – or to an economic system or culture (MacLure and Stronach 1993). The NVQ version of flexibility rests on the need to have transparent, universal and occupationally defined qualifications which follow a standardized progression route offering credit accumulation and transfer. It is attended by a panoply of words which are offered as both the aims of and a justification for, the new framework. Increasing flexibility, the view is, will provide skilled workers with transferable skills and is thus 'a way of raising people's aspirations and expectations in terms of what they can actually do' (Watts 1993). Alternatively, and this appears to be the previous Conservative government's view, it may mean equipping workers with portable skills, able to meet industry's needs wherever they might arise – so that they will be able to get on their bikes and get the jobs. This view, with its underpinning competitive individualist values, is flawed because of its narrow and vapid stipulation. To be flexible according to this account is to resemble a Ferguson tractor, which when tooled up with the particular items of equipment required, can perform most tasks on the farm. In this metaphor, the tractor (worker) provides the necessary power house (ability) to reliably and competently drive the specialist tools (skills) required to do the job in the variety of conditions which are presented (tasks). Each time a familiar or routine task is presented the particular tool is hitched up: in this way the worker is provided (trained in) with a tool-box of skills, all she/he has to do is to pick out the right one and use, i.e. apply, it. In this account of work there is no need for intelligence because work has been transformed into labour which, as Carr (1993) points out, 'is devoid of any intrinsic value with which the labourer can identify. Thus distinctive of labour is the absence of those standards of workmanship to which the labourer can aspire and of any concern for the quality of the finished product to which he or she can relate.'

When work is transformed into labour, when workers are neither expected to take responsibility nor to exercise autonomy, competence becomes 'the embodiment of a mechanistic, technically oriented way of thinking which is normally inappropriate to the description of human action, or to the facilitation of the training of human beings' (Ashworth and Saxton 1990). Grundy (1992) explains that this occurs because of the current dominance of positivistic thinking which attempts 'to develop more technically efficient and predictable decision-making systems which will decrease unpredictability and uncertainty and guarantee the desired outcomes.' If this was the Fordist view of work on the assembly line, then it seems that in contemporary, supposedly post-Fordist times, it has been successfully, if inadvertently, carried into the NVQ framework of vocational awards. What is deemed to be given therefore is a 'ready-made fixed self with given wants and predispositions' (Carr 1995). An alternative and preferable view to this highly deterministic and restricted view of the person, one which gives recognition and attention to fostering 'the open-ended formation of the human subject' (Carr 1995), is possible. This is a difficult notion but the experience of the MENYU trainers confirms both the validity of the claim and what is one possible version of it. To appreciate something of what is at stake between these two views invites further consideration of the nature and the value of work itself.

Recently Handy (1994) raised the contrast between two views of work: under capitalism, 'Business will look to the self development of their people only to enhance the business ability to make profits ... In all the organisation of a capitalist society, the individual is, in strict theory, the instrument not the purpose.' On the other hand is the view that all work is a vocation: 'that is the wealth creation of business is as worth doing and as valuable as the health creation of a hospital. We can and should, that argument goes, get our fulfillment out of work.'

This question is as pertinent today as it has ever been. If work is regarded as a means to some other end, and not as being 'a constitutive element of self-consciousness and development' (Maddock 1995), then the worker (and the trainee worker) will also be regarded, and will become, an instrument to some, or someone's, other purpose. One consequence will be that the way in which competence and the other qualities of workers are defined will reflect this view. For example, if economic competitiveness, as is presently claimed, depends on workers' flexibility, those abilities involved in dealing creatively and co-operatively with differing problematic tasks, then tooling up workers as the NVQ approach to work preparation adopts will be inadequate.

Cohen (1990) penetratingly argues that the words 'flexible' and 'flexibility' are in fact code-names for a much more insidious and disempowering intention, namely undermining 'the residual forms of control exercised by conventionally skilled workers by increasing the elasticities of substitution between different occupational categories.' This 'hidden agenda', he argues:

is to complete the disintegration of the apprentice-inheritance model and to strengthen all those forms of working-class individualism which can be articulated within the enterprise culture. This manoeuvre pivots on a redefinition of the functions and meaning of skill. First, skills are dissociated from specific practices of manual labour, or from general forms of mental co-ordination exercised by workers over the immediate labour process. Secondly, skills are divorced from their historical association with particular trades or occupational cultures ... Instead work practices are reclassified into 'occupational training families' defined according to a set of purely functional properties of co-ordination between atomised operations of mind-body-machine interfacing with the same 'information environment.' In this discourse skills have become abstract universal properties of the labour process ... training in transferable skills is essentially training for what Marx called abstract labour – that is labour considered in its generic commodity form as an interchangeable unit/factor of production. What transferable skilling corresponds to in reality is the process of deskilling set in motion by information technologies ...

Such a view seems well grounded given the repeated claim that competence acquisition under the NVQ rubric is 'independent of any course or programme of learning' (Jessup 1991). Something more is needed then than this acquiring of generalized skills and competencies in a mechanical way. And this is so because flexibility has at least two further sides to it each of which reflect the contrasting views of work and what it means to be a worker. On the one side there will be a context which requires flexible responses to be created. On the other, there will be workers who are flexible and who are willing and capable of exercising it. For these conditions to interact would seem to require that further considerations had been attended to.

First, on the context side, for flexibility to be needed implies that work tasks will increasingly cease to be routine and uniform. Given the growing emphasis on meeting individual customer demands, and on being able to tailor products to specialized market niches, this would seem to be becoming a more prominent feature of the workplace. It may also be the case that the newer the technology and the more tailored and more specialist goods and services become, the greater will be the need for effective teams, and not just individuals. The more difficult it becomes to prespecify what is required, the more participative will decision making become. These changes will require greater co-operation, better negotiating abilities and greater openness and creativity in the workplace. These in turn will need to be sought after and supported by employers and managers. What then additionally would be needed in the workplace are the conditions which would enable workers to respond to these challenges: they would need to find that they were valued, in ethical and not just in monetary terms. Personal affirmation would involve being listened to and being offered recognition, trust and respect. In other words, caring for the welfare of the workers, providing opportunities for active participation in designing the workplace, and removing the debilitating sense of their positions being precarious, would replace the current competitive and individualist emphasis in the workplace.

From the worker's side, flexibility requires an ability and willingness to be open and responsive to new challenges. Intellectual and emotional capacities are going to be required in addition to the ability to provide skilled performances. Grasping the nature of consumers' needs and responding actively to these, seeing new possibilities, creating new products, new ways of providing a service, requires cognitive flexibility, commitment, initiative and other personal qualities. Being willing to explore possibilities requires a willingness to extend one's horizons, a willingness in other words to experiment, to learn. These activities require the exercise of intelligence, including the ability to self-monitor and to modify one's practices in the light of subsequent consequences. Being willing to engage in these essentially risky activities requires a supportive context, where penalty and loss will be minimized, where a sense of personal security, of personal worth, self-esteem and respect, will be present. From both sides of flexibility then, different concepts of work and of careers guidance to the Fordist ones are needed.

To begin with, Gibson (1983) reminds us that: 'Work is all sorts of things: a livelihood, a source of job satisfaction, a way of passing the time, the interface for a variety of relationships.' McIntyre (1981) reveals that any practice, such as work, is a 'social practice' and as such is a:

> coherent and complex form of socially established co-operative human activity through which goods internal to that form of activity are realised in the course of trying to achieve those standards of excellence which are appropriate to, and partially definitive of that form of activity, with the result that human powers to achieve excellence, and human conceptions of the ends and goods involved are systematically extended.

This non-instrumental, social, and co-operative view of work is extended by Bowles and Gintis (1986) who explain how it helps build and develop personal identity and character:

> Individuals identify with others because others are integral to their individuality, and they act with others not only to get but to become. The key to collective action ... lies in the observation that ends are not pregiven and hence that there is a constitutive aspect of social interaction. In other words, individuals enter into practices with others not only to achieve common goals, but also to determine who they are and who they shall become as social beings ... To be brave is to act bravely. To be charitable is to act charitably ... These acts are not merely instrumental to the achievement of given ends, they register and create character. Action expresses identity and influences personal development, but action also is identity and is personal development. The motivation for participation in practices, despite the fact that instrumental rationality and the dominant values of the game militate against such behaviour is rooted in the constitutive character of action.

This self-defining, self-realizing, self-developing nature of action within a practice again means that work is more than 'the aggregation of simple technical skill domains' (Elliott 1991); it is more than improving specific, technical skills. It also involves 'having regard for the ends and the values which define the practice, and developing those powers which are necessary if they are to be realised' (Elliott 1991). The values and goals to which particular practices aspire also specify qualities and powers to be realized in the activities of the practice itself, and not just in their observable outcomes.

On the other hand in regard to careers guidance, Collin and Watts (1996) argued that, in a post-Fordist, post-modern context where globalization of the economy is being forged through the growth of new technologies, 'careers' guidance will need to be reconstructed into 'career' guidance. This reconceptualization is needed because of the break-up of the traditional concept of career. The concept of career originated, they claim, in the spread of industrialization and the growth of the industrial society where work became concentrated in large organizations. These 'opened up new and varied employment possibilities and, for some, a choice of occupation and opportunities for progression ... within a hierarchical organisation.' This progression came to be viewed as a career and hence careers guidance came to be associated with helping individuals 'choose between careers'. However, as 'the basic forms of the industrial age [become] radically transformed' so too will the present form of careers guidance, which 'allows the individual's characteristics to be objectivised, categorised ... measured, and then fitted to appropriate jobs within the organisation.' The growth in numbers of those employed in small companies, of part-time workers, and of those who are self-employed, together with the structural changes in the conditions of those employed in large organizations (downsized, delayered and outsourced), 'robs the individual of an observable pathway in which to invest, an awareness of the steps to be taken and the appropriate timetables for them.' As work becomes 'more task-focused, with individuals moving between a series of temporary projects ... [based on] a short term transactional contract,' then individuals 'have to depend much more on their own reflexivity as a means of identifying self-identity.' This will entail 'a radical shift from an "objectivist" view of the personality as a stable entity composed of traits and variables, to a constructionist view of self as story,' and will, crucially, require that the concept of career 'be reconstrued as the individual's development in learning and work throughout life.' So reconceived, career guidance would attend to the 'skills of career self-management ... self-awareness, self-promotion, exploring and creating opportunities, action planning, networking, matching and decision making, negotiation and political awareness, coping with uncertainty, development focus, transfer skills, and self-confidence.' Also, they argue, it would attend to 'helping individuals to develop their subjective career narrative ... helping them to "authorise" their careers by narrating a coherent, continuous and credible story, helping them to invest their career narrative with meaning by identifying themes and tensions in the story line, and learning the skills needed to perform the next episode in the story.'

These considerations raise the question of what it might mean to talk of the personal agency (the power to be and become, to choose and decide) of each trainee (and trainer?): are employees responsible just for doing what they are told to do; do they have rights/needs to decide or to contribute to the deliberations on what ought to be done? Agency raises consideration of the extent and manner in which individuals shape or are shaped by the 'structures' (the traditions, the organizations, the culture) in which they live and work. As Giddens (1984) claims: 'social structures are both constituted by human agency and at the same time are the very medium of this structuration.' What this orientates us to is the idea that social structures (schools, training organizations, government departments and agencies, work practices, etc.) are the outcome of actions and decisions taken by people and for and on behalf of people, which in turn provide the means and the influences whereby people come to be who they are and come to aspire to who they want to be. In other words, we and the organizations in which we live and work both reflect each other and set limits and offer opportunities as to who and what we are and can become. At the core of the theory of structuration is the idea that people are not passive beings: they may agree to believe in certain things, act in particular ways, accept sets of rules, but in so doing they are acting, shaping themselves and others, and not receiving passively, like a piece of clay, the influences and forces exerted upon them. So in asking the question about the meaning and value of work, we are asking: is it simply a 'means' of getting money to do other things with, and/or has it an importance in and of itself? If work is not to be understood solely in instrumental terms, but is to include intrinsic dimensions such as fulfilling personal needs (affirmation, development, friendship, realization and so on), and nurturing social values (citizenship, democracy, care, etc.), then a programme of training based on work tasks needs to attend to these other dimensions. A neo-Taylorist job analysis will continue to be an inadequate basis on which to provide for anyone's needs, including employers' as well as employees'.

Competence and democracy

The instrumental view of work signals a curtailment in what it means to be a worker and how work itself is to be understood. This in turn signals a potentially non-democratic pressure in vocational training and an abbreviation of citizen to employee: as such it represents, as Carr (1995) puts it, a major break with the Enlightenment Project which was 'in key part, an educational task to develop in all people the universal power of reason and thereby empower them to create a form of social life that would satisfy their aspirations and needs ... through education, individuals may become emancipated from the dictates of ignorance and superstition and so become rationally empowered to transform themselves and the social world in which they live.' Carr's point that rational autonomy can only be pursued in a society that has institutionalized the principles of rational justification and that such a society invariably seeks to be a democratic one, that is one which 'is governed by rational principles and which promotes the freedom of all individuals to exercise their powers of rational thought', highlights serious shortcomings in the lower levels of NVQ. (In Watts' recount of his meeting with government ministers who 'tried to control the debate', there is also revealed how those in power will inevitably use that power to secure attention to their agenda.) That these levels claim to reflect the workplace reveals firstly a contradiction between what competencies NVQ requires and what competencies employers say they need. One source, as a typical example, reports employers saying that they need employees who are reliable, trustworthy, and responsible (Field 1995), qualities which NVQ levels 1 and 2 rarely attend to. Wellington (1993) in any case reminds us that employers' definitions of their needs are often dysfunctional, confused and irrelevant.

Richardson (1993) summarized employers' views rather more bluntly: 'analysis of what employers say they want ... reveals a picture of incoherence, reinforced by a lack of knowledge and understanding.' But there is even more to it than that. If there is revealed a contradiction between what employers say they need and what they actually want, if they say that they need employees with these abilities but in reality they just want workers to be able and agreeable enough to simply do what they are told (Cohen's (1990) view of what flexibility really means), there is revealed a passive capitulative non-democratic image of the worker. This image reflects and reveals some of the limitations contained in the hidden agenda of the former Conservative government's ideological commitment to market values. Those on or below the bottom rungs of the economic ladder, i.e. those aspiring to NVQ levels 1 and 2, are not to enjoy the freedoms and benefits enjoyed by those richer and more powerful above them. Their identity is to mirror that of the slave (the tractor), rather than that of the citizen. Individual freedom is to be the prerogative of the few and is not to be seen as 'conducive to the growth of their intellectual potential and to the evolution of a more desirable form of social life' (Carr 1995). Carr (1995) reminds us that it was John Dewey who articulated the view that the growth of individuals and of society is a dynamic, transformational and dialectical process. For Dewey, democracy was neither dependent on maintaining individual rights nor was it a particular form of political structure: rather it was 'an experiment in "cooperation" and is justified only by a faith in the ability of ordinary men and women collectively to build and rebuild their communities in ways which will progressively increase and extend the opportunities for them to realise their freedom' (Carr 1995). Training methods and work tasks and situations which encourage obedience and self-interest and which use authoritarian methods such as direct instruction and the inculcation of fixed beliefs are therefore anti-democratic and non-educational. Field (1995) points out that this simply represents a modern version of what he called 'the pedagogy of labour ... the concept and practice of using work in itself as a didactic instrument', and he suggests that the NVQ framework has been developed not so much because of demand from employers, but more 'from the ideas and aspirations of a small coalition of modernising civil servants and highly-placed training professionals.' It is their views and their interpretations of employers' views which have structured the NVQ framework. At core, the definition of competence at NVQ levels 1 and 2 rests on a definition of work as labour. This in turn reflects a political economy where 'consumption is the greatest good and the ever-expanding production of commodities is an overriding political aim.' In this society 'the distinction between work and labour inevitably appears obsolete and the conception of work as a distinctively human and humanising activity becomes fragmented and begins to disappear' (Carr 1993).

This eventuality clearly denies the democratic impulse and, through its implicit concern with replicating the social hierarchy of the workplace, imposes a very restricted identity on young workers who aspire to climb the vocational qualification ladder. The NVQ documents are very explicit about this restriction and the experience of these MENYU trainers reveals it to be the case in practice. In other words, the NVQ aspiration of upgrading the skills of workers in the United Kingdom in order to make UK plc more economically competitive in world markets is in danger of shooting itself in the foot.

Competence and need revisited

What these considerations give rise to is the question of whether trainees' needs extend beyond job-defined, employer-prespecified, observable skills, to include personal and ethical needs/competencies/ qualities such as self-awareness, -respect, -determination, -control, -esteem, and others such as critical understanding, affirmation, responsibility, challenge, and independence. What for instance is inferred when it is claimed that some trainees need their confidence or their motivation levels increased? What is often inferred is that training ought to stimulate them to higher levels of motivation or confidence. Might it not be, however, that they want to become someone other than who they see themselves to be at the moment? If so they hardly need stimulation: what they need is opportunity, challenge and support. Also, it might be claimed that what one person needs another does not: or that everyone's needs change in priority due to the particular circumstances they find themselves in, or to the particular stage they have reached in their career or episode in their life. Given the likelihood that all of these are strong possibilities, is it improbable that a fixed list of personal needs can be predetermined, or if it could what its value would be?

It seems that what is required is the identification of some needs which are deemed essentially inherent to the idea of what it means to be a person and a citizen. Saying this, however, does not settle the question of who should decide on trainee needs. It seems that at present in the NVQ framework there is little room given to trainees to identify their own needs (the main assumption being that others, such as employers, know better than they what these are). At this point it is useful to recall that one of the key ideas behind the notion of 'open learning', one of the criteria the MENYU project proposal had to meet, is that a course is 'attuned to the needs and concerns of its users' (Tuckett 1988). Tuckett argues that this essentially requires that a curriculum is negotiated with its participants: he suggests that trainers need to examine 'how students' experiences, hopes, concerns can shape course design and how their voices can be heard in policy planning' (Tuckett 1988). This recognition of the value of identifying trainees' needs with rather than for them underpinned the aims of the MENYU project. The research approach emphasized encouraging their reflective participation in defining their needs while rejecting a unidimensional view of what these needs might be. What the trainers initially recognized was that their trainees needed to build their self-esteem and self-respect.

The MENYU experience

It was these personal qualities, encapsulated in the word confidence, which the MENYU trainers found underdeveloped in their trainees, and it was these which they hypothesized were contributing to the dependency the trainees brought to the training situation and placed on them: there is no point in thinking for yourself if you are neither given the support nor the opportunity to, nor are you listened to even when you do. It was making the connection between lack of confidence and dependency which set them on the road to finding practical ways of building competency and independence and thereby meeting the personal needs of their trainees. This they came to do in a variety of ways – all of which were discerned through a reflective process of trial and error which involved risk-taking by the trainers themselves. After going up some dead-ends, which helped clarify the route to be taken, Florence realized that by discussing with her trainees their previous experience of engaging in the tasks required by her Foundation Course, they developed self-respect and a better knowledge of themselves: with this enhanced self-awareness they became able to contribute to and to successfully complete the tasks she set. She attributed their gaining of independence, and ultimately her recognition that vocational training was based essentially on relationships of interdependency, to her giving space to her trainees to set their own agenda alongside hers and to discursively consider both. Moira eventually came to realize that for her child care trainees, learning the concepts and theories and practices of child care was greatly enhanced by her simultaneously inviting them to articulate their own views and to choose which particular defined competence they wished to observe, discuss and practise. These approaches provided opportunities for self-reflection and critical discussion of the specified competencies. They also allowed and supported her trainees in making personal connections between their own experience and abilities and what the NVQ prescriptions required. In this way, they became more critically self-reliant and better able to use their own initiative and judgement rather than depending on her to always be telling them what to do. Similarly Jeannie came to appreciate that instead of her trying to prepare and match her trainees to job vacancies, her task was to provide opportunities and support in enabling them to search out and apply for possible jobs for themselves. She began to learn how to orient her individual interviews and her group training sessions towards helping her trainees get to know themselves better. Establishing friendly relations she came to see as being properly directed to this task rather than solely to help her get to know them better in order to match them to vacancies. Self-knowledge in all cases came to be associated with self-evaluation, which in turn engendered self-awareness. As the trainees became more self-aware, of what they could do, of who they were, of what their interests were, of where they were coming from, they became able to better articulate what kind of a job or career they wanted. Self-awareness then contributed to clearer self-direction, more self-control and the possibility of greater self-determination and self-realization. What the members of the MENYU project had begun to construct was an integrative and holistic view of personal effectiveness. And what they began to reveal, as much to themselves as anybody else, was something of the ethical nature of relationships and actions in a training situation: being responsive to and taking others' experience and points of view into account is more than a technical concern – it involves paying respect to others.

Martin, one of Florence's last cohort of trainees while she was a member of the MENYU Project, confirmed something of the growth and development she had made. He came, in his own words, to her programme, 'shy', 'not able to talk to anyone', 'not sure of what I wanted to do', frightened of interviews and believing he made a 'real mess' of them. When nervous, he stuttered and stammered. By the end of the twelve-week programme, he claimed he felt 'more confident', 'more able to talk to anybody', had 'a definite career in mind', and, importantly, was 'able to think for myself.' He attributed this to the way Florence 'listened to you, it was not like at school, she made you think for yourself.' Martin volunteered to appear on one of the MENYU video programmes which was to be incorporated into a multimedia interactive package.

Two further anecdotes are pertinent here: firstly that of Geraldine, another trainer. Geraldine was both an NVQ trainer in keyboarding skills and a manager of an Action for Community Employment (ACE) scheme at the time that NVQs began to be trialled in these programmes. She was responsible for operationalizing the assessment of unemployed people on her scheme. As part of her action research she interviewed one ACE member, Sean, an experienced 42-year-old painter and decorator who had begun to submit himself for NVQ assessment. His experience was revealing: he told Geraldine that he felt he was being demeaned by the tasks NVQ set him – he was to take a Level Two assessment. As a mature experienced painter and decorator, he was being asked, for example, to show his ability to apply different kinds of paint and his ability to clean brushes, on three different occasions. He could already do these things with his eyes shut. He refused eventually to continue with NVQ assessment.

Moira had a similar experience with a young 20-year-old woman whom she regarded as one of the best trainees she had met in her child care course. This young woman, Susan, refused to pursue the available NVQ child care qualification, preferring to opt for the 'traditional' course and certificate in child care. This was because she had had prior experience of NVQ and had found it 'boring' and 'routine'. It might not be going too far to suggest that she found that an NVQ did not meet her needs for the reasons which Hartley (1991) suggested:

the government's rhetoric of purporting to meet the needs of individual pupils and teachers covers a deeper intention to justify greater central control of education on behalf of the proponents of economic liberalism. What purported to be a well-intentioned purpose to identify the needs of the individual ends up being a device by the government to ensure its own needs are met by individual teachers and pupils. Put another way: a declared democratic purpose (meeting the needs of the individual) will produce less democracy and more bureaucratic government control.

However, Richardson (1993) even casts doubt on the efficacy of such a move. He reported that: 'considerable doubts remain as to whether the national vocational qualifications structure will serve to increase skills demand; indeed, the likelihood is that the new system will certificate existing and historical skills needs in employment which by international standards have been, and remain, sub-standard.'

Carr (1993) makes the point that vocational education: 'should always incorporate opportunities for reflectively understanding and critically examining the cultural norms and values of the world of work.' When it is reduced to vocational training, it provides merely 'the knowledge and skills required for successful market participation.' Elsey (1993) extends this critique and likewise, in looking to the voluntary sector, offers a better alternative. He describes the essence of voluntarism as that of giving. 'At its most highly motivated,' he claims, 'the commitment is to giving to others in need as a moral and social responsibility, from the better to the least best placed as a social and community service.' Elsey went on to say that he believed that this giving was also 'to assist in the building and maintenance of supportive networks at local level and to foster integrative communities.' In this sense it is one of the key meanings of civil society where 'the individual [pursues] self-interests in a context of self-regulation underpinned by a collective morality ... the essence of the civil society lies in the value of social relations, founded on the free pursuit of personal and cultural interests and organised on a voluntary basis, located somewhere between the structures of the family and kinship, the market economy and the state, and serving as another dimension of social life with its own norms and values.'

Elsey warns us not to overplay some of these ideas but he does insist that, contrary to what actual positions and relationships may presently pertain, these ideas pick out a third and complementary way (civil society, state, free market economy) to maintain and develop the construction of society. Essentially he does reveal how other values than those of the market are essential to human activity and social relations. Handy (1994) goes further than Elsey and suggests that, rather than constituting a third alternative or additional dimension, voluntary organizations provide both an ethical and a practical model for manufacturing and commercial business. Their virtues, he claims are that they:

> are owned by no one. They have constitutions, members, boards of trustees as well as boards of management, sources of finance rather than shareholders and their purpose is their meaning. They are not properties, they cannot be bought or sold, although they can join forces, merge and make alliances. They have, in their doughnut, a core of professionals and beyond it, a space full of helpers.

Might not voluntary work also be the essence of what is meant by professional service, of manufacturing work itself, and might not the idea of being a volunteer, of being a voluntary organization, identify some of the desirable characteristics of people and organizations providing vocational education and training and career guidance?

Summary and conclusion

As presently conceived and structured, the lower levels of NVQ, their patterns of training and their associated careers guidance programmes prepare people for a life of dependence and powerlessness. Far from contributing to the strengthening of the democratic values of fairness, justice and equality, they deny them and replace them with benign exploitation, servitude and coercion. To retrieve the situation requires a reconceptualization of the nature of competence, of training, of work and of civil society. Work defined in terms of its intrinsic values predisposes the worker as actively contributing to, and participating in, the reconstruction and development of the social organizations and social mores in which s/he lives. The virtues which constitute civil society are constitutive of the workplace: their realization requires changes in structures and in practices. The MENYU project revealed the possibilities for such reconceptualization and practical reconstruction within the present vocational training format: it also revealed its debilitating limitations.

References

Ashworth, P.D. and Saxton, J.(1990) 'On Competence.' *Journal of Further and Higher Education 14*, 2.

Bowles, S. and Gintis, H. (1986) *Democracy and Capitalism*. London: Routledge and Kegan Paul.

Carr, W. (1993) 'Education and the world of work: clarifying the contemporary debate.' In J. Wellington *et al.* (eds) *The Work Related Curriculum: Challenging the Vocational Imperative*. London: Kogan Page.

Carr, W. (1995) 'Education and democracy: confronting the postmodernist challenge.' *Journal of Philosophy of Education 29*, 1.

Coffey, D. (1989) 'Vocational education: the way forward.' *British Journal of Educational Studies xxxvii*, 4, 358–368.

Cohen, P. (1990) 'Teaching enterprise culture: individualism, vocationalism and the New Right.' In I. Taylor (ed) *The Social Effects of Free Market Policies*. London: Harvester Wheatsheaf.

Collin, A. and Watts, A.G. (1996) 'The death and transfiguration of career – and of career guidance.' *British Journal of Guidance and Counselling 24*, 3, pp.385–398.

Crowther Report (1959) *15–18: A Report of the Central Advisory Council for Education*. London: HMSO.

d'Iribarne, A. (1987) 'New training and new skills in new factories.' *Vocational Training vol.1*, pp.7–12.

DOE (1988) *Employment for the 1990s*. London: HMSO.

Elliott, J. (1991) *Action Research for Educational Change*. Milton Keynes: Open University Press.

Elsey, B. (1993) 'Voluntarism and adult education as civil society and the "third way" for personal empowerment and social change.' *International Journal of Lifelong Education 12*, 1.

Eraut, M. and Cole, G. (1993) *Assessing Competence in the Professions*. London: Department of Employment.

Field, J. (1995) 'Reality testing in the workplace: are NVQs employment led?' In P. Hodkinson and M. Issitt (eds) *The Challenge of Competence: Professionalism Through Vocational Education and Training*. London: Cassell.

Gibson, T. (1983) 'Simulating production units in schools.' In J. Wellington *et al.* (eds) (1993) *The Work Related Curriculum: Challenging the Vocational Imperative*. London: Kogan Page.

Giddens, A. (1984) *The Constitution of Society*. Cambridge: Polity Press.

Grundy, S. (1992) 'Beyond guaranteed outcomes: creating a discourse for educational praxis.' *Australian Journal of Education 36*, 2.

Handy, C. (1994) *The Empty Raincoat.* London: Hutchinson.

Hartley, D. (1991) 'Beyond competency: a sociotechnical approach to continuing professional education.' *British Journal of In-Service Education 16*, No.1.

Hodkinson, P. and Sparkes, A.C. (1997) 'Careership: a sociological theory of career decision making.' *British Journal of Sociology of Education 18*, 29, 29–44.

Hyland, T. (1993) 'Competence, knowledge and education.' *Journal of Philosophy of Education 27*, 1.

Jessup, G. (1991) *Outcomes: NVQs and the Emerging Model of Education and Training.* London: The Falmer Press.

MacLure, M. and Stronach, I. (1993) 'Great accidents in history: vocationalist innovations, the National Curriculum and pupil identity.' In J. Wellington *et al.* (eds) *The Work Related Curriculum: Challenging the Vocational Imperative.* London: Kogan Page.

McIntyre, A. (1981) *After Virtue.* London: Duckworth.

Maddock, T.H. (1995) 'Science, critique and administration: the debate between the critical theorists and the materialist pragmatists.' *Educational Management and Administration 23*, 1.

National Council for Vocational Qualifications (winter 1995) *NVQ Monitor, 16.*

NICC (1994) *A Vocational Dimension in the Curriculum at Key Stage 4.* Belfast: Northern Ireland Curriculum Council.

Richardson, W. (1993) 'The changing nature of work.' In J. Wellington *et al.* (eds) *The Work Related Curriculum: Challenging the Vocational Imperative.* London: Kogan Page.

Schostak, J. (1993) 'Quality in education: who needs it? How to develop it.' *Journal of the Educational Research Network, Northern Ireland 7*, February.

Taubman, D. (1994) 'The GNVQ debate.' *Forum 36*, 3.

Tuckett, A. (1988) 'Open learning and the education of adults.' In N. Paine (ed) *Open Learning in Transition.* London: NCET.

Watts, T. (1993) 'Connecting curriculum to work: past patterns, current initiatives and future issues.' In J. Wellington *et al.* (eds) *The Work Related Curriculum: Challenging the Vocational Imperative.* London: Kogan Page.

Wellington, J. (ed) (1993) *The Work Related Curriculum: Challenging the Vocational Imperative.* London: Kogan Page.

Chapter 6

Ideology and Curriculum Policy under the Old and New Conservatives
GNVQ Revisited

Denis Gleeson and Phil Hodkinson

Introduction

For the first time in Britain, a large majority of young people are now staying in full-time education and training for at least one year after the end of compulsory education at 16. This significant reversal coincided with the introduction of a major new qualification – the General National Vocational Qualification (GNVQ) – by the then Conservative government. This chapter analyses the ideological rationale for and consequences of GNVQ as a means of restructuring mass education and training in England and Wales. The bulk of what follows was written in 1994 and first published in 1995 (see Gleeson and Hodkinson 1995). In writing it then, we were concerned to raise some wider issues around the context of GNVQ and the policy purposes envisaged for it. In re-presenting it for inclusion in this volume, we have left that early analysis largely untouched. It throws light on the political, social and economic contexts in which the introduction and early development of GNVQ took place, and there is now the opportunity for the reader to look back and make judgements about how accurate and/or relevant that early critique was. Towards the end of the chapter, we make our own attempt at that sort of hindsight by looking at the issues raised from our new vantage point in 1999. In doing so, we identify much of the existing analysis that still seems to ring true. Five years after the original article was written, there have been many changes relevant to GNVQ, but most of them appear to be relatively minor in their impact on the issues we raised. The Employment Department and the Department for

Education have been combined into the Department for Education and Employment (DfEE); the Dearing (1996) and Capey (1995) reviews have been completed; a new Labour government has been in power for two years and has given strong signs of its early policy development in this field (DfEE 1998), which we would characterize broadly as 'more of the same' – hence the possibly provocative title to this chapter; GNVQ has become bedded down in schools and further education (FE) colleges across Britain; and there has been a growing body of research and further analysis of the strengths and weaknesses of GNVQs in practice (Bates 1998; Edwards *et al.* 1997; FEDA 1997; Helsby, Knight and Saunders 1998; Bloomer and Hodkinson 1998). We began the original article by briefly examining the reasons why English post-16 education could not continue unchanged at the time GNVQs were introduced.

There have been numerous recent studies pointing out that English post-16 education and training lag behind equivalent systems in most other developed countries, summarized by Green and Steedman (1993). At long last, partly driven by this comparative evidence, there is now a consensus that post-16 education and training provision in England and Wales has not worked either for a majority of young leavers or in meeting the perceived need for a better workforce. Some, including the Conservative British government, see A-levels successfully facilitating HE entry, but a problem in producing a vocational qualification of similar status. A majority of academics follow Finegold *et al.* (1990) in viewing the longstanding division between high status academic courses and low status vocational courses as at the root of the problem. In apparent response the Conservative government introduced GNVQs as an attempt to solve these problems. Their hope was that GNVQs would have equivalent status to A-levels, encourage staying on and achieve reskilling, thereby bridging the academic/vocational divide (ED/DES 1991). But could GNVQ fulfil these multi-functions?

The positioning of GNVQs can only be understood through a complex combination of perspectives that are often treated separately. Here we focus on four: the ideological tensions and ambiguities within government policy and English cultural values surrounding GNVQ; the relationship between GNVQ development and the new managerialism which is currently rampant in British post-16 education; the relationship between the knowledge and content of GNVQs, the labour market and notions of upskilling the workforce; and the importance in GNVQs, as in all post-compulsory education, of addressing wider educational issues beyond current obsessions with economic rationalism.

GNVQ, ideology and tripartism

In promoting GNVQ as an 'alternative route' through post-16 education and training, the British Conservative government had boxed itself into a corner. On the one hand, rejection of the Higginson report (DES 1988), which proposed radical changes to the long-established and repeatedly criticized A-levels, legitimated continued pressure from right-wing groups for the retention of A-level essentially unchanged. On the other hand, the government remained committed to the continued development of competence-driven, essentially work-based National Vocational Qualifications (NVQs) as the central basis for its vocational training reforms. With a growing recognition that these two radically different types of qualification did not add up to an appropriate post-16 provision, GNVQ was a political solution, designed to satisfy the differential requirements of employers, labour markets and post-compulsory education itself. Failure to respond to calls for a unified system of qualifications, across the 14–19 age range, resulted in GNVQ filling the qualification gap.

The White Paper (ED/DES 1991) which first introduced GNVQ sought to establish a three-track, tripartite system for educational progression post-16: an academic full-time track based upon A-levels, a vocational full-time track based upon GNVQs, and a part-time, work-based training track based on NVQs. Part of a widespread 'common-sense' belief in tripartism is the division of people into Plato's men of gold, bronze and iron. The history of English education in the twentieth century can be seen as various ill-fated attempts to reproduce these 'natural' divisions in the educational system. Coffey (1992) shows that a tripartite hierarchy of educational provision in Britain was explicitly linked to class divisions in the late nineteenth century. There was professional education in the public schools which stressed leadership, general education for the middle class and skilled working class in grammar schools, and job-related training for the rest in the elementary schools, with an explicit reference to 'obedience'. By the twentieth century, the divide between grammar schools and public schools had narrowed, at least in curriculum terms, as the growing middle classes sought the same academic education as had developed originally for the sons of the aristocracy. Tripartism by then had become the division between academic, technical and practical. This is seen most clearly in the Norwood report of 1943, which was the precursor of the 1944 Education Act and the broad political consensus that followed it, a central part of which was the secondary tripartite system of grammar, technical and modern schools.

A belief in three clearly differentiated types of people is fundamental to one of the dominant ideological belief systems in British educational politics and especially the ruling Conservative government, which Skilbeck (1976) called 'classical humanism'. For those whose views are close to this ideal-type, such tripartism is seen as the natural order of things. There are four logically separate but commonly conflated assumptions within this tripartite 'common sense'. First, that people fall naturally (socially and genetically) into three distinct types: academic, technical and practical. Second, that these are closely correlated with 'ability' as it is generally understood. Thus the most able are naturally academic, the least able are practical and the technicians fall in the middle. The third assumption is that schooling and the curriculum should similarly be divided into different types of provision, to correspond to these different types of people and ability. The fourth assumption is that the opportunities and needs of the labour market also fall into the same neat divisions. None of these statements stands up to logical and empirical examination when taken in isolation, let alone together, but such ideological beliefs are notoriously resistant to rational challenges.

Once even a cursory examination is made of twentieth century English educational history, there is a glaring paradox. Despite the dominance of this tripartite perception, the middle strand of the three has always had a troubled and low-key existence. Until the 1960s, the focus was on three types of schooling. The 'top' and 'bottom' of the system are well known – the grammar schools that developed out of the public school tradition, and the various schools that evolved from the elementary school into the secondary modern schools of the 1950s and 1960s. There have been several attempts to develop technical high schools in the middle. Sanderson (1994) describes the growth of the Junior Technical Schools (the term 'Junior' is misleading, for they mainly recruited at 13+) and he and McCullough (1989) both describe the post-1944 secondary technical schools. Sanderson is an enthusiast, eulogizing what the schools could do, despite an often hostile environment. McCullough is more critical, suggesting that, in general, the technical schools never really established a coherent and credible vocational curriculum.

Both agree that these schools were always few in number and never catered for more than the tiniest fraction of children. In effect, the tripartite system was a myth, rhetorically labelling what was, in reality, dual provision. Following comprehensivization in the 1970s the focus largely changed from separate technical schools to technical curriculum provision. GNVQ can be seen as the latest in a long series of attempts to establish this middle, technical/higher vocational track, now seen as lying between A-levels and NVQs.

McCullough (1989) and Sanderson (1994) demonstrate the dangers of attributing simplistic explanations for the failure of technical education in Britain, and both list a range of interrelated, complex factors. We argue that part of this complexity can be explained by (i) an inevitable internal tension within classical humanist tripartism and (ii) conflicts between this widely held classical humanist ideology and other equally deeply held, though possibly less dominant, educational ideologies within English society.

The internal tensions in classical humanism arise because, in English society, very few people aspire to the technical route. For this reason, both technical schools and secondary modern schools began to ape the grammar school curriculum long before comprehensivization became the norm, whilst parents wanted their offspring to attend grammar, not technical, schools if they passed the 11+. In essence, middle class families saw anything other than grammar (or public) school as inappropriate, seeing both technical and modern schools as for the working class. In this context, the upwardly mobile working class were also more likely to aspire to the academic grammar school route than to a technical career that kept them firmly below the class equivalent of the glass ceiling.

This was reinforced by the common system of taking the young people with the best 11+ passes for the grammar schools, giving the technical high schools (where they existed) those who were left. Thus, a technician was identified not through a positive interest in or aptitude for technical studies, but simply as someone who was not judged capable of an academic career. This partly explains the lack of investment in technical schools, which were more expensive than grammar schools, for in such an élitist system, 'common sense' and the self-interest of the dominant groups suggest that most should be spent on the top level, not the middle.

Late twentieth century post-16 tripartism in England is complicated by separate institutions as well as a curriculum hierarchy. This is because of the anomalous position of sixth form colleges.

These had been originally set up within school regulations, to provide the traditional academic education based on A-levels as part of a reorganized comprehensive education system. It was often an old grammar school that was transformed into a sixth form college. The new post-16 funding arrangements abruptly moved them from the school sector in 1993, giving them independence from Local Education Authorities with funding provided by the Further Education Funding Council (FEFC). They exist alongside the predominantly vocational FE colleges, which have a very different history and ethos (Smithers and Robinson 1993). Research by Robinson and Burke (1996; see Chapter 10 by Robinson in this volume) suggests that many sixth form colleges are striving to preserve their élitist, academic ethos, based around provision of A-level to full-time 16–19-year-old students. Many will not offer more than a token GNVQ curriculum in one or two occupational areas. The risk is that if high status institutions like public schools and sixth form colleges do not take GNVQ seriously, the new middle vocational track will be squeezed every bit as effectively as were technical schools in an earlier age. Furthermore, a belief in a technical strand, for other people's children and for other educational institutions, reinforces the status and sense of well-being for those who have succeeded on the academic route. From this point of view, a middle stratum that is weak in practice but strong in rhetoric meets the status needs of the academic élite. To succeed where technical schools failed, GNVQ must break out of this ideological closed circle.

One of many other ideological conflicts relevant to GNVQ lies between classical humanism and what Skilbeck (1976) called reconstructionism. Within a reconstructionist ideology, the educational system is seen as a means of restructuring society, normally for economic ends. This can be seen in the repeated calls for more or better vocational or technical education, in order to close the skills gap between Britain and her rivals, to make industry more competitive and to ensure future prosperity. Such beliefs were almost as strong as classical humanism within the Conservative government, and are advocated by the influential Confederation of British Industry (CBI), amongst many others. Such a reconstructionist argument is frequently restated in the official rationale for GNVQ, which stresses the need to raise the standards of education and training across the board.

Such universalist views of attainment run counter to the classical humanist view that a norm-referenced, hierarchical distribution of ability and therefore of appropriate qualifications is part of the natural order of things. Talk of A-level as the gold standard has set GNVQ a difficult cultural and educational task. To succeed, at least in the terms of those government directives that brought it into existence, GNVQ must establish a credible vocational middle track whilst simultaneously raising levels of education and qualification in ways that are acceptable to the mass of the English public, be they parents, young people, teachers, employers or politicians. It is our belief that success will be more likely if the rigid three-track system is abandoned, in favour of the type of unified curriculum structure advocated by Finegold *et al.* (1990).

Quality and managerialism in the post-16 curriculum

Another key question relates to the nature of learning experiences in GNVQs and what counts as quality learning. Quality is the buzz-word of the currently dominant 'new managerialism' in British education. As attempts are made to import industrial procedures, such as Total Quality Management, into schools and colleges, there is a widespread assumption that what counts as quality in education is straightforward and unproblematic. Thus the FEFC or Office for Standards in Education (OFSTED) inspectors read mounds of documentation, watch some classes, talk to staff and ascribe a teaching quality rating to a teacher, course and institution.

What is more, the income of educational institutions is being ever more closely linked to simplified and unexamined assumptions of quality, measured through performance indicators. Two approaches to funding are currently dominant. First, income follows students, so schools and colleges are rewarded for recruiting. Marketing and the hard sell become more important than either good teaching or good student relations in determining success and defining 'quality'. To balance such distortions, proportions of funding are now being awarded only on successful course completion and student certification. In this way, 'quality' becomes synonymous with passing and the intrinsic value of the course followed becomes marginalized. From this perspective, all that matters about GNVQ is (i) how many young people can be persuaded to enrol and (ii) how many of them can achieve successful completion. While such measures might satisfy some politicians and policy makers, they deflect attention from the really important issues about educational quality within GNVQ and even undermine it (Gleeson 1992).

Yet the reality is that educational quality, far from being simple, agreed and measurable, is problematic and highly contested. Once more, Skilbeck's analysis of ideological positions helps make the point, for the nature of quality varies between each. Skilbeck (1976) identifies three conflicting ideologies, 'progressive' as well as 'reconstructionist' and 'classical humanist'. Progressivism is well known as a label, drawing on a student-centred and individually developmental view of education. For progressives, the process of learning, assessment and decision making should be shared between student and teacher, so that negotiation becomes a central concept. Progressive views of education have influenced post-16 provision in Britain in two ways. There has been a growth of student-centred approaches in many A-level subjects, with a greater emphasis on learning processes, group work, project-based course work and the like. In parallel, pre-vocational education has developed similar approaches with an explicit work preparation focus. From either progressive viewpoint, the test of educational quality is the developmental needs of the individual student.

As we have seen, reconstructionism is arguably the dominant ideology in the development of GNVQ. From this perspective, the test of quality is the value of educational provision to employers and the economy. Since Skilbeck wrote, this reconstructionist approach to education has developed a radical formulation, worthy of the separate ideological label of market forces. Numerous variations of this ideology have developed, but in the post-16 context the ideas of the CBI (1989, 1993) are dominant. They argue for individual students to become the purchasers of education and training, through the issue of a voucher. In such a market system, quality would be defined by the choices made by the purchasers, as colleges and schools are supposedly forced to improve in order to compete.

In contrast, the classical humanist position on educational quality supports high academic standards for the more able élite and better quality vocational training for the rest. This view of quality can be seen in the fight to preserve A-levels, insistence on written external examinations and the development of separate vocational and academic educational pathways. Our main point here is not to debate the relative merits of these ideological positions, but to demonstrate that the new managerialism is based on a fallacy, for there is no agreed, unproblematic notion of what educational quality is. The inevitable result is that despite the broad overall consensus about the need for change in post-16 provision, the nature, purpose and content of education remains contested and the subject of struggle.

As we have seen, one result of such conflicting pressures, in the English context, has been the repeated failure to establish a credible middle road between high status academic education and low status vocational preparation. Can GNVQ succeed where other initiatives failed? For Halsey *et al.* (1991) the danger is 'academic drift', whereby provision originally designed as vocational copies the higher status academic curriculum in order to acquire some of that status for itself. If this happens to GNVQ, driven by the ever-elusive parity of esteem with A-level, the practical and technical will remain marginalized in English and Welsh education.

There are two further problems. The current obsession with outcomes and qualification achievement means that the explicit focus on learning processes within GNVQ specifications may be lost. The worries of Smithers (1994) and others about the reliability of GNVQ assessment reinforce the marginalization of educational experience *per se*, so that measurable attainments become all important. But many of the most important aspects of (vocational) education are not directly measurable.

Also, current managerialist approaches to education risk reducing teachers to technicians, who simply 'deliver' the official curriculum to young people. This ignores the fact that:

> teachers don't merely deliver the curriculum. They develop, define it and reinterpret it too. It is what teachers think, what teachers believe and what teachers do at the level of the classroom that ultimately shapes the kind of learning that young people get. (Hargreaves 1994, p.ix)

If GNVQs are to be successful, ways must be found to reinforce and protect the professionalism of teachers rather than attempting to control their actions through ever-tighter specifications, inspections and performance-related funding.

GNVQ, upskilling and economic rationalism

In looking at the relationship between GNVQ and post-compulsory education there is also a need to consider the connection between employers, labour markets and the knowledge content of the vocational curriculum. Essentially, two competing perspectives circumscribe the English and Welsh debate: the need to provide young people with high quality education and training to improve their job prospects, and the question of whether employers have an equal need to employ highly educated and trained young people. Three further policy implications arise: the first is that without adequate inducement in the form of tax breaks or tax levies (depending on political viewpoint) employers may remain committed to training only those already in work. The second is that the longer they are away and further removed young workers become from the workplace, either through unemployment or off-the-job training, the less employable they may become. The third concerns the content and underlying assumptions of the GNVQ curriculum which on the one hand promises parity, progression and reskilling while on the other is locked into a youth labour market characterized by unemployment, casualization and low pay. In such circumstances, the danger is that GNVQ will become either another substitute for employment or a conduit to service sector employment. Traditionally, industries such as engineering, construction and energy had the highest concentrations of young people with formal recognized qualifications. With the decline of such industries, the need for formal training may increasingly be determined by the demands of the expanding, mainly casualized, service sector (Gray, Jesson and Tanner 1993). If this bodes well for improving training levels in a sector with the lowest incidence of high quality training, it may well fail to address national and local skill shortages.

There is an assumption in much writing about post-16 education and training that better skilled and qualified young people are a necessary condition for economic prosperity. Implicit in such a view is the belief that if young people become better skilled and qualified, they will be more able to acquire good jobs. For many, this notion is linked to views of a post-Fordist labour market where all workers require higher levels of skill and flexibility compared with the past. While there remains disagreement about the extent to which this shift to post-Fordism has taken place, there are those who see radical potential for education in such change (Brown and Lauder 1992; Young 1993). The argument runs that increasingly hierarchical systems of managerial control and surveillance are being replaced by flexible organizational structures, involving adaptable machinery, flexible workers, flatter hierarchies and the breakdown of the division between mental and manual labour. It is argued that, in the twenty-first century, new skills of learning, abstraction, team-work, independent thinking and experimentation will be required by increasing numbers of workers (ED/DES 1991).

It is not difficult to see how this radical and universal conception of the knowledge worker finds appeal across a broad and diverse spectrum including government, opposition, CBI, Trades Union Congress and examination bodies. For different ideological reasons, each retains different interpretations of what post-Fordism will bring in terms of innovation, profit, work organization, labour, and self-development. Such is the flexibility of the post-Fordist vision of society that it has become highly chameleon-like. For the Left it legitimates critiques of old models of hierarchy which offered false promises of choice, classlessness and freedom. For the Right it legitimates market-led reforms in modernizing Britain's work and education institutions on more flexible and competitive terms. In so doing, both perspectives are able to idealize education and the quality of teaching and learning as a necessary co-determinant of economic change. Moreover, modernizers (of all political persuasions) anticipate a progressive and humane conception of the worker as an autonomous rather than as an alienated being. Thus, not only does the post-Fordist vision of society suggest that education and work are synonymous, but also that the creation of the knowledge worker implies radical changes both in the content and form of the curriculum. For Young (1992) this necessarily involves challenging divisive specialization associated with academic–vocational divisions, insulated subject boundaries and the separation between education and training. However, it is also the case that successful 16–19 education and training provision is dependent on a buoyant youth labour market. The commitment of young people to the vocational curriculum offered within GNVQ will be strongly linked with their perceptions of the likelihood of a good job at the end of it.

GNVQ, progression and careership

Most current research on the transition from school to work stresses the stratification of inequality (Furlong 1992; Banks *et al.* 1991; Bates and Riseborough 1993; Kerckhoff 1993). This contrasts sharply with policy assumptions based on individualism and free choice (CBI 1989, 1993; Bennett, Glennester and Nevinson 1992; ED/DES 1991). Ostensibly, GNVQs are designed with the intention of enabling young people to progress either to HE or into employment, allowing virement and freedom of movement between academic and vocational courses. Yet both routes and virement are problematic. It is unlikely that GNVQs will provide ready access to popular, high status HE courses. Currently, over 70 per cent of the year group are now entering full-time post-16 education. At the same time, intake into HE has been capped at around 33 per cent. It is, therefore, unlikely that more than a third of GNVQ Advanced students will progress to university. For the majority of students recruited to GNVQ, the enormous efforts currently being devoted to ensuring progression to HE may be largely irrelevant.

However, the progression routes direct to employment via GNVQ are plagued by uncertainties. Traditionally, most British employers looking for school leavers took them at 16+, whilst a small group of major employers, such as banks, recruited at 18+. Recently the 18+ recruitment has largely dried up, partly in response to recession and partly as employers react to the recent expansion of HE by recruiting exclusively from that sector. Moreover, traditional 16+ recruiters are being forced to change because there are fewer young people looking for jobs and training places at that age. Even if, in future, employers recruit at 18 or even 19+, there remain progression problems for those leaving with GNVQ. Many employers traditionally disregarded qualifications altogether (Moore 1988). Furthermore, many small and medium sized employers are unlikely to know what GNVQ is. These difficulties are exacerbated by a growing gulf between GNVQ and NVQ (Hodkinson and Mattinson 1994). Unless students have topped up GNVQ with NVQ units, they may have little relevant work-based skill.

Because the launch of GNVQ has been so closely linked with employment needs, it is likely that many of the young people flocking to take these new courses are doing so in the hope of getting into HE and/or of getting a good job. But education does not create jobs for students. Unless there are widespread changes to the ways in which labour markets, industry and the City are organized, progression for many GNVQ students will be undermined no matter how good the actual course provision may be (Finegold and Soskice 1991). There is a risk that the GNVQ bubble will burst if, regardless of the quality of actual provision, inflated expectations of progression are dashed, to be replaced by disillusion. Mass post-16 educational provision must be based on wider and more substantial foundations than this.

The wider purposes of education

From being a relative backwater of research and education policy, post-compulsory education and training has become strategic in the official discourse of social and economic reform. The situation of the 1950s to 1970s has changed, with the influence of unemployment, markets, changing technology and work organization, global and geopolitical factors. Such factors have brought into question traditional distinctions between schooling, education and work, academic and vocational knowledge, and mental and manual labour in work and education. International comparisons associated with a knowledge revolution have exposed weaknesses in post-compulsory education and training in England and Wales. These include overly behaviourist models of training, lack of investment in intermediate skills, and an inability to translate knowledge and innovation into growth. Such factors, often overlain with traditional suspicions about theory and thinking skills in Britain, have maintained narrow and arbitrary distinctions between academic and practical modes of thought. Increasingly, there is a need to challenge the dependency culture engendered by instructional discourse in favour of a pedagogy of work and self-learning, embracing what has recently been described as the predeterminants of a knowledge-based society (Reich 1991). According to Lyotard (1984) '... the old principle that the acquisition of knowledge is indissociable from the training (Bildung) of minds, or even of individuals, is becoming obsolete and will become ever more so.'

In England and Wales, the tension within a policy which encourages prescriptive pedagogical discourse and, at the same time, demands a pedagogy of empowered self-learning has been a major obstacle to progress. Is there a unifying way forward? There is a need to go beyond both the 1944 and Thatcherite positions: the challenge being to generate a new way forward which combines conceptions of social unity with competitiveness and productivity. According to Donald (1990) such a way should be based on '... participation and distributive justice rather than simple egalitarianism and on cultural heterogeneity rather than a shared humanity.' For Whitty (1993) the new way should combine conceptions of unity and a common good with differentiation and recognition of individual needs. This not only has crucial implications for the future of mass schooling and vocationalism, exemplified in GNVQ, but also for the nature of knowledge which underpins new policies and practices of teaching and learning. If Donald and Whitty's accounts challenge both the 1944 and 1988 settlements, the emphasis on equality and civic restructuring retains much in common with earlier post-war policy assumptions (Newsom 1963; Crowther 1959; Robbins 1963). The difference lies in the determination and transition from an instructional pedagogy to a learner-oriented pedagogy which, though still circumscribed by economic rationalism (after all, capitalism hasn't changed that much), radically redefines the social relationship between learning, earning and competitiveness (Husen 1986).

Perhaps now is the time to address long-overdue questions about the nature and purpose of education in a social democracy. As we increase staying-on rates post-16 and effectively raise the school-leaving age to 18 for most young people, we need to revisit the difficult problem of past educational failures. From the 1960s onwards, study after study showed the educational system, be it based on grammar and secondary modern schools (Hargreaves 1967; Lacey 1970) or on comprehensive schools (Ball 1981; Hargreaves 1982; ILEA 1984), failing large numbers of young people, especially the less able of working class origins. More recently, the focus has shifted to problems for young women and young people of minority ethnic origins (Arnot and Weiner 1987; Troyna 1987). Contributors in Bates and Riseborough (1993) paint graphic pictures of inequality in post-16 education just prior to the introduction of GNVQ. Though we are in favour of expanding educational provision post-16, more does not necessarily mean better. It is interesting that in the USA, where staying-on rates are much greater than in Britain, similar concerns about poor quality provision are frequently expressed (Brause 1992).

Missing in current policy discourses in England and Wales is any broader vision of citizenship and learning – in terms of the kind of people the new post-16 education system is designed to produce – including images of 'human nature' which GNVQs (or A-levels) presume to develop. The question arises, is there a way of rescuing the reform process from itself, and in what direction should we be looking for a broader vision of post-16 education and training?

Genuine alternatives must embrace a socially constructed view of education and citizenship which inter-links partnership and empowerment in personal, education and economic relations, beyond market, qualification and employer-led considerations. For example, Hodkinson (1994) suggests that education for all young people should include three overlapping dimensions – personal effectiveness, critical autonomy and community. By personal effectiveness he means the ability to do things for oneself and with others. The emphasis is on being practically proactive, be it running a play group, making jewellery, or raising funds for a charity. Critical autonomy refers to the importance of thinking for oneself, including the ability to critique common assumptions. Community is about developing one's place in a diverse society – about understanding conflicts of interest and struggle, about recognizing and respecting the rights and opinions of others, and about contributing to society, through individual and communal effort. Too often educational provision has fallen well short on some or all of these, as when vocational courses were/are typically uncritical, so that important issues of social justice and inequality were/are not even discussed. Education should include attention to economic and commercial issues. However, analyses such as this demonstrate the narrowness and sterility of basing a curriculum exclusively on the economic agenda. As ever, principles of democracy and justice are involved here, which render holistic conceptions of education and training a right of all citizens and a precondition of citizenship.

According to Tomlinson (1993), the new model must necessarily offer the development of intellectual capacities, economic skills and personal qualities that every individual has a right to acquire and the obligation to put these to the service of society. This not only demands rethinking teaching and learning, but also the content and process of the curriculum as it affects knowledgeable adult development in a learning society. As Lee *et al.* (1990) point out, leaving youth training to market forces has resulted in under-provision, skill shortages and a waste of young people – tantamount to their civic exclusion. This phenomenon, recently associated with cuts in benefit, homelessness, poverty and single-parent families, has further marginalized some young people, both in societal and educational terms. The danger here is that alienation and anomie become overlain, effectively creating an underclass.

Conclusion

In these different but interlinked ways, our original paper saw the future for GNVQ as rather bleak. So how well has that analysis withstood the test of the last five years? Despite our prediction, GNVQ has not yet been squeezed out of existence. However, it still looks pretty sickly compared to good old academic A-levels and even the newer forms of work-based youth training, such as the Modern Apprenticeships. There is now abundant evidence that GNVQ has failed to achieve parity of esteem with A-levels (Edwards *et al.* 1997). A-levels continue to attract the most able young people and GNVQs are, by and large, populated by those who lack the qualifications, self-confidence and cultural capital to succeed on that high status route. Indeed, any sense of clear purpose or identity for GNVQ, apart from this fall-back, second best, second chance opportunity is very hard to discern. Despite, or more likely because of, this, recent Labour policy has been to make GNVQs even more like A-levels (similar numbers of modules, one GNVQ to be the same size as one A-level, same grading procedures used, increased amounts of external testing), rather than to emphasize their distinctive qualities. It could be argued that we are, in this way, reverting to a two-track provision – full-time education and part-time training. What GNVQs have arguably done is allow a larger number of people to stay on the full-time route, whilst protecting and preserving the élitism of A-levels. The marginalization of the practical and work-based within this full-time track continues apace, and the counter-balancing lack of any academic breadth or criticality on the vocational route also stubbornly survives, despite some spirited attacks (Evans *et al.* 1997). The vocational continues to be associated with the less able, its low status being effectively reinforced.

The new Labour government seem much less committed to a rigid three-track system than were their Conservative predecessors. Post-Dearing recommendations and policy changes fall well short of establishing a single, holistic curriculum, but do seem to be concerned with blurring boundaries between A-levels and GNVQs. The recent introduction of AS levels that are now seen as the first stage of a full A-level, combined with the introduction of GNVQs that are the same size as A-levels, gives some hope that significant numbers of young people will study more than three subjects, and that many will take a mixture of A-levels and GNVQs. It is too soon to know whether either of these things will happen or not, but history is not on the government's side. Whilst it is possible to see why some GNVQ students might like to add an A-level to their curriculum, there is far less incentive for A-level students to reciprocate. Furthermore, if large numbers of mixed diets do emerge, an inevitable effect will be that a far larger number of young people are taking at least one A-level. If that happens, there will almost certainly be further attacks from those classical humanists who equate wider access with lowering standards. Just like their predecessors, the conservative new Labour appears to want exclusivity of standards and widening of access simultaneously. Preserving a GNVQ that remains separate in practice, but not in expressed intention, allows them to square that ideological circle, whilst failing to address the underlying contradictions.

What is clear is that, despite some pretty rhetoric in the introduction to the Green Paper *The Learning Age* (DfEE 1998), economic rationalism and the new managerialism remain rampant. The only purpose of lifelong learning, let alone GNVQ, appears to be to improve economic competitiveness and to enable (force?) people to get jobs. Everything else is subservient to that. Thankfully, unlike their predecessors, the Labour government is targeting youth unemployment, through a whole series of initiatives around the New Deal. For the purposes of this chapter, there are two noticeable features of this policy crusade. First, it is assumed, as we argued in the original paper, that education and training is all that is needed to get recalcitrant people into work. Second, the unemployed and educationally unsuccessful are seen metaphorically as having something missing which can be replaced. Education and training provide the missing bit: get people repaired in this way once, and everything will be all right ever after. At the time of writing, these policies are having a relatively easy time. They are only just beginning to be put in place and unemployment in Britain is dropping. Their real test will come a little way into the future. If our original analysis was correct then, once the next recession arrives, it will become apparent that (i) young people cannot be forced to learn and (ii) giving them 'learning' will not of itself create jobs or ensure that everyone gets one. The deep-seated inequalities in British education and British employment, related to class, gender, ethnicity and geographical location will continue, unchallenged. For these reasons, it still seems appropriate to conclude with the original ending only slightly rewritten, despite everything that has happened since ...

In challenging the problems surrounding and bedevilling GNVQ and the tripartism it represents, it is necessary to address a broader vision of citizenship and learning, in fact a different polity (Ranson 1994), which will sustain the personal development of all. In addressing this issue, four preconditions are essential. First, the professionalism of teachers and lecturers needs to be enhanced rather than destroyed, as a lethal combination of school-based initial teacher training, growing centralized government control of education and, ironically, repressive neo-Fordist school and college management approaches (Hodkinson 1997) threaten. Second, the FEFC needs to re-examine its funding regime in terms of the broader educational issues addressed here. The current obsession with performance-related funding, focused on student numbers and completion rates, reinforces a narrowing of choice, removal of flexibility and loss of unfunded 'curriculum extras' such as non-examination adult and general education studies (Ainley and Bailey 1997). Third, educational purpose must range beyond economic performance and markets. This is not a matter of either/or. Ironically, the much-cited evidence from our European partners also suggests that a broader, more general education which will bring us closer to the wider agenda advocated here might also better fit the economic imperative (Green 1995). Even some advocates of a three-track system (Smithers and Robinson 1993) see a need for a broader general technical/vocational education, with a greater emphasis on mathematics and science education to underpin practical skill development. Finally, the issue of inclusion and exclusion which has bedevilled British education must be abandoned in favour of a unified approach to 14–19 education and training. A common certification for years 14–19, along the lines outlined by the National Commission on Education (1993) and Evans *et al.* (1997), is a necessity. Its introduction would make parity of esteem for A-level and GNVQs as 'alternative routes' a redundant concept (Sweetman 1994). The types of curriculum approach advocated by Young (1993) would be valuable in providing a general education that is flexible and less divisive, broader whilst still specialized. Given some or all of these changes, some of the developments that have taken place under the GNVQ banner may yet play a part in the reconstruction of post-16 educational provision. Without them it offers little hope of real and lasting reform and, like so many previous attempts to redefine the middle ground of tripartism, may eventually wither on the policy vine. In the meantime, Crowther's (1959) recommendations for universal post-school provision remain on the table, still unaddressed.

References

Ainley, P. and Bailey, B. (1997) *The Business of Learning: Staff and Student Experiences of Further Education in the 1990s.* London: Cassell.

Arnot, M. and Weiner, G. (eds) (1987) *Gender and the Politics of Schooling.* London: Hutchinson.

Ball, S.J. (1981) *Beachside Comprehensive: A Case Study of Secondary Schooling.* Cambridge: Cambridge University Press.

Banks, M., Bates, I., Breakwell, G., Bynner, J., Elmer, N., Jamieson, L. and Roberts, K. (1992) *Careers and Identities: Adolescent Attitudes to Employment, Training and Education, their Home Life, Leisure and Politics.* Milton Keynes: Open University Press.

Bates, I. (1998) 'The empowerment dimension in the GNVQ: a critical exploration of discourse, pedagogic apparatus and school implementation.' *Evaluation and Research in Education 12*, (1), 7–22.

Bates, I. and Riseborough, G. (eds) (1993) *Youth and Inequality.* Buckingham: Open University Press.

Bennett, R., Glennester, H. and Nevinson, D. (1992) *Learning Should Pay.* Poole: BP Educational Service.

Bloomer, M. and Hodkinson, P. (1998) *Moving into FE: The Voice of the Learner.* London: FEDA.

Brause, R.S. (1992) *Enduring Schools: Problems and Possibilities.* London: Falmer.

Brown, P. and Lauder, H. (1992) 'Education, economy and society: an introduction to a new agenda.' In P. Brown and H. Lauder (eds) *Education for Economic Survival.* London: Routledge.

Capey, J. (1995) *GNVQ Assessment Review* (The Capey Report). London: NCVQ.

CBI (1989) *Towards a Skills Revolution, Report of the Vocational Education and Training Task Force.* London: Confederation of British Industry.

CBI (1993) *Routes for Success – Careership: A Strategy for all 16–19 year old Learning.* London: CBI.

Coffey, D. (1992) *Schools and Work: Developments in Vocational Education.* London: Cassell.

Crowther Report (1959) *15–18: Report of the Minister of Education's Central Advisory Committee.* London: HMSO.

Dearing, R. (1996) *Review of Qualifications for 16–19 Year Olds: Full Report.* London: SCAA.

DES (1988) *Advancing A Levels* (The Higginson Report). London: HMSO.

DfEE (1998) *The Learning Age: A Renaissance for a New Britain.* London: The Stationery Office.

Donald, J. (1990) 'Interesting times.' *Critical Social Policy 9*, (3), 39–55.

ED/DES (1991) *Education and Training for the 21st Century.* London: HMSO.

Edwards, T., Fitz-Gibbon, C., Hardman, F., Haywood, R. and Meagher, N. (1997) *Separate but Equal? A levels and GNVQs.* London: Routledge.

Evans, K., Hodkinson, P., Keep, E., Maguire, M., Raffe, D., Rainbird, H., Senker, P. and Unwin, L. (1997) *Working to Learn: A Work-based Route to Learning for Young People.* Issues in People Management, No. 18. London: IPD.

FEDA (1997) *GNVQs 1993–97: A National Survey Report.* London: FEDA.

Finegold, D., Keep, E., Milliband, D., Raffe, D., Spours, K. and Young, M. (1990) *A British 'Baccalaureat': Ending the Division Between Education and Training.* IPPR Education and Training Paper No. 1. London: Institute of Public Policy Research.

Finegold, D. and Soskice, D. (1991) 'The failure of training in Britain: analysis and prescription.' In G. Esland (ed) *Education, Training and Employment, Volume 1: Educated Labour – the Changing Basis of Industrial Demand.* Wokingham: Addison-Wesley.

Furlong, A. (1992) *Growing Up in a Classless Society? School to Work Transitions.* Edinburgh: Edinburgh University Press.

Gleeson, D. (1992) 'Legislating for change: missed opportunities in the Further and Higher Education Act.' *British Journal of Education and Work* 6, (2), 29–40.

Gleeson, D. and Hodkinson, P. (1995) 'Ideology and curriculum policy: GNVQ and mass post-compulsory education in England and Wales.' *British Journal of Education and Work 3* (3), 5–19.

Gray, J., Jesson, D. and Tanner, M. (1993) *Boosting Post-16 Participation in Full Time Education: A Study of Some Key Factors.* ED Research Series, Youth Cohort Report No. 20. Sheffield: Employment Department.

Green, A. (1995) 'The European challenge to British vocational education and training.' In P. Hodkinson and M. Issitt (eds) *The Challenge of Competence: Professionalism Through Vocational Education and Training.* London: Cassell.

Green, A. and Steedman, H. (1993) *Educational Provision, Educational Attainment and the Needs of Industry: A Review of the Research for Germany, France, Japan, the USA and Britain.* Report No. 5. London: National Institute of Economic and Social Research.

Halsey, A.H., Postlethwaite, N., Prais, S.J., Smithers, A. and Steedman, H. (1991) *Every Child in Britain.* Report of the Channel Four Commission on Education. London: Channel 4 Television.

Hargreaves, A. (1994) *Changing Teachers, Changing Times: Teachers' Work and Culture in the Postmodern Age.* London: Cassell.

Hargreaves, D.H. (1967) *Social Relations in a Secondary School.* London: Routledge and Keegan Paul.

Hargreaves, D.H. (1982) *The Challenge for the Comprehensive School.* London: Routledge and Keegan Paul.

Helsby, G., Knight, P. and Saunders, M. (1998) 'Preparing students for the new work order: the case of Advanced General National Vocational Qualifications.' *British Educational Research Journal 24*, (1), 63–78.

Hodkinson, P. (1994) 'Empowerment as an entitlement in the post-16 curriculum.' *Journal of Curriculum Studies 26* (5), 391–508.

Hodkinson, P. (1997) 'Neo-Fordism and teacher professionalism.' *Teacher Development 1* (1), 69–81.

Hodkinson, P. and Mattinson, K. (1994) 'A bridge too far? The problems facing GNVQ.' *Curriculum Journal 5* (3), 319–332.

Husen, T. (1986) *The Learning Society Revisited.* Oxford: Pergamon Press.

ILEA (1984) *Improving Secondary Schools.* (The Hargreaves Report). London: Inner London Education Authority.

Kerckhoff, A.C. (1993) *Diverging Pathways: Social Structure and Career Deflections.* Cambridge: Cambridge University Press.

Lacey, C. (1970) *Hightown Grammar.* Manchester: Manchester University Press.

Lee, D., Marsden, D., Rickman, P. and Duncombe, J. (1990) *Scheming for Youth: A Study of YTS in the Enterprise Culture.* Milton Keynes: Open University Press.

Lyotard, J.F. (1984) *The Post-Modern Condition: A Report of Knowledge.* Minneapolis: University of Minnesota Press.

McCullough, G. (1989) *The Secondary Technical School.* London: Falmer.

Moore, R. (1988) 'Education, employment and recruitment.' In R. Dale, R. Ferguson and A. Robinson (eds) *Frameworks for Teaching.* London: Hodder and Stoughton.

National Commission on Education (1993) *Learning to Succeed: A Radical Look at Education Today and a Strategy for the Future.* London: Heinemann.

Newsom Report (1963) *Half our Future.* London: HMSO.

Ranson, S. (1994) *Towards the Learning Society.* London: Cassell.

Reich, R. (1991) *The Work of Nations.* London: Simon and Schuster.

Robbins Report (1963) *Committee on Higher Education.* Vol. 1. London: HMSO.

Robinson, J. and Burke, C. (1996) 'Tradition, culture and ethos: the impact of the Further and Higher Education Act (1992) on Sixth Form Colleges and their futures.' *Evaluation and Research in Education 10* (1), 3–21.

Sanderson, M. (1994) *The Missing Stratum: Technical School Education in England, 1900–1990s.* London: Athlone.

Skilbeck, M. (1976) 'Three educational ideologies.' In The Open University *E203 Curriculum Design and Development, Unit 3: Ideologies and Values.* Milton Keynes: Open University Press.

Smithers, A. (1994) *All our Futures: Britain's Education Revolution.* Dispatches Report on Education. London: Channel 4 TV.

Smithers, A. and Robinson, P. (1993) *Changing Colleges: Further Education in the Market Place*. London: The Council for Industry and Higher Education.

Sweetman, J. (1994) 'Examining new options.' *Guardian Education*, 1 April.

Tomlinson, S. (1993) 'No future in the class war.' *Times Educational Supplement*, 20 August.

Troyna, B. (1987) *Racial Inequality in Education*. London: Tavistock.

Whitty, G. (1993) 'New Schools for New Times? Educational Reform in a Global Context.' Unpublished paper presented to an International Conference on Educational Reforms: Changing Relationships between the State, Civil Society and the Educational Community. University of Wisconsin – Madison, USA, June 1993.

Young, M. (1992) 'A Curriculum for the 21st Century.' Paper presented at the International Workshop on Mutual Enrichment and Academic and Vocational Education in Upper Secondary Education, Institute for Educational Research, University of Jyvaskyla, Finland, 23–26 September 1992.

Young, M. (1993) 'A curriculum for the 21st century? Towards a new basis for overcoming academic/vocational divisions.' *British Journal of Educational Studies 41* (3), 203–222.

Chapter 7

Inclusive Lifelong Learning or Stratified Lifelong Training?

Educational Policy Developments in Late Modernity

Martin Dyke

Introduction

In some respects debates about vocational education and training correspond with the parallel discourse of late modernity in current social theory. In the last few years there have been a wealth of policy documents that directly advocate educational change as a means of responding to the economic particularities of our time. Will these educational policies and structures facilitate learning, democratization, and a third way politics? Or will policy simply provide an infrastructure for lifelong vocational training rather than lifelong learning? It is argued that reflective learning is central to the needs of a reflexive economy and society in the new millennium. A high skill, high quality economy is dependent on knowledge creativity and innovation of its workforce. The form of vocational education and training required in a reflexive economy is provided by reflective learning, or perhaps more accurately reflective learning in lifelong education. The changing needs of capitalism could lead to a framework for lifelong education, a tradition associated with empowerment and democratization. A more reflexive form of vocational education and training is required in late modernity. If achieved it is likely to characterize the ambivalence of the times; to represent both a potential source of empowerment and economic control.

This chapter provides an analysis of the social and economic context for post-compulsory education. The analysis presents a late modern perspective and sets the argument for reflective learning in vocational education and training. In the second part of the chapter the policy response to late modernity is examined. The policy agenda has been set in reports by Dearing (1996), Fryer (1997), Kennedy (1997) and the Green Paper *The Learning Age* (DfEE 1998). The final part of the chapter examines possible consequences related to lifelong learning policy. There is optimism with reference to the prospects for an overarching advanced level award or British Baccalaureate and concern that (despite it being a mantra of policy makers) the promise of empowerment presented in lifelong learning may only result in narrowly defined lifelong training.

Social, economic and educational context

The current epoch has been characterized as a period of rapid and wide-ranging change, a period where people are forced to reflect on new information and perhaps reassess their taken-for-granted knowledge and experience of the world. Past experience, custom and practice is less reliable as a source of guidance and decision making. Education has a key role in enabling people to navigate new routes through a modernity where what may have seemed universal, regulated and secure appears more complex, diverse and uncertain. Theorists have described these changes as late modern (Giddens 1998), reflexive modern (Beck 1992), post-modern (Bauman 1997) and neo-modern (Szerzynski 1996). Whichever variety of prefixed modernity used, all these authors recognized the uniqueness of our times. A similar discourse of change and transition has been adopted by political leaders, with Prime Minister Blair freely using the language of modernity in advocating, curiously, the need to modernize.

The 'modern' can be said to have originated in ideas of the eighteenth century Enlightenment (Hall and Gieben 1992). Reason, science, empiricism and universal understanding provided the foundations that defined the modern world. The Enlightenment philosophies placed a tremendous confidence in the human progress being gained by science. The more reflexive late modern critics would seem to have replaced this faith and confidence in science with scepticism and doubt, Zygmunt Bauman simply defining 'reflexivity as scepticism' (Bauman 1993, p.201). In place of the Enlightenment belief in universal law and understanding, there is a late modern awareness of the complexity of the natural world, the unforeseen consequences of human action and risk. A loss of faith in science has emerged that in part has been nurtured by a catalogue of ecological and health crises. Witness the controversial responses to genetically modified food or BSE in beef. The modernity belief that the application of science and reason would inevitably produce progress has also been called into doubt. Modernity or the 'progress guided society' (Bauman 1995, p.21) has been recast as the 'Risk Society' of Ulrich Beck (1992) – a society where humankind has manufactured risks that are incalculable, risks that are manifest in the nuclear, biological and chemical technologies.

Another element in the late modern perspective is the information society discourse, where abundant and rapidly changing information is mediated through extensive communication technologies (Castells 1996). Anthony Giddens acknowledges the importance of information in guiding decision making and reflection:

> Reflexivity has two senses, one very general, and the other more directly relevant to modern social life. All human beings are reflective in the sense in which thinking about what one does is part of doing it ... Social reflexivity refers to a world increasingly constituted by information rather than pre-given modes of conduct. It is how we live after the retreat of tradition and nature, because we have to take so many forward orientated decisions. In that sense, we live in a much more reflexive way than previous generations have done. (Giddens and Pierson 1998, p.15).

Continuous reassessment of experience, and information as part of experience, is therefore central to living with the rapid change of late modernity. Earlier forms of modernity could more frequently use custom and tradition to guide action. In economic terms capital needs to adapt to the rapid pace of change by using labour that is more reflective, creative, innovative and autonomous. These skills had become necessary to profit making in high skills sectors of the economy. Lash and Urry (1994, p.60) go as far as to argue that the current period is one that depends on 'reflexive accumulation', where responding to new and changing knowledge and information is essential to economic growth. If knowledge and cognition are central to work in a system of reflexive accumulation, what then are the policy implications for vocational education and training?

The language of reflexivity has a strong resonance with that of reflectivity in learning (Kolb 1984; Schon 1987). Indeed when interviewed, Giddens quite explicitly defined the concept of reflexivity in terms of reflection:

> I use it to mean just the generic fact that we are reasoning beings who reflect on the conditions of our activity, and that all human

> beings are like that; but I also use it in the sense of social reflexivity or institutional reflexivity … essentially a world where you have constant or organised reflection on the conditions of our existence as a means of living those conditions. (Chignell and Abbott 1995, p.11)

In education this 'reflexive monitoring of action' is referred to as a 'basis for reflective learning' (Jarvis 1992, p.37). Lash and Urry also refer to the critical reflection of individuals in their account of reflexivity (1994, p.32). Reflexivity and reflection are therefore at the heart of the theoretical approaches that described new forms of modernity (Beck 1992; Giddens 1991; Lash and Urry 1994). The concept of reflexivity is central to sociological and economic accounts of late modernity and has strong parallels with the concept of reflective learning. Beck clearly argues that freedom of information and education for uncertainty is central to the democratization of a risk society (IPPR 1996). Such education for uncertainty is best expressed through reflective learning. Lifelong learning that enables individuals, organizations and communities to navigate their way through late modernity in a risk society therefore needs to nurture reflective learning.

The language of complexity, uncertainty, risk, diversity and even chaos has shaped the contemporary late modern discourse. Reflexivity and scepticism provided a late twentieth century critique of the Enlightenment and presented an agenda for change. These ideas are not necessarily new; indeed, a close reading of the Enlightenment (particularly David Hume) suggests they were acknowledged then. However, the ideas seem more pertinent, more powerful as explanations of contemporary experience. As a discourse the late modern critique may be capturing hegemony. It is the discourse that provides the theoretical background for the following exploration of vocational education and training in late modernity. Two aspects of recent policy discussion will be explored: first, reform of the qualifications framework; and second, lifelong learning.

Qualification frameworks

A new 'settlement' (Avis 1993) is said to have emerged in post-compulsory education, a political settlement that has progressive educationists, unions, business, the New Right and government sharing a similar vision of vocational education for the twenty-first century. The settlement is consistent with the late modernity perspective and third way politics. An end to the vocational academic divide is a key aspect of the policy consensus in post-compulsory education. Parity of esteem is also a key aspect of progressive post-Fordist education (Brown and Lauder 1992) and implicit in the policy reforms proposed for post-compulsory education such as the British Baccalaureate (Finegold *et al.* 1990) and the General Education Diploma of the National Commission on Education (1993). The Dearing Report (1996) calls for 'Equal acceptability of achievement at the relevant level in the A level, GNVQ, and NVQ pathways, and combinations of these' (1996, p.65). As outlined below, the Fryer Report also advocated greater parity of esteem between academic and vocational qualifications.

Discussion of reform at advanced level has been evident for decades from the Crowther Committee over forty years ago through to the Robbins Committee on Higher Education and more recently the Higginson Committee in 1988. The debate has intensified since Higginson proposals promoted a limited form of modularization with a call for the development of AS levels (Ball 1990, pp.194–95). In 1990 the Institute for Public Policy Research published proposals for a more fundamental reform of A-level and advocated a 'British Baccalaureate' (Finegold *et al.* 1990) a proposal not dissimilar to the General Education Diploma suggested by the National Commission on Education (1993). The AEB has experimented with modular A-levels with the Wessex project, while the Oxford and Cambridge Examining boards have reported success with modular maths at A-level that can transfer credit to GNVQ (Holdsworth 1994, p.x).

The Labour Party in opposition had also proposed a similar reform of A-level with the proposed introduction of a 'General Certificate in Further Education (GCFE)' (*TES* 29.7.94, p.7). The GCFE would be a single examination system for post-compulsory education, modular in approach and combining the academic and vocational, available to all students including adult returners and part-time students. The proposals had the support of the CBI and the Committee of Vice Chancellors and Principals (*TES* 29.7.94, p.7). The GCFE proposal provided a logical rationalization of the New Qualifications Framework in extending the principles of comprehensive education post-sixteen.

Support for a merger of the three qualifications' pathways had also come from the leading organizations representing Head Teachers and College Principals, including the traditionally conservative bodies such as the Headmasters Conference (*TES* 14.10.94, p.10). The Head Teachers and Principals view evolutionary reform of the government's New Qualifications Framework (DfEE 1994) as necessary to 'remove artificial boundaries between academic and vocational education' (Nash 1994, p.10). The Head Teachers and Principals' proposals were reported to have the support of industry and the predecessor to the Qualifications and Curriculum Authority the NCVQ. Once again it is the political settlement and a modular approach to study that holds the key to change.

It has been argued (Dyke 1996) that by promoting the modularization of courses the New Qualifications Framework may provide a stepping stone to further rationalization of qualifications post-sixteen. Such a development would facilitate the demise of, or at least chip away at, the academic and vocational divide that has stifled equal opportunity within state education for half a century. The modularization of courses could provide a form of credit accumulation and transfer that has been promoted in higher education (Lester 1994). Demand for a system of unit-based credit accumulation and transfer in further education was taken up by the Kennedy and Fryer reports and will be discussed below. NVQ and GNVQ are already unit based; it could therefore be possible for individual students to mix and match the balance of their portfolio evidence with academic, vocational and specific work-related qualifications. Add to this the possible modularization of A-level (Holdsworth 1994) and the potential to mix and match vocational and academic achievement can be reduced to individual units. Students would be able to gain advanced level qualifications made up of many possible combinations of A-level, GNVQ and NVQ units. If such a scenario emerged the vocational/academic divide would be relatively invisible; it could disappear in the complexity of different configurations of advanced level qualifications. Matriculation would focus on the number of advanced level units or points achieved, rather than attempt to unravel the academic, vocational and occupationally specific origins of the award. The traditional A-level gold standard would remain only in name, emptied out of its original meaning, with the evidence of 'Advanced level/NVQ level 3' achievement becoming the new gold standard.

Two strands of the New Qualifications Framework, NVQ and GNVQ, already possess a modular structure. For the above scenario to emerge it requires A-level to be reformed and provide greater breadth of study. The modularization of A-level provides a key to the reform of the New Qualifications Framework, and its replacement by an overarching Advanced Level Award made up of units from NVQ,

GNVQ and A-level subjects. The exact combination of units for an Advanced Level Award is less important than the possibility of one overarching award at Advanced/Level Three provided by modularization. Possible configurations have been discussed elsewhere (National Commission on Education 1993; Dearing 1996; Dyke 1996). An overarching Advanced Level Award could replace A-level as the standard for matriculation and thereby blur the distinction between academic and vocational qualification pathways. Adults in work seeking the award may opt for more NVQ work-related units, while the 16–19 age group may prefer less specialist units and follow general vocational or academic interests.

The modification to the New Qualifications Framework, outlined above, presents relatively modest changes to the award structure, providing incremental change to what already exists rather than a radical overhaul of the system, and building on the strengths of existing awards. This reform is easier to achieve without threatening the current settlement in post-compulsory education and will if necessary provide a stepping stone for more fundamental policy changes. Support for such reform is evident in recent policy documents on post-sixteen qualifications. A similar proposal for incremental change was recommended by the Dearing *Review of Qualifications 16–19* (1996).

Dearing acknowledged the widespread demand for reform at advanced level. Dearing's research also canvassed the views of students and noted demand for a broader curriculum at advanced level (Dearing 1996, p.61). The Dearing Report recommended an optional overarching advanced level award with its proposal for a 'National Advanced Diploma' (Dearing 1996, p.60), the requirements for which were as follows:

> Advanced level: two A level passes, or a full GNVQ at Advanced level, or a full NVQ at level three plus competence in communication, the application of number and information technology demonstrated through the NCVQ units at level 3 or through the new AS in the three key skills … (Dearing 1996, p.60)

The aim of the National Advanced Diploma is to provide breadth of study while maintaining the normal university requirement for depth. As noted above, parity of esteem between vocational and academic pathways is a key characteristic of the proposal for an Advanced Diploma (Dearing 1996, p.65).

Rationalization of post-sixteen qualifications gained further support from the Kennedy Report on widening participation in further education. The credit accumulation and transfer arrangements similar to those suggested above are recommended in the Kennedy Report with calls for a 'National Framework for Credit' (Kennedy 1997, p.86). A more flexible model that recognizes learning achieved at a unit level is recommended: 'The "UCAS profile" acting as the database of lifelong learning, will enable learners to record the credits achieved and enable them to present evidence of credit accumulation' (Kennedy 1997, p.86). These recommendations made in the Kennedy report are argued to be consistent with those provided by the Dearing Review.

The need for a unit-based system or credit framework was also emphasized in the Fryer Report, *Learning for the 21st century* (Fryer 1997). The Fryer Report revisits many of the issues identified in Dearing (1996) and provided a lifelong learning rationale for a credit framework. Fryer identified a number of advantages of a unit-based credit framework; these include:

- Encourage parity of esteem between academic and vocational qualifications

- Facilitate recognition of the fact that an overarching certificate or qualification may be built up of units at different levels.

- Ensure that the qualifications formed from agreed combinations of mandatory and optional units will meet the diverse needs of employers and individual learners.
  (Fryer 1997, p.82)

The debate had sharpened with the election of the Labour government in May 1997, committed to broadening A-levels. By February 1998 the newly formed Qualifications and Curriculum Authority (QCA) were advising Ministers on the outcomes of the consultation exercise on the future of post-sixteen qualifications referred to as 'Qualifying for Success' (QCA 1998). Qualifying for Success established the growing demand for an overarching certificate at advanced level. The QCA recommended that the government should move towards an overarching certificate at advanced level in the longer term. 'The actual date at which such a certificate might be introduced would depend on the form adopted, but it is unlikely to be 2002 at the earliest' (QCA 1998, p.2). The QCA presented a welcome phased programme of implementation, which has been given the go-ahead by government. The Ministerial response to QCA advice was positive:

That is why we agree that QCA should undertake further work on the implications of a unit-based credit framework. We are also inviting QCA to examine further the possible development of an overarching certificate at advanced level, which would reflect A level and vocational results. (Blackstone 1998, p.3)

At the time of writing (March 1999), the government is awaiting a QCA report on the introduction of an overarching certificate. The Education and Employment Minister Baroness Blackstone announced a broadening of A-levels consistent with the proposals outlined by Dearing and the provision of an overarching certificate at advanced level (DfEE 1999a). As noted above, the reports by Dearing, Fryer and Kennedy support transfer between qualification pathways. The reports do not, however, appear to acknowledge the critique and problems identified with the competence-based education and training that underpins GNVQ and NVQs. For a transition to occur the Qualifications and Curriculum Authority (QCA) would need to address the critique of competence-based education and training presented by Smithers (1993), Hyland (1992) and Wolf (1995). Unless there is a satisfactory response to the serious theoretical and practical problems identified, a Qualifications Framework will lack credibility. The transfer between modules within the qualification pathways would not be possible. In such a scenario there can be no parity of esteem between awards; the synthesis out of tripartitism represented by the New Qualifications Framework will remain elusive. Even Dearing appeared cautious about the contribution of NVQs when he stated: 'If NVQs are to contribute fully to this new award, as described above, work will need to be undertaken to establish their size relative to A levels and GNVQs' (Dearing 1996, p.67).

There are two other problems associated with the modularization of courses, which are not fully addressed in the policy documents referred to. How will an overarching award built upon diverse units and modes of assessment provide coherence and progression in learning? It is noted that awards need to be made up of agreed combinations of units if an award is to be coherent. Will such 'agreed' combinations of units be compatible with meeting diverse needs of employers and individuals, and incorporating community-led learning initiatives? Both Fryer and Kennedy argue:

An expansion of learning in the workplace and outside conventional institutions and progression between learning programmes and different providers will follow. (Kennedy 1997, p.86)

... a range of achievements from work, college, open, and distance learning and community based learning activities to be brought into a common format which can be added to throughout life and provide progression opportunities across further education and into higher education. (Fryer 1997, p.82)

The whole gist of widening participation and lifelong learning is the accreditation of learning where: 'There are many providers and locations, including the home and the workplace, training and enterprise councils, and schools and community centres, where people expand their horizons and extend their capabilities' (Kennedy 1997, p.8).

Will a National Framework of units from such diverse backgrounds follow the A-level, GNVQ or NVQ assessment criteria? How can the range of learning activities identified above be fitted into any of these or another common format? There is a risk that aspects of the NVQ experience may be repeated. The credit framework could result in a highly bureaucratic centralized assessment system, one that seeks to make all learning, be it at work, in the community or college, fit the needs of the framework rather than the local needs of the learner. Yet in order to be credible, advanced level awards that are built upon the unit-based framework need to be credible, coherent and provide for progression. This requires agreement on acceptable combinations of units and a common system of grading and assessment. Such a National Framework of credit transfer requires centralized control of the curriculum. This creates potential conflict with the local needs of learners. Initiatives that widen participation and create opportunities for lifelong learning tend to thrive on autonomy and flexibility. The adult education tradition, for example, has been more focused on empowerment and the needs of the learner rather than any centralized systems and procedures aimed at national standards and control of the post-sixteen curriculum.

A strong case for reform of the post-sixteen qualifications framework has been presented in a number of recent policy documents. There is government support for a national framework of credit transfer and the overarching certificate at advanced level. These initiatives do have a number of possible advantages, which are well documented by Fryer (1997, p.82). The National Credit Framework envisages wider participation and accreditation of alternative units of learning from work or the community. It remains to be seen if quality assurance systems and procedures associated with national awards can meet the needs of small-scale work and

community-generated education and training. The system introduced for National Vocational Qualifications does not give rise to
optimism, as it was bureaucratic, complex and written in a language
not easily understood by users. The centralized, prescriptive and
bureaucratic system introduced with NVQ resembles the assembly-
line processes of scientific management referred to as Fordism (Dyke
1996). Late modernity requires rationalization that provides flexible,
responsive and democratic structures.

As outlined above, attempts to break down the academic vocational
divide through reform of the post-school qualifications framework is
consistent with a late modernity perspective, and a neo-Fordist
analysis of economy (Kumar 1995). In *The Third Way*, Giddens
(1998, p.25) calls for harmonization of educational practices and
standards that enhance portability. The Fryer report, *Learning for the
21st Century*, loosely attempts to connect changes in the wider
socio-economic context to the need for lifelong learning. Aspects of
the late modernity analysis can be found in Fryer with discussion of
challenges in the economy and labour market and '... wide ranging
changes to be addressed in families, communities, relationships and
in people's aspirations and very identities' (Fryer 1997, p.3). As with
the earlier reports from Dearing, Kennedy and Fryer the letter from
the QCA to the Secretary of State for Education and Employment
shares *fin-de-siècle* discourse of late modernity:

> First, several of the recommendations aim to extend the scope for
> learners to study breadth, improving their adaptability and keep-
> ing options open to help them progress in a rapidly changing
> world. (Stubbs 1998, p.1)

The challenge to policy makers seeking reform of the post-sixteen
qualifications framework is to provide a more reflexive or post-Fordist
structure. The post-Fordist analysis, perhaps more accurately
described as neo-Fordist, recognized that successful organizations
need to harness the creative and cognitive energies of labour. A
national framework for post-sixteen qualifications requires credible
standards and assessment procedures, but also needs to facilitate
diverse, flexible, responsive, learner-centred innovations in education
and training.

Lifelong learning?

Fryer then moves on to discuss quality assurance issues and credit
frameworks. The consequent emphasis on purchasers, providers and
the mixing and matching of units in a credit framework connects with

the market orientation to provision noted by Peter Jarvis in this volume (Chapter 4). The credit framework suggested paints a picture of units of lifelong learning being consumed and collected like commodities, with learning increasingly defined in terms of accreditation. Will such structures equip people with the values and reflective learning skills required to successfully navigate their route through a more reflexive world?

Before directly returning to this question, a brief examination of the key terms of the debate is necessary. Fryer does provide a brief definition of learning from the Campaign for Learning as:

> what people do when they want to make sense of experience. It may involve an increase of skills, knowledge, understanding, values, and capacity to reflect. Effective learning leads to change, development and a desire to learn more. (Fryer 1997, p.16)

This definition is consistent with the concept of reflective learning. Fryer's definition is broad ranging – it has not defined learning in narrow behaviourist terms and gives pride of place to reflection on experience. It is similar to the definition of reflective learning presented by Peter Jarvis: 'Learning, then, is of the essence of everyday living and conscious experience; it is the process of transforming that experience into knowledge, skills, attitudes, values and beliefs' (Javis 1992, p.11). At face value there is cause for optimism amongst those who believe that reflective learning has come of age and needs to be at the heart of policy making. However, Bob Fryer (1997) and for that matter the government Green Paper *The Learning Age* (DfEE 1998) discuss at length issues such as credit frameworks, learning at work, standards, quality, learning accounts, learning providers and information and communication technology. Is this really central to the learning defined above as the 'transformation of experience', that part of everyday life that is essential to living and indeed to being? The policy makers of the 1990s risk promoting a familiar conceptual fallacy, one noted by Peter Jarvis's (1992) account of lifelong learning in the 1970s and 1980s. The contemporary discourse on lifelong learning confuses learning with education:

> Learning is wider than education ... But all the social institutions together cannot contain learning, since learning is fundamental to human being and to life itself. These institutions exist only to facilitate the smooth functioning of the social system, and they may often constrain learning. Without them though, there would be a

lot less opportunity for human learning and development. (Jarvis 1992, p.10)

At the risk of being pedantic, the lifelong learning of Fryer (1997) and which DfEE (1998) refers to is generally organized or institut-ionalized learning. It may be more accurate to describe the lifelong learning of current policy documents as lifelong education. A more inclusive institutionalized and organized learning perhaps, but isn't that by definition education?

As noted above, both the Fryer report and the Kennedy report provide a wide agenda for lifelong education, one that acknowledges the variety of life contexts in which learning occurs. Both promote diversity in the provision of inclusive lifelong education and argue passionately against social exclusion. Democratic traditions in education are referenced along with strategies for learning for all, at home, in the community and in traditional educational organizations such as schools, colleges and universities. The government's response to these reports is articulated in the Green Paper *The Learning Age* (1998).

The Learning Age

The Learning Age opens with a statement by the Prime Minister:

> Education is the best economic policy we have. (DfEE 1998, p.9)

The views expressed in the Foreword by the Secretary of State are clearly consistent with a late modern perspective:

> Investment in human capital will be the foundation of success in the knowledge-based global economy of the twenty first century. This is why the Government has put learning at the heart of its ambition ... This Green Paper sets out for consultation how learn-ing throughout life will build human capital by encouraging the acquisition of knowledge and skills and emphasising creativity and imagination. (DfEE 1998, p.7)

Economic necessity provides the dynamic that is driving educational policy. Elements in the Secretary of State's aim resonate with themes associated with the much maligned progressive education. However, a risk with this economic orientation is that a narrow vocationalism comes to define and dominate learning opportunities. The wider commitment to learning, and the recognition that the desired learning process can be achieved through diverse means and initiatives, could be stifled by an instrumental orientation to the needs of industry. In a period of rapid change these perceived needs of industry have proved notoriously difficult to define and predict (Dyke 1997, p.6). Transferable abilities such as to learn, reflect, adapt, think and innovate are, in the long term, more likely to equip an individual more adequately than any narrowly defined vocational skills that are here today and gone tomorrow. The transitory nature of many vocational skills may in part explain the enthusiasm for transferability in the key skills of communication, numeracy and information technology in Dearing (1996, p.3).

The Learning Age Green Paper argues that 'the Learning Age is about more than employment' (DfEE 1998, p.10). The word 'learning' is said to include 'formal study, reading, watching television, going on a training course, taking an evening class, at work, from family and friends' (1998, p.10). Despite such inclusive aims the economic arguments about skills, employment and a changing global market dominate the Green Paper. There are occasional references to a wider educational agenda, but the balance of the arguments presented have an economic and training orientation. The funding principles point towards a new partnership between government, individuals and employers where: 'Individuals enhance their employability and skills, businesses improve their productivity, and society enjoys wider social and economic benefits' (DfEE 1998, p.25). The stated benefits of 'learning' to individuals primarily emphasize the work ethic. We are instructed: 'Individuals should invest in their own learning to improve employability, professional competence and earning potential or for leisure' (DfEE 1998, p.26). There are more direct and explicit vocational aims in *The Learning Age* that argue:

> the Government's role is to provide incentives for training. (DfEE 1998, p.26)

The Learning Age is peppered with educational ideals and visions yet even in the chapters which are not devoted to work or administration, such as the chapter 'Realising the Learning Age' (DfEE 1998, pp.45–56) there is a constant reference to skills, employability, traineeships, work, economic performance. It is difficult to avoid the conclusion that, for government, business and economics will drive the Learning Age.

The central risk of the economic rationale that dominates the Green Paper is that lifelong learning, while arguably lifelong education, is in practice reduced to lifelong training. The ethos of empowerment, inclusion, community, even democracy, risks being subsumed within narrowly defined vocational ends. What could be the consequences if a narrow vocational agenda comes to dominate the Learning Age? One consequence could be that inclusive lifelong education is emptied out of its original meaning and simply becomes another element of hegemonic control in the form of lifelong training. As Foucault (1979) argued, those in power seek to control behaviour and gain knowledge through surveillance. Lifelong learning that in practice was only experienced as the accreditation of approved (funded) training has Orwellian connotations. In such a pessimistic scenario the main contribution of the Learning Age would be to nurture the work ethic and the production of 'Compliant-Creative workers' (Esland 1990a). The Learning Age would contribute to what Beck referred to as the 'individualisation of social inequality' (Beck 1992, p.87), part of the process where 'individuals become agents of their educational and market-mediated subsistence' (Beck 1992, p.90). Ulrich Beck argued that such individual agency should not be confused with emancipation. It refers to a process whereby individuals become more dependent on education and training in a world that has 'tendencies toward the institutionalisation and standardisation of ways of life' (Beck 1992, p.90). More centrally controlled systems and frameworks thereby limit individual decision making. Usher *et al.* also recognized this dilemma, and noted that individuals are encouraged to take active responsibility for their own learning. In practice these 'active' learners are forced to comply with pre-defined skills and competencies, such as those specified in NVQs, that in effect subject their learning to close regulation and control (Usher, Bryant and Johnston 1997, p.80).

In a sense the mix of central control with increased degrees of individualism replicates a late modern account of globalization. Giddens argued that with globalization a concentration of power occurs at the same time as a transformation at the local level (Giddens 1998). In economic terms Lash and Urry (1994, p.124) describe a tendency for economic power to remain concentrated and centralized while production and work becomes more fragmented and flexible. In the pessimistic lifelong-training scenario sketched above, government controls the 'production' of what is defined as learning. Government can effectively brand what counts as learning through control of qualifications, curriculum and through funding and quality assurance mechanisms. Alongside this centralization there may be diversification in the provision of what is centrally defined as learning. Such learning could well take place in local communities, at work, at home or anywhere a person has access to information and communications technology. Learning, education or training has the potential to be provided relatively free of time and place. Who provides learning and in what context may be less important than who controls the information that counts as knowledge, the knowledge included in qualifications and the curriculum. In the context of the information and communications revolution the work of Young (1971) on Knowledge and Control has renewed relevance. The Learning Age could herald a centralization in the production or branding of learning with a diversification in the provision of that product. A central issue remains: who defines, supports and accredits learning? The University for Industry aims to provide brokerage, to act as an agency that links learners and business to education and training provision. Through this process the University for Industry is likely to gain more control over the supply of education and training programmes. The University for Industry's (UfI) Pathfinder Prospectus stated: 'The UfI will ensure that the products and services which benefit from UfI branding are relevant, cost-effective and of high quality' (DfEE 1999b, para.4.10). Will the University of Industry nurture an inclusive approach to lifelong learning as articulated by Fryer and Kennedy? One that empowers the learner by providing control and choice as to how they learn and what they learn. Flexibility should not simply be confined to where and when learning takes place, but include what and how individuals and groups choose to learn.

A broad-based inclusive response to lifelong learning could indirectly meet the needs of the economy as well as the individual. By nurturing the learning in itself, and particularly reflective learning, people will develop transferable skills that can benefit work and employment. The Ford motor company recognized the economic benefits of broadly defined non-vocational learning. Ford, together with the trade unions representing its workforce, established an Employee Development and Assistance Programme (EDAP) in 1988. The Ford scheme has been endorsed by the National Institute for Adult Education (NIACE):

> All Ford employees are entitled to up to £200 per year for learning and health/fitness activities so long as these are **not** related to their work. Annual uptake is in the region of 30%. A further feature is that independent advice and guidance is provided by Local Education Advisers who report to (and are managed by) local joint committees but who are employed by an external agency (currently the University of East London). This feature means that the

Advisers are completely separate from the company's industrial relations apparatus. (NIACE 1997)

The Ford scheme meets the criteria for Employee Development Programmes as defined by NIACE. Participation is voluntary, learning takes place primarily in the learner's own time and participants have few restrictions limiting their choice of learning. With the Employee Development Programme the Ford Motor Company would appear to be sponsoring a post-Fordist form of education and training (Brown and Lauder 1992, p.4). The above example illustrates that broadly defined and inclusive lifelong learning that is learner controlled can have economic benefits. Press reports (Baty 1997) suggested that such an approach was supported by the Prime Minister as a model for the University for Industry. If that is the case, the University for Industry may provide a vehicle for more lifelong learning and not simply lifelong training. It remains to be seen whether or not the University for Industry in practice supplies, or brands, programmes that promote lifelong learning or merely acts as a broker for lifelong training.

Conclusions

The inclusive lifelong education that is advocated here is included in Giddens' account of Third Way politics. Giddens also acknowledged the primacy of cognitive competence over training in specific skills:

> Governments need to emphasise life-long education, developing education programmes that start from an individual's early years and continue late in life. Although training in specific skills may be necessary for many job transitions, more important is the development of cognitive and emotional competence. (Giddens 1998, p.125)

A breakdown of the vocational academic divide through reform of the qualifications framework is one means of facilitating inclusive lifelong education and providing greater harmonization of vocational education and training practices. The difficulty lies in providing a credible system that is easily understood and nurtures educational diversity. Proposals for an overarching award have received widespread support and a positive response from government, with the year 2002 recommended as the earliest date for introduction of such an award (QCA 1998, p.2). In terms of qualification frameworks there does appear to be some cause for optimism that policy will support inclusive lifelong education and challenge the academic vocational divide.

The powerful economic rationale for the Learning Age presents a paradox. The economic arguments provide the *raison d'être* for expenditure and investment on education and training. It also risks undermining inclusive lifelong education, replacing a diverse educational provision with narrowly defined lifelong training. Such risks should not be oversimplified: it is all to easy too equate training with control, education with empowerment. Empowerment and control are not exclusive to either education or training, but as Usher *et al.* note:

> Increasingly adult learning is equated with training, moreover a training defined as the acquisition of pre-defined skills and competencies and the development of certain kinds of attitudes defined in relation to the current needs of the economy (Usher *et al.* 1997, p.80)

The benefits of diversity in education, with parity of esteem, are widely acknowledged (Fryer 1997; Kennedy 1997; Giddens 1998). If the Learning Age is to facilitate democratization in late modernity such diversity needs to be nurtured, with individuals and groups given maximum choice in terms of where, when, how and what they learn.

In a world full of conflicting and changing information, individuals need to learn how to interpret, apply, evaluate and synthesize information. They need to transform information into knowledge that can enable informed decision making. If education and training is to help individuals live in late modernity, reflective lifelong learning needs to be a central theme of vocational education, training and assessment (Dyke 1997). The centrality of reflection as a response to reflexive modernization is evident in the Jansen and Van der Veen (1992) analysis of risk society and critical adult education. They argue that adult education needs to adapt to reflexive modernization, and that such changes would stand in 'a long tradition of reflective adult education' (Jansen and Van der Veen 1992, p.285). Despite the centrality of reflection and reflexivity in social and educational theory, reflective learning remains peripheral to policy in vocational education and training.

In *The Politics of Risk Society* (Franklin 1998) Anna Coote argued that public policy must engage in 'a new political culture which supports an informed and reasonable scepticism about scientific or expert knowledge' (Franklin 1998, p.127). Decisions relating to current scientific developments in nuclear, biological and chemical technologies, for example, can affect all our futures. Late modern theorists (Beck 1992; Giddens 1990; Franklin 1998) argue for more public involvement in decision making. Prescriptive lifelong training alone is not likely to meet the needs of individuals, work or democracy, whereas reflective learning within lifelong education can facilitate the process of democratization, economic development and decision making in Risk Society. It will enable people to plan and make judgements in an age of uncertainty, as Anna Coote suggests:

> Planning for uncertainty involves realistic appraisal of the evidence at our disposal, a deep understanding of the present (not marred by a rose tinted view of the past). It involves knowing that we cannot go back. (Franklin 1998, p.130)

Reflective learning in lifelong education has a role to play in enabling individuals, organizations and communities to engage with expert opinion and make informed decisions about all aspects of living in late modernity. Reflective learning and lifelong education are essential elements in the possible democratization of Risk Society.

References

Avis, J. (1993) 'A new orthodoxy, old problems: post-sixteen reforms.' *British Journal of Sociology of Education 14*, 3, 245–260.

Ball, S. (1990) *Politics and Policy Making in Education*. London: Routledge.

Baty, P. (1997) 'Ford model for UFI plan.' *Times Higher Education Supplement*, 13.6.97.

Bauman, Z. (1993) *Postmodern Ethics*. Cambridge: Polity.

Bauman, Z. (1995) *Life in Fragments*. Cambridge: Polity.

Bauman, Z. (1997) *Postmodernity and its Discontents*. Cambridge: Polity.

Beck, U. (1992) *Risk Society: Towards a New Modernity*. London: Sage.

Blackstone, T. (1998) 'Blackstone announces A Level improvements.' *DfEE Press*, 170/98, 3 April 1998. London: DfEE.

Brown, P. and Lauder, H. (1992) *Education for Economic Survival: From Fordism to Post-Fordism*. London: Routledge.

Castells, E. (1996) *The Information Age: Economy, Society and Culture Vol.1.* Oxford: Blackwell.

Chignell, H. and Abbott, D. (1995) 'An interview with Anthony Giddens.' *Sociology Review 5*, 2, 10–14.

Dearing, R. (1996) *Review of Qualifications for 16–19 Year Olds*. Middlesex: SCAA.

DfEE (1994) *The New Qualifications Framework*. London: HMSO.

DfEE (1998) *The Learning Age: A Renaissance for a New Britain*. London: The Stationery Office.

DfEE (1999a) 'A level curriculum will guarantee standards.' Baroness Blackstone, 19 March 1999. http: //www.dfee.gov.uk/news/125.htm.

DfEE (1999b) *University for Industry: Pathfinder Prospectus.* http: //www.dfee.gov.uk/ufi/download.htm.

Dyke, M. (1996) 'The New Qualifications Framework: towards post-Fordist reform.' *International Journal of Lifelong education 15*, 4, 266–275.

Dyke, M. (1997) 'Reflexive learning as reflexive education in a risk society: empowerment and control?' *International Journal of Lifelong Education 10*, 1, 2–17.

Esland, G. (1990a) *Education Training and Employment, Vol. 1.* Wokingham: Addison-Wesley.

Finegold, D., Keep, E., Milliband, D., Raffe, D., Spours, K. and Young, M. (1990) *A British Baccalaureate.* London: Institute for Public Policy Research.

Foucault, M. (1979) *Discipline and Punishment.* Harmondsworth: Penguin.

Franklin, J. (1998) *The Politics of Risk Society.* London: Polity Press/IPPR.

Fryer, R. (1997) *Learning for the 21st Century. First Report of the National Advisory Group for Continuing Education and Lifelong Learning.* London: Stationery Office.

Giddens, A. (1990) *The Consequences of Modernity.* Cambridge: Polity Press.

Giddens, A. (1991) *Modernity and Self Identity.* Cambridge: Polity Press.

Giddens, A. (1998) *The Third Way.* Cambridge: Polity Press.

Giddens, A. and Pierson, C. (1998) *Conversations with Anthony Giddens.* Cambridge: Polity Press.

Hall, S. and Gieben, B. (1992) *Formations of Modernity.* Cambridge: Polity Press.

Holdsworth, N. (1994) 'Module answer to a decline.' *Times Educational Supplement,* 2.6.94.

Hyland, T. (1992) 'Expertise and competence in Further and Adult Education.' *British Journal of In Service Education 18*, 1, 23–27.

IPPR (1996) Politics of Risk Society' (speakers Ulrich Beck and Anthony Giddens). IPPR Conference 26 March 1996, London.

Jansen, T. and Van Der Veen, R. (1992) 'Reflexive modernity, self reflective biographies: adult education in the light of risk society.' *International Journal of Lifelong Education 11*, 4, 275–286.

Jarvis, P. (1992) *Paradoxes of Learning.* San Francisco: Jossey-Bass.

Kennedy, H. (1997) *Learning Works.* London: FEFC.

Kolb, D. (1984) *Experiential Learning.* New Jersey: Prentice-Hall.

Kumar, K. (1995) *From Post-industrial to Post-modern Society.* Oxford: Blackwell.

Lash, S. and Urry, J. (1994) *Economies of Signs and Space.* London: Sage.

Lester, L. (1994) 'Crediting the learning company.' *Training and Development Journal of ITD*, January, 22–24.

Nash, I. (1994) 'Radical aims for A-level successor.' *TES*, 29.7.94, p.7.

Nash, I. (1994) 'Heads look beyond fourth horizons.' *TES*, 14.10.94, p.10.

Nash, I. (1994) 'Reforms creep closer for A Level.' *TES*, 25.11.94, p.3.

National Commission on Education (1993) *Learning to Succeed.* London: Heinemann.

NIACE (1997) *Working People and Lifelong Learning: A Study of the Impact of an Employee Development Scheme.* London: NIACE.

QCA (1998) *The Future of Post-16 Qualifications: The Response of the Qualifications and Curriculum Authority to the Government's Consultation on Qualifying for Success.* http://www.qca.org.uk/shframes.htm.

Schon, D. (1987) *Educating the Reflective Practitioner: Toward a New Design for Teaching and Learning in the Profession.* San Francisco: Jossey-Bass.

Smithers, A. (1993) *All Our Futures.* London: Channel 4 TV.

Stubbs, W. (1998) Letter to DFEE 17 February 1998 from Sir William Stubbs, Chairman of Qualifications and Curriculum Authority. http://www.qca.org.uk/shframes.htm.

Szerzynski, B. (1996) In S. Lash, B. Szerszynski and B. Wynne (eds) *Risk, Environment and Modernity.* London: Sage.

Usher, R., Bryant, I. and Johnston, R. (1997) *Adult Education and the Postmodern Challenge.* London: Routledge.

Wolf, A. (1995) *Competence Based Assessment.* Buckingham: Open University Press.

Young, M.F.D. (1971) *Knowledge and Control.* Middlesex: Collier Macmillan.

PART III

Management and Funding

Chapter 8

The Management of Teaching in Further Education
Issues from a Case Study

Geoffrey Elliott

Overview

Changes in the economic and political context of further education (FE) have supported a managerialist culture within colleges, but the response of lecturers has not been uniform. Many lecturers retain a student-centred style of teaching and, in contrast to the emerging managerialist culture, a democratic ideology. The market and incorporation have brought about: new terms and working conditions (imposed by the College Employers' Forum); new quality assurance arrangements; the introduction of the Training and Development Lead Body assessor and verifier awards for lecturers; lecturer appraisal; college performance indicators. Not all of these are seen in negative terms by lecturers, but criticism has been levelled at the way in which they have been introduced. The implications of the introduction of competition and business models into FE are major concerns of lecturers. Whereas the market is seen as lessening equalities in access to education and a barrier to social justice, education is viewed not as a means of producing compliant individuals, but learners who can be critical of the system.

Introductory comments: the national policy context

For so long the 'Cinderella' of the education service, FE has now come of age. Government spending on FE for 1998/99 is set to exceed £3 billion. The high profile of the sector is underpinned by the Fryer Report on Lifelong Learning (NAGCELL 1997), the report of the Kennedy Committee on widening participation (FEFC 1997), and the Green Paper *The Learning Age* (DfEE 1998). Whilst this increase in the visibility of the FE sector has led to some increased funding, there are nonetheless economic tensions which have led some FE colleges to conclude that they must merge in order to remain operational. These same tensions are highlighted by the requirement upon all colleges to move towards an average level of funding, which has introduced economic instability to some of the most successfully proactive corporations.

In light of such root and branch changes in the political and economic context of FE, it is commonly assumed that the incorporation of FE has brought about major changes in the working practices of lecturers. However, after working with lecturers in the FE sector, it seems to me that they had often developed a range of strategies to thwart attempts to impose external systemic and specific changes perceived to be at variance with their core values. In other words, lecturers do not seem to respond unthinkingly to externally imposed new curricula or administrative tasks. As key stakeholders (Harvey, Burrows and Green 1992) in the educational institution and system, they seemed to assess and evaluate proposed changes and innovations against a benchmark described by their experience and their practice. Furthermore, and crucially, they played a decisive part in filtering and adapting externally generated reform and innovation. A key influence upon lecturers' practice appeared to be their orientation towards their students and their commitment to a student-centred style of teaching which takes for granted:

- that lecturers and students worked together as equal participants in the educational process

- the relevance of learning to the students' needs as well as vocational contexts

- the centrality within the curriculum of opportunities for the development of a questioning, critical, active intelligence in students.

The evidence of my personal experience as a lecturer in the FE sector, conversations with colleagues, discussions with other practitioners, some previous academic work in the field, and the evidence of the data reported in this study, supports a perspective which points to the possibility of tensions between policy and practice in FE; between the reality and rhetoric of policy and its implementation. This tension is, in part, a consequence of the often contrasting and contradictory demands on, and expectations of, those who work in a complex and changing FE sector. These demands include political pressure, through the National Targets for Education and Training (NTETS) and the emergence of a government-backed widening participation agenda for the sector, for 16–19 participation and achievement rates to match those of other European countries; calls by the FEFC for increased efficiency and inspection arrangements designed to give greater accountability; action by college managers to introduce Human Resource Management (HRM) strategies, including the imposition of the new College Employers' Forum (CEF) 'professional contract' for FE lecturers; the radical curriculum reforms of the NCVQ and the successor body the Qualifications and Curriculum Authority (QCA); and the everyday engagement of lecturers, support staff and students in varied and flexible teaching and learning processes. It is the tension between these influences and the ideological orientation of FE lecturers which has provided the theme for this research.

The case study upon which this chapter is based was carried out in a large FE college during the period in which the sector became incorporated. Sources of data included college publications, policy statements, strategic plans, meetings, conversations with staff and open-ended interviews with a group of lecturers in one department of the college. The findings of the case study suggest that the cumulative effect of reforms of the structure and curriculum of the sector has been to create contradictory and oppositional forces within FE. In the case study college this is evidenced by a pervasive market ideology, willingly imposed by senior managers who embrace a managerialist culture, and actively resisted by lecturers who hold an alternative and competing democratic ideology underpinned by a commitment to a student-centred pedagogic culture. The external demands of quality assurance systems and lecturer accreditation experienced by the lecturers in this study are felt by them to be imposed by senior managers who were responding to governmental pressure to implement wide-ranging reforms, many of which were designed to increase efficiency and meet quantitative performance indicators (Elliott and Crossley 1994).

The lecturers' alternative world view leads them to voice strong criticism of government policies that they see as imposing an inappropriate market ideology upon educational practice. At the same time, however, they well understand the structural and system demands upon the college posed by incorporation, and are ready to acknowledge the need for realistic, efficient and effective management strategies that are required to ensure survival in an increasingly competitive market.

Policy, the market and incorporation

The findings discussed in this chapter are largely drawn from the qualitative interviews which took place during the academic session in which colleges of further education became incorporated. Incorporation brought about major structural changes which included a new funding body and new inspection arrangements. A major influence upon the way in which colleges dealt with human resource issues was the establishment of the CEF to act on behalf of college managers in framing and introducing new terms and conditions of service for lecturers in the sector, replacing those formerly negotiated between NATFHE and the local authorities, their former employers. Other significant externally imposed initiatives current at the time of the study included the introduction of new quality assurance arrangements in colleges, notably the British Standard (BS) 5750 (now ISO 9000); the introduction of the TDLB assessor and verifier awards for lecturers; lecturer appraisal; and increasingly sophisticated college performance indicators, which required college managers to collect and submit a broad range of data to the funding council. These initiatives were live issues in the case study college at the time of the interviews, and were seen by most lecturers as inspired by central government, and experienced by them as implemented and imposed by an ill-prepared but compliant college management. At the same time, there is evidence within the interview data that the lecturers were open to and welcomed many aspects of these initiatives, but were unhappy about the way in which they were implemented, and the emphasis that tended to be placed upon a formalistic interpretation. The number of such initiatives, and the speed with which they were introduced, also appears to have been a significant factor in bringing about negative responses by the lecturers. Many of the initiatives were required to be in place in order for colleges to continue to receive FEFC funding for their core work, which gave college managers little opportunity – even if they wanted to – to resist them. The implication that central government policy for education was out of sympathy with the concerns of educational practice led one lecturer to argue that government is imposing an economic paradigm upon education:

> ... under the current climate, there are so many aspects of education that are being pushed down from central government, from a distance, from people whose contact with practical education is minimal.

Another lecturer foreshadowed one of the dangers inherent in the emerging view of colleges as businesses:

> ... the college as it stands at the moment is a business, or we've been told it's a business and if it is a business then, if we see it in those terms, then this business is going to go down the pan because you always have a head team of management who knows who their customers are, what their customers want ... and this company doesn't know ...

There was evidence to suggest a concern that the desire by government to move colleges towards a business orientation, and to subject them to increased competition within an educational market, had taken place without adequate preparation and ground laying at the college level. One lecturer, for example, liked the idea of colleges as 'autonomous organizations who offer something and attract students to it', but insisted that the policy had been undermined by the lack of adequate development support for college managers.

Another noted that the imposition of policy-driven changes upon colleges may have brought with it a lack of ownership of external initiatives on the part of educational managers, making the important point that by this strategy 'you're encouraged to have a negative attitude, even by the people who are presenting it.'

For most lecturers, incorporation had simply not delivered what had been promised. The following view was typical:

> Well I have to say I've found it very difficult to see any tangible benefits in terms of the kind of promised land that was held out to us when the discussions originally took place. In terms of funding I've not seen any huge benefit, I mean there was a great deal of talk about there not being sticky fingers from the local authority or whatever, most of the monetary advantages that were perceived to exist don't seem to have turned into anything you can touch, feel or use, so I mean at the chalk face or whatever I can't see that there has been a huge benefit.

The idea of competition, and the introduction of an increasingly competitive ethos following incorporation, emerged as a strong issue of concern to the lecturers in the study. They felt under pressure from college managers to make efficiency gains, for example by employing more part-time staff who came cheaper than full-timers, in order to become more competitive. Staffing and equipment budgets were continually being reviewed and trimmed, and an internal bidding system was introduced for capital expenditure. This competitive ethos was regarded by lecturers with caution. Most lecturers disliked the idea of the college being placed in competition with schools, and had even greater reservations about internal competition. As one put it:

> One has become very aware within the college that there is a cake and you're competing for the slices of it; competing for the bigger slices, that's obviously out of one's hands.

Competition had a clear effect upon staff's relationships with each other, and promoted 'challenges about resources and about which area's more important.'

Most lecturers rejected in strong terms the notion of applying a business model to education, which might be considered surprising, given the assumed business orientation of the sector as a whole:

> I hate it! I hate the idea! It's what sort of college plc is, it's forcing the college even more, it's forcing colleges to operate as businesses. They shouldn't be, they should be subsidised to a huge degree.

There was a strong sense of blame attached to the government, which introduced reforms without adequately preparing those whose task it would be to implement them. In the view of one lecturer, the creation of a newly independent FE sector and the government expectation that college managers should somehow be equipped to deal with the new circumstance in which they find themselves, was flawed:

> I think a lot of the problems are stemming from their ignorance, and I don't use that as a negative – that's a point of fact – they are ignorant about how to operate in that sector.

The removal of responsibility for education from the state into private hands strikes against a strongly-held ideological position of most lecturers. Almost all lecturers in the study expressed the strength of feeling on this issue, signified in the ensuing extract, during the interview cycle:

> Education should be the responsibility of government or the state, I suppose (by the state I mean us as a democratic state) – it is within that province, it shouldn't be a private enterprise. The idea of it being a private enterprise is anathema to me, and that's the way it's moving at the moment … the sense that the resources that a student can count on are dependent on the business efficiency, and the competitive business efficiency, of an educational organization is appalling. It makes me angry – I get inarticulate about it because I get so angry.

FE lecturers and student learning

A major theme, which was returned to frequently by all lecturers in the study, was that of the need to keep students at the centre of the educational process. Whilst recognizing the need for efficient and effective management in colleges, they were increasingly fearful of a shift in the core business and focus of colleges, from the development of students' potential to a preoccupation with balancing the budget. The majority of the lecturers in the study, on the other hand, expressed the view that 'the students should be priority'. This led them to share a concern that the vocationalization of the FE curriculum was endangering the educational character of FE provision, shifting the focus of provision away from serving the needs of the students to serving the needs of the labour market. As one lecturer put it:

> ... I have a concern about the move to totally competence based and vocationally based focus within the FE sector. I regret there is some loss in losing that kind of general educational background that always – did exist ... I mean I do recognize the need for a skills based workforce in the country, but my perception of the successful economies is that they are not only skills based but they also have a level of understanding and awareness across a range of issues ...

Another condemned the drift within vocational education towards basic, vocational skills, and away from a more rounded, higher level, education:

> ... some of that critical edge is being lost and a lot of courses are much more to be concerned, I suppose, with how to use those manipulative skills rather [than] ... to understand why that process of persuasion is taking place and to understand something about the ideological notions that are ascribed to certain forms of communication etc.

All lecturers in the study perceived that they had a facilitative, enabling role in working with students, and typically expressed this role in terms of a student-centred pedagogy:

> ... enabling students can be a simple process of orientation through delivery and then they start to use themselves and any kind of physical and library resources and yourself as a resource, and they're up and running.

The high value placed by the lecturers upon creativity led them to a highly democratic notion of the lecturer/student relationship:

> I find the easiest way for a student to understand is for them to cre-
> ate themselves, whether it's a product – you know a large scale
> production or whether it's a scale model of something – or
> whether it's their own ideas. I mean I always say to students none
> of your ideas are wrong.

Thus were students encouraged to develop a critical, questioning
intelligence which enabled them to 'understand what processes
they're being subjected to'.

The emphasis within this model of lecturing, highlighted by most
lecturers, was not upon the omnipotent and all-knowing lecturer, nor
upon the content of what is taught. It was, rather, upon the process in
which lecturers and students equally engage. In this engagement, the
relationship is not expressed as one which involves lecturers filling
students with subject knowledge. One lecturer described his role as
one of a facilitator in an educational setting providing access to
knowledge – which is not the same as providing knowledge – and also
ensuring essential feedback into the process. Another put it in terms
of his responsibility for creating an appropriate learning environment,
which provides progression opportunities.

Lecturers are required to apply the same standards to their own
practice as they do to students:

> I don't see lecturers as omnipotent and knowing everything. I
> think a good lecturer always admits when they don't know some-
> thing. If they don't know they'll go away and find out, because you
> expect a student to do that so why shouldn't you do that?

An alternative approach to management: a bottom-up model

This primary focus of the case study was upon the lecturers' world-
view. The hostility expressed by many lecturers towards the top-down
style of management practised in this college was strongly evidenced
within the interview data. Yet there was an equally strong theme
emerging from the data which pointed to a viable, alternative model
of management, derived from the lecturers' perspective and
grounded in pedagogical culture. At the same time, it is a model
which is realistic, in that it recognizes a competitive environment and
the consequent need for the college to be well-run. Whilst most
lecturers voiced strong opposition to the idea of the college as a
business, they well appreciated the extent to which it was necessary
for the organization to be efficient, and to be run in a businesslike
manner, in order to be effective:

I believe in efficiently run organizations, but I don't believe in 'efficiency' and 'in business' being a priority which overrides the
concerns and the needs of students and, in fact, of staff as well …
There is a place for this, business management is important.

The position represented by this lecturer, and others, was not that
management is unnecessary, but that 'progress has to be linked to
what is best for the student, not to what's best for the business, [so]
that managerial team needs to bear in mind all the time what that
business is for and who the business is for.'

The key point is the differential emphasis placed by lecturers and
managers upon business and educational values. Lecturers felt that,
for the college managers, business methods had become an end in
themselves, sustaining a control ethos and a managerialist culture. A
common complaint was that college managers seemed to have lost
sight of the core business of student learning and achievement – they
no longer saw students as students, but as units of funding. On the
other hand the lecturers in this group prioritized learning and
teaching processes. Crucially, however, they were not unaware of the
need for the college to be competitive in the newly created
quasi-market, or naive about the need for management efficiency.
One lecturer showed a sharp sense of realism in relation to the
funding of his curriculum area:

I know that funding is going to be tight and therefore you try and
do the best you can within that circumstance to try and do the
things you want to do within a particular department, and if you
can't do it one way you find another way to achieve it.

Another considered that whilst the college management did not know
where to contract, 'it knows where to expand but is very cautious
about putting the money forward (quite rightly – that's good business
practice).'

A third acknowledged that colleges should be externally
accountable, but with the enigmatic caveat that accountability must
be consistent with high standards:

Part of me says yes, I mean any industrial body who are investing
money into colleges should expect a certain standard when they
have people trained by the college. My other half says that's fine
but if the college has got to cut corners to try and meet those standards or if the college standards were above that which the
industry were expecting I don't think they should cut them. I believe they should try and acquire the highest standard possible for
the students.

Whilst incorporation had heightened, and to a large extent symbolized, the encroachment of a market in further education, it is important to note that its effects were not uniformly regarded negatively by this group of lecturers. There was a view, which the following extracts illustrate, that independence could bring certain advantages:

> I suppose that as far as experience goes in practice it is rather early days ... freedom from various changes in political control could be an advantage.

> I think there are advantages in institutions having the freedom to decide what they should do without artificial constraints and without the mix and match funding that you've had before. In theory I think it was an excellent idea and I was strongly in favour of it ...

Even for some of the lecturers with major reservations concerning incorporation, some of the effects are regarded as potentially short-lived. A poor response to staffing requests led one lecturer to express a 'hope that that was simply a matter of incorporation and it just happened and they were sorting out themselves, and that now that would have happened a lot better this time.'

A benefit of incorporation was thought by one lecturer to be the extent to which it could foster ownership of strategic planning by management:

> Now if under incorporation they're free to a certain extent to decide what changes to take place you can expect a sense of ownership from the management, which might result in them presenting it more positively.

One lecturer identified the lack of training and development received by college managers to prepare them for change, rather than incorporation itself, as the underlying issue:

> I think senior management of all institutions have been well dropped in it by the government ... because they've had no training, because they've had no development.

There was a widely shared view that managers should communicate their own values to lecturers:

> You know it's perfectly likely that there are people here who are very sympathetic to the needs and aims of the college senior management ... if anybody ever told us what they were.

This gives further weight to the argument that the lecturers were not operating in an isolated or idealistic context; they understood the demands made by incorporation upon management, but found their own value orientation undermined by the way in which senior managers embraced the use of a new educational management jargon, which reflected the needs of accountancy rather than pedagogy, and exacerbated the problem of communication of management purposes:

> It may be a problem in educational management that our changes are never presented that well ... I have to say that part of their problem is that they don't communicate very well with the staff ...
> I mean I don't think they communicate what their plans are, they don't actually have a presence in the college.

Many of the management failings that were mentioned by the lecturer group were seen to emanate from their inconsistent and unclear approach to the management of the college. The model of management that is being rejected is one which does not assume responsibility for the effective communication and implementation of its policies. A 'dialogue' is expected, even assumed, and it was largely the absence of opportunities to engage in dialogue which drove wedges between lecturers and senior managers. The formalized management style adopted by senior managers, their use of business jargon, the use of confrontation politics in the run-up to incorporation, and the sense which the lecturers had that management did not understand, care about, or value the curriculum activity, all contributed in a major way to stifling dialogue, or even beginning to build upon the areas of commonality which existed.

Discussion and conclusion

The evidence of emergent and oppositional cultures within the interview data directed analysis towards the existence of a shared lecturer culture and its characteristics. This territory seemed a fruitful one to pursue, since lecturers themselves clearly felt that the cultural dimension was important to the successful implementation of their role within the incorporated college. It also appeared significant to the writer, since the extent and degree of change which college managers were asking lecturers to take on, including acceptance of new contracts with more flexible working arrangements, and the operation of a new qualifications framework, appeared to be in jeopardy for as long as cultural-political differences between lecturers and college managers were allowed to persist unaddressed. There did seem to be common ground between lecturers and managers, which was not being recognized and therefore capitalized upon by managers.

However, underpinning the real differences in culture within the college is the stark reality of the politics of education in modern Britain. The unceasing government-led drive towards a radical right wing orientation within education has brought with it a new orthodoxy which is legitimated and supported by a new vocabulary. The orthodoxy is one of transience and contingency. There is no place within such a vision for traditional values of the right or the left. Thus New Labour, by committing itself to the spending targets of the former Conservative government for the first two years of its life, seemed to allow itself little choice in terms of post-compulsory education reform. Although the damaging consequences of the market in further education, in terms of the establishment of a culture of competition rather than collaboration, were fully recognized in the Kennedy Report (FEFC 1997), the government response to that report, and to the Fryer report on Lifelong Learning (NAGCELL 1997), has been disappointing. The evidence is that in the first years of Labour government the market continues to dominate FE decision making. The customer still pays, and education becomes a service industry whose product is experienced by purchasers and providers as a commodity. National Targets for Education and Training are a quantitative indicator, to be recalibrated to suit current administrative convenience. Colleges close when they have been squeezed dry by a funding mechanism which does not recognize that lifelong learning, awkwardly, cannot be attributed a tariff value. Whilst part-time students are still denied the opportunity to study through vigorous application of new benefits criteria, increased staff workloads ensure that those who are on courses in colleges experience less and less contact with those who teach them.

It is within this context that the lecturers and managers in this study work out their separate agendas. Both in a sense are victims of a system which is determined by government interventionism. Yet at the same time, the possibilities of varying responses and proactive strategies are clearly indicated by this study. The market paradigm offers, at one and the same time, constraint and opportunity. However, these two dimensions do not divide simplistically along the line between managers and managed. Lecturers respond in both positive and negative ways to the unfolding manifestations of the market in their college. As for the managers, they seem to be more closely bound by the chaotic but manipulative imperatives that they face as business managers who appear to be willing but unprepared victims of incorporation.

The crisis of reform in the college is deep-seated, having both cultural and political manifestations. The resulting disorder becomes a metaphor for the collisions between rationalistic managerialism and negotiated collegiality. Pfeffer and Salancik characterize an organization as 'a coalition of groups and interests, each attempting to obtain something from the collectivity by interacting with others, and each with its own preferences and objectives' (Pfeffer and Salancik 1978, p.36). To the extent that this notion conjures up a picture of competing rationalities and unintended consequences, it strikes many chords in relation to the management of teaching and learning in the case study college. However, the interests, preferences and objectives of lecturers and managers in the incorporated FE sector need to be understood and interpreted within the context of political influence and control. By accepting the rules of competition within a marketplace, those within the institution are, arguably, making an attempt to preserve the learning and teaching environment which they value. Increasingly, however, the rules of discourse within the college make it more and more difficult for lecturers to maintain continuity. Appealing to a moral principle or an educational aim represents an inappropriate discourse for a college focused on the fashionable management objectives of 'downsizing', 'flexibility' and becoming 'leaner and fitter'.

The vigour with which college managers embrace the market paradigm suggests that for them the opportunities of incorporation were long overdue. In dealing with HRM issues during the 1980s, managers felt that their hands were tied, in that they were subject to the authority of the LEA and thereby unwilling signatories to the Silver Book agreement which guaranteed a range of entitlements including a specified national maximum number of teaching contact hours. During the period immediately leading up to incorporation day itself, managers and lecturers were locked in dispute, with strike action over conditions of service threatening to dampen the celebrations which were planned. Subsequently, the power, influence and membership of the main college lecturers' union declined dramatically. The lecturers' so-called 'professional contract', local pay bargaining, performance related pay, the introduction of casual part-time staff and technician-demonstrators to replace lecturers, are well-established throughout the sector. The discourse of the marketeer has become an orthodoxy, with customer service, total quality and performance indicators maintaining a high profile.

What is to be done? It is necessary to move beyond the data of the study to look for an answer to a political question. The presence within the college of a circle of contradiction and tension has been noted. By accepting the rules of a technocratic discourse, both lecturers and managers have become locked into a cycle of decline, just as all colleges in the sector have become engaged into a competitive spiral in which the losers are taken over by the winners. Within this discourse, the needs of students are secondary to the needs of the market. Market forces demand that colleges compete, in order to demonstrate ever-increasing efficiency gains. Whilst both the present and previous governments have claimed to be widening participation through the implementation of their respective policies, there is a silence from opposition parties and from the sector as to alternative strategies. No-one can imagine dismantling the market that has been created, and putting in place government of post-compulsory education in the true sense of the word. West (1996), writing about the schools sector, argues for a locally accountable democratic model of educational policy:

> ... the problems of modern society can only be resolved by the fostering of new civic partnerships: the involvement of education's stakeholders. The political voice and skills of governing bodies and local communities are important elements in this: the only elements at present perhaps that can lift schools out of the sterile concentration of administration and technique: there is in other words a need for the concept of self-management to extend to that of self-governance and co-governance, for without political voice and participation, at the local level the skills of government could so easily be replaced by a tier of technocrats – the accessories of hegemony. We have to begin again in building the democratic process and in unearthing civic awareness from traditional assumptions, paternalism and market silences. (West 1996, p.92)

The political context of further education is indeed one of hegemonic influence and control, where debate is constrained within a technocratic market discourse, to the point where many lecturers are experiencing the fundamental contradiction of educational practice: 'the experience of holding educational values, and the experience of their negation' (Whitehead 1989, p.44). There is some growing disquiet at the Labour government's muted response to the significant reports by Kennedy, Dearing and Fryer cited earlier which were commissioned by its predecessor (DfEE 1998). Further and higher education institutions are becoming used to the idea that whilst they are certainly not free to operate in an open market free of governmental interference (if that were possible), there is going to be no golden future for state-governed post-compulsory education. At the institutional level, Louis and Miles (1990) suggest that managers have a particular strategic responsibility for bringing about a shared vision. Theirs is the specific responsibility of putting procedures in place which are effective in promoting communication in all directions, in harnessing existing strengths, and in recognizing core values shared by front-line employees. The management-of-change literature suggests that alliances, albeit sometimes fraught with tension and difference, are an essential prerequisite for the effective management of learning and teaching (see, e.g. Fullan 1991, p.349). There would appear to be only a single way forward, and that is to find strategies to replace the dominant discourse with one which is predicated upon collaboration rather than competition. Whether or not this is possible within the current political climate is open to debate. There is an emerging swing away from conflict to consensus models in education (Lawton 1992; Hall and Wallace 1993; Bridges and Husbands 1996). Funding incentives are beginning to be offered to FE and HE institutions that can demonstrate a commitment to a strategic collaborative approach to widening participation. Whether these in themselves have the force to influence current directions to a significant extent is another matter.

References

Bridges, D. and Husbands, C. (1996) *Consorting and Collaborating in the Education Marketplace*. London: Falmer.

Department for Education and Employment (1998) *The Learning Age* (Green Paper). London: HMSO.

Elliott, G. and Crossley, M. (1994) 'Qualitative Research, Educational Management and the Incorporation of the Further Education Sector.' *Educational Management and Administration 22*, (3) 188–197.

Fullan, M. (1991) *The New Meaning of Educational Change*. London: Cassell.

Further Education Funding Council (1997) *Learning Works: Widening Participation in Further Education* (The Kennedy Report). Coventry: FEFC.

Hall, V. and Wallace, M. (1993) 'Collaboration as a subversive activity: a professional response to externally imposed competition between schools?' *School Organisation 13* (2) 101–117.

Harvey, L., Burrows, A. and Green, D. (1992) *Criteria of Quality: Summary.* Quality in Higher Education Project. Birmingham: University of Central England.

Lawton, D. (1993) *Education and Politics in the 1990s: Conflict or Consensus?* London: Falmer.

Louis, K. and Miles, M. (1990) *Improving the Urban High School: What Works and Why.* New York: Teachers College Press.

National Advisory Group for Continuing Education and Lifelong Learning (1997) *Learning for the Twenty-First Century: First Report of the National Advisory Group for Continuing Education and Lifelong Learning* (The Fryer Report). London: NAGCELL.

Pfeffer, J. and Salancik, G. (1978) *The External Control of Organisations: A Resource Dependence Perspective.* New York: Harper and Row.

West, S. (1996) 'Competition and collaboration in education: marriage not divorce.' In D. Bridges and C. Husbands (eds) *Consorting and Collaborating in the Education Marketplace.* London: Falmer.

Whitehead, J. (1989) 'Creating a living educational theory from questions of the kind, "How do I Improve my Practice?"' *Cambridge Journal of Education 19*, (1), 45–52.

Chapter 9

Cinderella FE – You Shall Go to the Ball!

Markets, Funding and Growth in Further Education

Don Bradley

Introduction

Government attention and focus upon the further education sector since the 1950s has been sparse and spasmodic. Many people both within and outside the sector have long regarded it as the 'Cinderella service'. The phrase itself was coined by Kenneth Baker, the ex-Minister of Education, in a speech to the Association of Colleges of Further and Higher Education (ACFHE) (Baker 1989). In many respects such a designation reflected the neglect which politicians themselves had shown towards the sector.

As one writer noted, it was 'undervalued by politicians with little contact and with little experience of non-advanced FE' (McGinty and Fish 1993, p.3). Unlike in the university sector, politicians themselves had not tended to pursue courses at their local college and they may therefore have had a limited understanding of FE: 'They had not attended these colleges themselves nor had they sent their children to them' (Hall 1994, p.20).

The Further and Higher Education Act (1992) and the subsequent formation of the Further Education Funding Council (FEFC) therefore marked a new departure. It heralded a significant change in the position of FE within the education system. Through the Act it was now recognized and acknowledged that such an inferior status needed to be addressed.

In the White Paper and the subsequent Act a new legislative environment for further education would represent: '... the first concerted attempt since Crowther (1959) to provide a legislative framework for post 16 education and training' (Gleeson 1993, p.30). To achieve these objectives, in the proposals there was a political assumption, as Maclure (1991) points out, that all students and trainees should continue in education and training to at least eighteen and this aim needed to be linked to the planned expansion of FE and HE.

This chapter will explore the consequences of incorporation for colleges in relation to their changed status and more particularly the funding methodology which facilitated independence. It will examine the business and market-related context of financing in which colleges now find themselves and compare this to the previous 'regime' operated through Local Education Authorities. Outlining the FEFC's rationale for the funding approach it has adopted, it will explore the explicit steers which it has introduced. It will go on to see whether in practice what has happened in colleges is what the originators of the methodology intended. Using one college as an example the chapter will examine the funding implications in terms of the effects they have had on middle managers.

The discussion will draw upon the author's own field research into the policy-making aspects of the FHE Act through the views of the politician who steered the Act through Parliament (Bradley 1997). Similarly at the other end of the policy-producing chain are the middle managers who are the policy implementers at a college level. Again, utilizing field research findings, we will explore how their position as finance managers as well as curriculum managers has affected their roles and responsibilities. Many of the issues can be generalized to most colleges. At a general and specific level the background question will be what have been the intended but also the unintended results of the funding methodology.

Finally, we are now entering a new era for FE. There is a fresh emphasis on collaboration rather than competition within the sector. Funding opportunities are being geared to partnerships of colleges and other providers. Colleges are being encouraged to recruit from groups in the population which have previously excluded themselves from FE. The introduction of this new 'widening participation' agenda will be explored in relation to the operation of the funding methodology. What changes are being proposed and implemented and what might be the likely consequences?

The market context

The rationale for granting independence to colleges was that it would free them to engage in entrepreneurial activity and to enter a 'market place' of education where they could compete with other colleges to attract students. The overall aims were to increase the level of participation in FE, to raise the levels of attainment and to do so in a way which encouraged institutional efficiency. There was a common theme in the two volumes of the White Paper, in terms of both the need for institutional autonomy and an overwhelming commitment to the efficacy of 'the market'.

Statements reiterating this theme were peppered throughout the documentation and speeches made by government officials. 'It means giving schools, colleges and universities the institutional freedom and the necessary incentives to develop and respond to the demands of young people and of employers' (Clarke 20.5.91). 'With the move to independence, the need for FE colleges to be able to respond rapidly and flexibly and to grasp opportunities will be even greater' (Eggar 1991).

The official view was that the Act would provide a framework in which corporate status would drive the new market mechanisms. There was here in many respects, as Gleeson (1993) noted, a fascination with markets. This fascination needs to be referred back to the desire of its advocates to reskill and upskill the workforce. The ideological agenda behind the Act was an attempt to break the public service elements of FE. The legislation would mean that FE would be in the 'market place', unfettered by bureaucracy and more responsive to market needs. This deregulation process had been mirrored in many other areas of local government and within the education service itself.

The overall aim was to make colleges more competitive through independence and more entrepreneurial in their actions. This was essentially seen in terms of a greater responsiveness to the business, industrial and commercial infrastructure, rather than local community-based initiatives. The Bill and the Act were therefore less about curricular and qualification framework changes and more about 'repositioning' FE in a policy framework which enabled this reorientation to occur (Gleeson 1993).

However, it is questionable whether the FE sector can be equated with a medium sized business which is located exclusively in the private sector. Rather, in many respects it is in a more 'quasi market' position, not completely free to plan its own development. Most college funding comes from the FEFC and thence from government where national priorities for skills training are laid out. This is irrespective of any local circumstances that may militate against their implementation.

Furthermore, planning may be difficult in a sector that remains unsure about how many customers it will have each year right up to the main September enrolment period. Colleges are therefore not completely free to respond to the market as they would wish at a local level. They must always have one eye on national directives and steers in order to maintain their level of funding.

There may therefore not be a free market operating in the FE sector. Can there be, where the Secretary of State for Education still determines what products are available in the market? He has the final decision-making powers regarding which post-sixteen curriculum policies to pursue. Similarly he decides who shall be allowed to enter the market and on what terms, for example in relation to the approval of local reorganization proposals.

The FE market: the perspective of a policy producer

The perspective of a policy producer supports this emphasis which was placed upon fostering competition between colleges in a new market place for education post-incorporation. The Minister in question was Tim Eggar, who piloted the FHE Act through Parliament and was interviewed at length by the author during field research. He saw market forces as beneficial in terms of 'weeding out' the less efficient and effective colleges in the sector.

The insertion of competition was viewed by the Minister as a necessary development, which concentrated colleges' minds on the 'customers' that it needed to attract and the market that it needed to develop. As a result the consumers of the service, that is the students, are receiving a better deal from their local colleges: 'I have no doubts at all that in the overwhelming majority of colleges a better opportunity is being given to larger numbers of students than would otherwise have been the case.'

He considered that market principles have improved practice in FE. He made this explicit when discussing the market and competition in relation to the flexible provision which colleges were now providing:

> By and large yes they are providing flexible provision. At any one point in time you can always find particular examples which you can argue have not led to improved delivery. But if you look across

the country as a whole and across colleges as a whole then I think the answer to that is yes. It's certainly led to much more flexible methods of provision. It's led to I would say a more imaginative set of options available to students.

The language of business and the use of marketing terms to describe aspects of further education provision have become a commonplace in the sector. The introduction of business practices and procedures has concentrated managers' minds on how they should market the college.

Referring to the way in which colleges have attempted to attract new students whilst using business-derived methods the Minister noted that this responsiveness had been due to:

... a combination of things. It's a change in the structure of the governing bodies, it's a recognition that the college can use its assets to redevelop itself. The need for competition or for market responses has meant that they have been much more attentive to the needs of their customers who are the students.

The notion of competition as a powerful tool which would motivate institutions and individuals to offer and market their wares was reiterated throughout by the Minister:

we undoubtedly thought that by giving independence, by allowing colleges to compete, they would come up with a wider spread of options, more innovative approaches from the students' point of view.

The Minister was clearly in no doubt regarding the efficacy of introducing market principles and practice into the new FE sector.

The funding context

In order to enable this reorientation of the FE sector to occur, a new system of funding colleges was introduced. The FHE Act transferred the funding and control of FE, tertiary and sixth form institutions from the local authority sector and passed it to the colleges themselves. They were granted corporate status and would henceforward be responsible for their own budgets in terms of, for example, staffing, marketing, course planning and provision.

These developments have driven many changes in the management of colleges and the consequent cultures of many institutions. New working methods for both staff and students have resulted and there have been increasing pressures, as identified by some writers (e.g. Elliott and Hall 1994), for colleges to adopt a much more proactive business orientation in their operations.

A number of writers (e.g. Hyland 1992, Bottery 1994) pointed to the finance-driven context in which colleges found themselves. There has also been a long debate over whether colleges, as essentially non-profit-making organizations, could be compared with commercial ones in terms of their aims and objectives (e.g. Morgan and Murgatroyd 1994).

Colleges, using language adopted from the commercial sector, now talk of competition, making 'surpluses' to plough back into the business and satisfying a diverse range of 'customers' with various constituencies. Colleges often adopt financial and business practices which are similar to those in the commercial sector. They seek to satisfy performance criteria to meet targets set both internally and externally.

On a general level, then, the context of funding and the establishment of the FEFC in terms of fostering a business-oriented climate in colleges was very important. There was a clear intention to create an 'environment in colleges which would encourage institutions to be enterprising, flexible and responsive to their students, potential students and employers' (FEFC 1994, p.4). In this respect the sector has seen a greater degree of competitiveness between institutions to recruit students.

Many managers in FE have found it hard coming to terms with these significant changes, developing new systems, structures and processes to expand student numbers and compete with other institutions in the 'market place'. Within colleges Human Resource Management strategies have come to play a significant part. There is a relationship between the incorporation of colleges and the introduction of HRM. It is about the influences of a market and business ideology upon colleges and the practices within them. However, as will be discussed below, some of the middle managers in colleges have been cynical and even hostile about the introduction of these finance-driven imperatives.

Funding: the perspectives of college managers

With the flatter management structures adopted by many colleges following incorporation, much of the new financial responsibility was devolved to middle managers. These managers needed to be able to manage budgets, prioritize and effectively deploy resources. Middle managers were granted a degree of budgetary autonomy, albeit within particular parameters.

However, at the time of the FHE Act many managers in colleges were unused to having significant financial responsibilities and certainly not to the extent that financial decisions on their part could have crucial consequences for a college in terms of its future. Nevertheless, post-incorporation, managers had to take on board new ways of working. They had to adopt new systems and strategies for maintaining the financial viability of a college.

As evidenced through the field research previously referred to, there could be a dichotomous relationship between the priorities which the FE sector as a whole now gave to financially managing colleges efficiently and effectively compared to some middle managers' views. Many of them had not taken on board the market and competitive ethos which, as the Minister stressed, was at the heart of the new FE. During the author's research one middle manager, for example, commented on the general moves in the sector: 'I feel very unhappy about it. I see decisions being made for purely financial reasons and things happening which are actually educationally unsound.'

Some managers were sceptical and at times hostile to the predominance of monetary concerns despite the fact that these were the dominant ones which tended to generally drive the FE sector. To one middle manager there was almost a disdain for the financial aspects of education and his own financial role:

> It's the role that I absolutely detest. I like dealing with people; I hate dealing with money. It's the role I feel least confident about and I know it's always a source of tension because people never have enough money and they always think that you are always holding back on them and that they should be having more.

To another there was no doubt that there was a lack of confidence in relation to financial budgeting:

> It's because its not a strength of mine, budgeting, finance and fig-ures all round. I don't feel as confident with it as I do dealing with other things. I am not a terribly numerate person. Also because I have a lot of disdain for money. I don't like talking money.

This was ironic at a time when financial considerations were affecting all aspects of colleges and some of the operational managers who could influence the direction felt inadequate with regard to this crucial part of their role.

The reluctance of some middle managers to prioritize financial aspects also related to their own personal histories and value systems. Like many other colleges, all of the middle managers in this college had been full-time teachers who were promoted out of the classroom. They considered themselves to be essentially curriculum managers. They often felt happier dealing with staff and students rather than money. Their values were not business ones, concerned with markets and competition.

Their own self-perceptions and motivations may not have been congruent with the notion of a highly charged competitive environment. If their values and beliefs were not in tune with this new orientation then they might in practice be resisters or oppositionists.

Funding background

The FE sector had, up until 1992, been funded through LEAs. Essentially the allocation of resources to colleges was based on the notion of a full-time equivalent (FTE) student. The main part of a college's budget was thereby decided by the number of students that were enrolled. The allocation to a college was set by a LEA after all local FE institutions had submitted their plans. However, the value attached to a 'mythical' FTE student could vary widely between LEAs. There was no nationally agreed standard of provision and resource allocation formula (Birch, Latham and Spencer 1990).

In this model a college's budget, determined under specific expenditure headings, was based on a historical and incremental system. There was little planning activity connected with the determination of these budgets. The lines of responsibility which might exist for any planning and control were complex and often overlapped each other (Birch *et al.* 1990). Therefore the financial resources which a college might be able to draw upon depended on both geographical location and historical precedent.

How much a particular student allocation attracted depended upon the type of course programme and the level of work, which was weighted to reflect the need for extra resources for particular students. So, for example, special needs work attracted an increased weighting compared with many other programme areas. Importantly for the later discussion in this chapter, the mode of student attendance also affected how much a college might receive from its LEA. How much money a part-time as opposed to a full-time student might attract was crucial to college funding. The total student number allocation was then converted into FTEs (Levacic 1993).

Nevertheless, many colleges had excellent working relationships with their LEAs. More than this, they were also locally accountable through the local authority which determined their budgets. Some colleges pointed to how cost-effective and economical some LEA services were compared with having to finance them at a college level (Evans 1994). An instance of this is that insurance cover has become a burden for some colleges. These 'extra' costs, it is sometimes stressed by college principals, are not reflected in the funding formulae operated by the FEFC.

The operation of the FE funding methodology

The formation of the FEFC and its funding methodology were designed to address many of the perceived faults of the previous LEA funding system. Funding was put on a national basis with a common funding methodology applicable to all colleges. In essence it could be said that the FEFC became the largest LEA in the country!

In this new market system the rewards for colleges were related to gross volume of turnover. As in the school sector, the number of students which an individual college could recruit would determine its overall budget allocation. The aim was to make colleges more responsive to market forces. Top-up funding for enrolments over targets would be an incentive to increase student numbers and reduce unit costs. The funding formula was driven by student numbers and programmes offered. There would be a bidding process linked to corporate requirements laid down by the FEFC.

In reviewing the later operation of the funding methodology, it was noted that it was: 'intended to ensure that successful institutions which are attractive to students and use their funding effectively, are able to secure significant increases in budgets each year to support expansion' (Prime Research 1995, Appendix 5, p.1). The market operation and ethos of the process was here made explicit.

In the White Paper prior to the Act it was said that colleges would have greater freedom to respond to the country's education and training needs and be able to raise participation and boost achievement. This was despite the fact that a central funding body was established to regulate the market through its funding objectives. In some respects the funding agency was here acting in the role of 'regulator as policeman'.

The methodology was designed to match the complex nature of FE and consisted of key features which the FEFC aimed to implement (FEFC 1994). Its advantages were that it was aligned with a college's need to incur expenditure at different points of a student's progress through college, unlike the old scheme which was based purely on enrolments and historical precedent. There was, through this new methodology, a block allocation of recurrent funding to each institution each year which could vary between programme areas.

In addition there was an element of funding which was 'demand led', based on a college's estimate of their future growth in the forthcoming year. The FEFC, through the funding methodology, guaranteed to fund the core elements to allow for sufficient year-on-year stability for each college. The DLE (demand-led element) of the allocation was based upon previous performance in terms of growth in student numbers (FEFC 1994).

The education and training provision which each college provided was expressed as a total of standard funding units, which allowed comparison between institutions. Each category and aspect of provision which the Council funded was assigned a value of funding units in a tariff (FEFC 1994). So in any one year institutions received ninety per cent of their previous year's allocation and they were able to apply for additional funding units at a standard rate of funding. Each institution's total funding allocation was the sum of its core funding and marginal funding allocation. Throughout there was monitoring by the FEFC of the core and demand-led funding. If an institution's value of units achieved was less than set out in its funding agreement a corresponding reduction would be made to the institution's recurrent funding allocation.

Funding units

The funding units are then broken down into tariff values which each attract a particular level of funding for a student's time at college. First, the 'entry element' which encompasses all the activities leading to the enrolment of a student on a learning programme (FEFC 1994). This is essentially concerned with the initial guidance and assessment which a student receives. Second, the 'on programme' element which encompasses 'all activities of learning and accreditation of achievement, general and specific support services and enrichment activities' (FEFC 1994, p.20). Finally, the 'achievement' element which is the funding of student achievement in terms of nationally recognized qualifications.

As can be seen, this is a much more comprehensive funding methodology compared with the previous LEA model. One of its principal originators, Roger McLure of the FEFC, stressed that there was a conscious move to depart from a system based purely on student numbers to one based on the 'funding units' making up an individual's student programme (McLure 1994). As it is a national funding mechanism, there was said to be a common currency, i.e. funding units, so that when the FEFC evaluated the volume of activity at institutions it was able to compare apples to apples. Under the LEA system, due to the different funding mechanisms and values, apples might be attempted to be compared with pears!

The 'steer' then from a national perspective was a guarantee of baseline funding with a bonus of further funding if a growth in student numbers occurred in a college. However, this simplistic scenario, as will be seen later, had a number of intended, but also some unintended, consequences for many colleges.

Planned consequences of the recurrent funding methodology

There is no doubt that many of the now visible consequences of the methodology were envisaged by the FEFC. They may sometimes not have been explicitly stated, but the rationale of the new funding system was such that it would inexorably lead to some of the developments in the sector which have now occurred.

On the credit side, as Hyland (1992) explained, the formation of the FEFC was aimed at freeing colleges from what were perceived by many to be often inept and incompetent LEAs. The move also paralleled those taking place in the school sector, where there was an encouragement for schools to 'opt out' of LEA control and become grant maintained.

In this process there was, as previously discussed, an intention to raise the status of FE in the country. The sector is often seen as the most directly work-related area of education. The National Targets for Education and Training (NTETs) were clearly written into the 'achievement' elements of the funding methodology. Colleges would receive funding if and when students successfully achieved NVQs and other equivalent qualifications.

There has been some concern that the establishment of the FEFC has meant that colleges are therefore finance and numbers driven, to the detriment of qualitative factors. They are geared to fulfilling national targets determined by others. This means that 'resources spent at a local level have to tally with nationally defined objectives' (Cook and Crook 1991, p.61). However, it has always been the case that the FE system has been a responsive one. It has had to respond to government, economic and industrial developments and at the same time serve its local community.

The clear intention of the scheme was to address the issue of retaining students throughout their programmes of study at college. Under the LEA funding system there was no incentive to keep them until they had completed their studies, in a methodology based purely on enrolments. The new funding methodology, with its entry, on programme and achievement units rewarded colleges for student retention and their final qualification achievements, related to their 'learning goals'.

On a general level then the context of funding and the establishment of the FEFC in terms of fostering a business-oriented climate in colleges is very important. There was a clear intention to create an 'environment in colleges which would encourage institutions to be enterprising, flexible and responsive to their students, potential students and employers' (FEFC 1994, p.4). In this respect the sector has seen a greater degree of competitiveness between institutions to recruit students.

This competitiveness has also been extended to competing with school sixth forms where the same 'pool' of students is often being targeted. The consequence has been that to become competitive some institutions have had to merge to reduce costs and offer students a more comprehensive programme. Like commercial organizations operating within the market place they have seen mergers and closures. Many in the FEFC made no secret of the fact that they expected or intended this to occur for there were seen to be too many colleges in the sector. One commentator noted that one in five colleges could collapse as a result of changes sweeping the sector (*Education* 6.1.95, p.2). As recently as December 1998, the Secretary of State for Education made clear that there was 'a continuing drive to rationalise provision (notably through mergers), particularly where such rationalisation has the potential to improve cost-effectiveness' (Dawe 1998).

A crucial explicit intention in the recurrent funding methodology was to tackle the differential funding base which colleges inherited from the time when they were under LEA control. For as McLure (1994) pointed out, colleges were receiving different amounts of money for doing the same work as for example a neighbouring college. The FEFC's aim was to narrow that range of differences in college funding until a 'convergence' occurred.

Inevitably there have been gainers and 'also rans' in that process. The result has meant that some colleges have had to be more efficient in terms of spending for the funding allocation which they receive. Efficiency in this sense may mean more teaching from individual lecturers, larger classes and a shrinking of college's resource bases. Many of them have undergone a difficult transition to achieve these objectives. The colleges which met growth targets with a relatively low level of funding have been the ones which have benefited.

The other major directive and intention by the FEFC and the government was for the FE sector to grow progressively over a 'convergence' period. To do this colleges were allowed to bid for extra 'growth' funding units in the first few years in the life of the new funding methodology. Unfortunately many were not as successful as they might have hoped, with a series of consequences, many of them not unexpected, although maybe not intended by the FEFC.

Ironically the current funding backcloth is that the FEFC will now no longer fund unlimited growth in colleges. There is a 'cap' upon funding through the methodology and an increased stress upon the need to economize. Many colleges thus find themselves in financial difficulties and mergers are a feature of the FE sector. The consequences of some of these changes are discussed later in the chapter.

Unplanned consequences of the recurrent funding methodology

Some of the external factors which influence colleges' potential for growth were not taken into account when their funding was determined. As a result some college principals have said that the funding formulae has been too mechanistic and insensitive to differences between colleges (*TES* 26.5.95).

A number of colleges, for example, were in a more advantageous position to achieve growth numbers. They could for instance 'poach' students from another college, which although it is growth for that college may not be growth in the way the FEFC intended it to mean. Similarly, due to geographical location some colleges may be faced by more post-16 institutions attempting to recruit students from the same catchment area.

Very few observers foresaw the battle for students which has occurred between colleges and schools with sixth forms. Students in school sixth forms are funded more generously than those in colleges and the FEFC through its funding methodology takes no account of this fact.

Equally, some colleges were in a more favourable position to 'franchise' programmes to other agencies, claim FEFC funding and pass a proportion of it to the actual deliverer of those courses. This has occurred in relation to both training on employers' premises and delivery in community settings by locally based organizations. The FEFC, although it might applaud the ingenuity of such moves, did not intentionally see this as an explicit aim.

Similarly the growth elements of some colleges have been achieved by increases in the 'units of activity' of students. As the formula is not enrolment driven, but activity driven, further units could be claimed for the extension of the range of programmes which a student might undertake. However, there may have been no growth in actual student numbers, although these have been the 'activities' which they pursued. The FEFC clearly did not intend the methodology to attract such intricate and ingenious moves to sidestep its intended aims.

At a more general level there was no account taken of the socio-economic environment in which a college found itself and therefore its actual and potential intake (Akker 1995). Such parallel debates have occurred in the school sector in relation to the 'value added' concept. Traditionally, particular socio-economic groups do not take up the offer of further education or training and a college may find itself in a catchment area where such groups predominate.

A further factor of 'external' influence which might affect a college's growth target and over which it has little control are the financial support mechanisms provided for students. The predominant growth in college student numbers has been achieved through an increase in adult enrolments. However, there is a fear that issues of financial support for such students affect enrolments. Discretionary awards, for example, administered by LEAs to help students financially, have disappeared in many parts of the country.

Widening participation

Since the initial first few years of funding unlimited growth in colleges, there has been a progressive claw-back in the funding stream. In some respects this was not unexpected in the sense that some colleges had a 'blank cheque' in that whatever growth they achieved would be funded by the FEFC. However, that is now not the case. The DLE was in reality a lifeline for colleges for it was an additional source of income. That aspect of funding has now disappeared, for the Treasury was not prepared to finance unlimited growth. Ironically many colleges that were in a position to respond more readily to government encouragement for rapid expansion are the colleges that now face the biggest losses. Many FE colleges are now coping with a double disadvantage in that they have to maintain a low level of price per funding unit whilst facing a real reduction in their funding through the absence of this growth element.

The funding scenario has in some respects changed from one of overall college growth targets to one of much more emphasis on targeting particular groups of potential students. As one principal has noted, in some respects this situation mirrors other funding in the post-compulsory education sector: 'FE from now on will be planned like higher education. Where in the past you had unbridled growth, in future growth will be finely tuned and targeted' (FE NOW! 1997, p.6). This is the point at which the widening participation agenda enters the funding methodology equation.

During the last 2–3 years there has been an increased stress upon 'widening participation', which in practical terms means attempting to reach groups of the population who have been traditionally under-represented in FE. These include, for example, people without qualifications, unemployed people and people on low incomes. Reaching and retaining these students on college programmes is sometimes problematic for, as has been noted, 'some groups of learners are more difficult to recruit, more likely to drop out and less likely to achieve at all stages of their learning' (Kennedy 1997, p.61). There have been various reports which have highlighted and stressed the need for a 'lifelong learning' process to include these under-represented groups in post-compulsory education (e.g. Kennedy 1997; Fryer 1997).

There is a new stress on lifelong learning and a myriad of initiatives which are aimed at encouraging the development of a lifelong learning culture beyond compulsory schooling. Some involve, for example, employers, a soon to be launched UfI (University for Industry), funding schemes to encourage institutional collaboration and partnership, a national learning grid, enhanced basic skills provision and other schemes to encourage adults to return to education.

In relation to colleges in its plans for funding FE 1999–2002, the Secretary of State for Education announced in the Comprehensive Spending Review (CSR) of November 1998 that an extra £225 million would be available for FE in 1999/2000, rising to an extra

£470 million in 2000/01. He stated that this funding would mean year-on-year increases in student numbers of 178,000 in 1999/2000, 109,000 in 2000/01 and 340,000 in 2001/02 (Dawe 1998).

However, this is not a return to unqualified growth. As the Director General for Further and Higher Education at the DfEE stated: 'FE has a critical contribution to make to the realization of "The Learning Age" vision and a central role to play in meeting the National Targets. Success in achieving these will entail a major widening of participation which is vital to the nation's economic and social wellbeing' (Dawe 1998).

The Kennedy report *Learning Works*, in particular, had addressed the actions necessary to widen participation. Some of these actions revolved around the need to develop new funding arrangements which would assist and enable the widening participation agenda. It was recommended that changes should be made in the distribution of funds to provide incentives for and to recognize the costs of drawing under-represented groups into learning.

In the short term these recommendations were about altering the monetary value of the funding units which colleges receive in order to reflect the extra costs involved in teaching these client groups where, for example, more support and guidance may be required. So, for example, part of the incentive process for colleges would be an increased monetary value for entry units on the basis of the relative levels of social and economic deprivation of students.

The methodology to be employed would be to ascertain the postcode areas from which these students were drawn and award entry units to colleges according to the relative levels of deprivation for those students. The rationale for this approach is that students with low levels of prior achievement are more likely to be poor and to live in economically disadvantaged areas. There are links between poor levels of retention and achievement, low income and living in areas of social and economic disadvantage. These students must be 'unit rich' in terms of the funding methodology so that colleges have clear incentives to recruit them to ensure that they succeed in their learning.

In the long run Kennedy stressed that the aim should be to simplify the funding system. Similarly, more emphasis should be placed on a partnership approach to widening participation. The funding methodology should be utilized to reward institutions which adopted this approach. There was here both explicitly and implicitly much criticism of the competitive approach in FE and its encouragement since the 1992 FHE Act. This characteristic has been discussed throughout this chapter and forms the backcloth to much of the discussion of funding FE.

The Secretary of State has taken many of the *Learning Works* recommendations on board. He asked the FEFC to move towards funding a 'widening participation factor' by 2001/02 on the basis of an average 10 per cent premium per relevant student (Dawe 1998). This 'uplift factor' to funding units should encourage colleges to recruit from under-represented groups in the population.

However, there are emerging issues involved in the implementation of the widening participation agenda as it relates to the funding methodology. So, for example, on the surface the scenario of targeting under-represented groups via postcode information and rewarding colleges accordingly for attracting such students seems to offer a way forward. However, the scheme which is now operating in practice means that there are very wide variations in the funding which colleges receive via this scheme and some college principals argue that it is unfair. As one commentator noted: 'a widening participation (WP) index is applied which brings in extra money ranging from an additional 60 per cent down to 0.1 per cent of student funding' (Kingston 1998).

This is because the process for identifying these individuals is based on postcode information which places them in a particular ward. Each ward has a deprivation index which is calculated by the Department of the Environment according to a set of indicators such as type of housing and children in low-earning households. The difficulties are that first the information is based on the 1991 national census, much of which is now out of date. Second, the postcode can be an imprecise indicator for identifying students from the target groups. This may particularly be the case in rural areas where the wards tend to cover more ground than in the cities. Such a methodology may therefore be a blunt instrument.

There is a concern that colleges have developed ingenious systems for interpreting the funding guidance. *Learning Works*, for example, highlighted that 'an analysis of additional support units claimed by colleges shows wide variation in practice' (Kennedy 1997, p.60). These additional units are linked to students who need extra support of some kind whilst in college due to their particular extra learning needs. The report did not want to see the same thing occurring in relation to widening participation funding for it should be a matter of right, not dependent on providers' imaginations.

The FEFC funding formulae has been seen by some as being too complicated and unworkable. One commentator described the system as 'a dizzying and intricate panoply of units, load bands, costs factors, and percentages' (*Furthering Education*, Autumn 1994, p.6). It is true that the formula is a complex one but the FE system is complicated. Some colleges have been ingenious and imaginative in interpreting the funding guidance from the FEFC. There have been many years of defining and refining funding eligibility criteria. A new twist in relation to widening participation may result in a new round of such redefinitions.

Conclusion

The first discussion in this chapter was around the notion of colleges as being in a market place, in competition with each other for students. This was encouraged by a policy producer and the language which has been developed in the sector is often centred around ideas borrowed from the business world. However, at a national level the FHE Act itself represented some internal contradictions. Any promotion of a pure market ideology was circumscribed by the fact that FE, like other former local government arenas, was transformed into a quasi market.

On the one hand colleges as individual units were encouraged to compete with each other and in so doing attract more customers. On the other hand they were financed by a quango, the FEFC, which determined many educational priorities which colleges should be adopting through a strict and deterministic funding methodology. As one writer noted: 'the changes in the 1992 FHE Act have demonstrated yet again the tensions between a government's desire to establish and control planning levers and its wish for an untrammelled market economy' (Gray 1992, p.89).

Such a dichotomous relationship was mirrored through the various perspectives of the actors involved in the enactment and operation of incorporation. The introduction of a market place philosophy and competition into the FE sector represented a significant reorientation for many college managers. Incorporation attempted to introduce a new culture in a short space of time. College managers were expected to embrace this culture that emphasized the role of markets and a market ideology with all the accoutrements which that might entail.

Not all managers were convinced of the efficacy of the market place. As a result many did not accept the consequences of operating such a system within their own colleges. The finance driven, competitive ethos of the new FE was sometimes at odds with the motivations and intentions of some of these managers. There was a 'loose coupling' (Weick 1976) in terms of the relationship between policy proposals and policy implementation.

As a result, 'sites of resistance' were sometimes established in colleges. An illustration of this was given through the words of some college middle managers. It might take the form of opposition by managers to the operation of market forces in a college environment. However, a more common response was the accommodation and dilution of ideas into a form which could be operated at a college level.

As can be seen, the FEFC funding methodology, as the principal means by which colleges are funded, had and has a fundamental effect upon them in terms of orientation and operation. Some of these have been intentional and have been made explicit by its proponents. However, as we have seen some of these consequences have often had effects not envisaged by the FEFC or colleges themselves. Many of them were unplanned but they have become as important as the planned aims. Perhaps inevitably with such a new scheme there would be winners and losers. But there is no doubt that both much of the FE sector and the FEFC itself had not envisaged the equally complicated mixture of intended and unintended consequences of the methodology which has resulted.

External and internal influences all play their part in the operation of the funding methodology. There is no doubt that the methodology has in many ways been successful. The National Audit Office, in a report published in 1997, concluded that it has encouraged colleges to achieve government targets for growth and efficiency. In addition it has provided stability, has assisted planning and has encouraged colleges to pursue business opportunities (National Audit Office 1997).

The new emphasis on widening participation will have its effects on the funding methodology. More crucially it will have an effect on the operation of colleges. *Learning Works* noted many of the consequences of how colleges are funded. With funding related to successful outcomes, namely qualifications attained by students, there was a tendency to go in pursuit of students who were more likely to succeed. A national stress on growth resulted in a tendency to go for the easier targets. The new agenda and challenge is for colleges to encourage through their doors 'those for whom learning is a daunting experience' (Kennedy 1997, p.3). There will undoubtedly be twists and turns on this new funding pathway.

References

Ainley, P. (1997) 'The Crises of Colleges.' *Education Today and Tomorrow 49*, 2, 14–15.

Akker, J. (1995) Dear Kenneth Clarke. *Education, 3* March, p.10.

Baker, K. (1989) *Speech to the Association of Colleges of Further and Higher Education* (ACFHE). 15 Feb.

Birch, D., Latham, J. and Spencer, A. (1987) 'Joint Efficiency Study of NAFE: Non-Teacher Costs.' *Coombe Lodge Report 19*, 12. Blagdon: Further Education Staff College.

Birch, D., Latham, J. and Spencer, A. (1990) 'Financial Delegation for Further Education Colleges: A Case Study.' *Coombe Lodge Report 21*, 8. Blagdon: Further Education Staff College.

Bottery, M. (1993) *The Ethics of Education Management.* London: Cassell.

Bottery, M. (1994) 'Education and the convergence of management codes.' *Education Studies 20*, 3, 329–343.

Bradley, D. (1997) *The Impact of Incorporation on Further Education Studies.* Unpublished Ed.D Dissertation. Bristol: University of Bristol.

Cook, C. and Crook, G. (1991) 'Changes in Funding: A College Response' In P. Raggatt and L. Unwin (eds) *Change and Intervention: Vocational Education and Training.* Falmer Press.

Dawe, R. (1998) (Director General of Further Education DfEE) Letter to D. Melville, Chief Executive of FEFC. 8 December.

Eggar, T. (1991) 'Speech to National Conference for Chairmen of Further Education College.' *Governing Bodies,* 26 September.

Elliott, G. and Hall, V. (1994) 'Business orientation in further education and the introduction of human resource management.' *School Organisation 14*, 1.

Evans, R. (1994) 'Further vision.' *Education,* 14 Jan, 27.

FE NOW! (1997) Issue 35, 6.

Fryer, R. (1997) *Learning for the Twenty-First Century.*

Further Education Funding Council (1993) *Guidance on the Recurrent Funding Methodology.* Coventry.

Further Education Funding Council (1994) *Council News 19.* Coventry.

Further Education Funding Council (1994) *How to Apply for Recurrent Funding 1995–96.* Coventry.

Furthering Education (1994) Winter, 31.

Gleeson, D. (1993) 'Legislation for change: Missed opportunities in the further and higher education act.' *British Journal of Education and Work 6*, 2, 29–40.

Gorringe, R. (1993) 'The future looks bright for FE.' *Education*, 10 September, 190–191.

Gray, L. (1992) 'Competition or collaboration – the tensions in colleges of further education.' In T. Simkins, L. Ellison and V. Garrett (eds) *Implementing Educational Reform: The Early Lessons*. Harlow: Longman.

Hall, V. (1994) *Further Education in the United Kingdom*. London: Collins.

Hyland, T. (1992) 'Reconstruction and reform in further education.' *Educational Management and Administration 20*, 2, 106–110.

Kelney, B. and Davies, T. (1995) 'Cost reduction and value for money.' *Coombe Lodge Report 24*, 6. Blagdon: Further Education Staff College.

Kennedy, H. (1997) *Learning Works*. Coventry: Further Education Funding Council. Coventry.

Kingston, P. (1998) 'The cheque's in the postcode.' *The Guardian*, 8 December.

Levacic, R. (1993) 'Financial management in education: An emerging function.' In R. Levacic (ed) *Financial Management in Education*. Milton Keynes: Open University Press.

Low, G. (1995) 'Bye-bye to Gung-ho.' *Education*, 24 Feb, 14.

McGinty, J. and Fish, J. (1993) *Further Education in the Market Place: Equity, Opportunity and Individual Learning*. London: Routledge.

McLure, R. (1994) 'FEFC Funding and the Implications for Colleges.' The Further Education Programme. Educational Broadcasting Services Trust: FEU.

Maclure, S. (1991) *Missing Links: The Challenge for Further Education*. London: PSI.

Morgan, C. and Murgatroyd, S. (1994) *Total Quality Management in the Public Sector*. Buckingham: Open University Press.

National Audit Office (1997) *The FEFC for Engalnd*. London: HMSO.

Powell, B. (1994) 'Going for growth with the FEFC.' *Adults Learning 5*, 10, 248–250.

Prime Research and Development Ltd (1995) *Mapping the Further Education Sector*. Harrogate: Department for Education and Employment.

Times Educational Supplement (1995) 26 May, 12.

Utley, A. (1995) 'Hopes of 6% growth.' *Times Educational Supplement, 26* May, 8–9.

Weick, K. (1988) 'Educational organisations as loosely coupled systems.' In A. Westerby *Culture and Power in Educational Organisations*. Milton Keynes: Open University Press.

Chapter 10

Ethos as Tradition and Ethos in Practice

Sixth Form Colleges After Incorporation

John Robinson

Introduction

Although they are few in number (around 100) sixth form colleges (SFCs) form a significant element of the provision of post-compulsory education in England and Wales. Recent New Labour thinking suggests that their futures are bright indeed with SFCs 'solv[ing] the trickiest problem it [the Government] faces in its radical reform of post-16 education' (Kingston 1999, p.13, commenting on the White Paper *Learning to Succeed* (DfEE 1999)). The main reason for their attractiveness lies in the fact that students in SFCs are generally academically successful whilst at the same time SFCs themselves are more cost-efficient than school sixth forms. SFCs are the only sector of state-funded education which can rival the independent sector for academic success and the funding basis for their students provides better efficiency gains than general further education and school sixth forms. The basis of this success lies in the origins of SFCs as former grammar schools and their academic ethos is deeply rooted.

In this chapter I want to explore briefly the origins of that grammar school background and then explore, by drawing on data derived from interviews with nine sixth form college principals, how that tradition and ethos influenced the ways in which SFCs responded to the changes which the post-16 sector faced as a consequence of the implementation of the Further and Higher Education Act (1992) in April 1993 (normally referred to as Incorporation) (see Robinson and Burke 1995 and 1996 for details). In doing so, some comparisons will be drawn with further education (FE) colleges from data from an earlier interview sweep with lecturers immediately prior to the Act coming into force (see Robinson and Burke 1994 for details). Then by drawing on data derived from interviews with a sample of students in one of the SFCs included in the first round of college principal interviews I want to examine to what extent the ethos identified actually exists in practice in the minds of the students themselves. The purpose of this critical examination of the ways in which SFCs responded to their changes in status which Incorporation brought about is to explore how SFCs have achieved the sorts of academic and cultural/social success which they have and to test how real these achievements are for the students themselves.

According to Gleeson (1993) the FHE Act (1992) had its origins in the 1991 White Paper *Education and Training for the 21st Century*, which recognized a failure to invest in post-16 education and training and which had left Britain with not only a vicious circle of low skills, low wages and low productivity, but also with one of the least educated and trained workforces in the industrialized world (Gleeson 1993, p.29). The Act transferred funding and control of FE, tertiary and SFC institutions from LEAs to the colleges themselves. This meant that post-16 institutions became responsible for their own budgets, staffing, marketing, personnel issues, and course planning and provision, all of which had been undertaken previously to a greater or lesser degree in partnership with the LEA. The mechanism for funding and control passed from the LEAs to the Further Education Funding Council (FEFC), a central body with delegated Regional Advisory Committees. Funding was based on a formula which was primarily driven by student numbers and courses offered. As Gleeson (1993) noted, the Act had both political objectives and administrative objectives: political in the sense that local democratic links were broken; administrative in placing the newly incorporated institutions in new market arrangements (which obviously had ideological objectives as well).

The Act, combined with changes which were taking place within the education sector and wider society as a consequence of an embedding of Thatcherite principles concerning competition, choice and the role of market forces, brought two very disparate types of educational institutions into one newly created sector. The histories of the two different sorts of colleges has meant that the management and tutorial staffs of the FE and SF colleges approached Incorporation with differing sorts of preparedness and expectations. The dominant ideologies of both sets of institutions differed. Their origins in Workers and Mutual Improvement Societies which responded to working men's demands for some sort of education on the one hand (FE colleges) (Burgess and Pratt 1970), and a combination of the comprehensive ideals following on from Circular 10/65 and attempts to uphold the tradition of high academic educational achievement on the other (SF colleges) (MacFarlane 1978), has meant that the two types of colleges developed with different ideologies, patterns of work, students, courses, management structures and expectations (see Smithers and Robinson 1993). FE colleges developed within a sector which 'grew' into the Polytechnic and Higher Education system (Burgess and Pratt 1970; Pratt and Burgess 1974) whereas SFCs operated under 'schools regulations' enshrined in the 1944 Education Act almost as if they were 11–18 schools without pupils under the age of sixteen. Additionally, Incorporation brought about changes in funding arrangements which involved SFCs, mainly for the first time, being engaged with Training and Enterprise Councils (TECs) and both sorts of colleges with the FEFC.

For many, these transitions were not welcome and have not been smooth. Earlier research attempted to capture some of these anxieties by interviewing lecturers and tutors in FE and SF colleges using semi-focused interviews in seven colleges in the period between November 1992 and February 1993 (Robinson and Burke 1994), that is just immediately prior to Incorporation (which came into effect on 1 April 1993). The research which is reported here involves data collected from semi-focused interviews with nine SF principals between April and June 1994 (that is a year after Incorporation) and a sample of students from one of the sample SFCs in 1996 and 1997. This data is reported in detail in Robinson and Burke (1995) and Bloomer and Hodkinson (1997). Although the samples are relatively small in absolute numbers, as a proportion of the total numbers of SFCs it is a relatively large sample. Furthermore, the conclusions drawn are relatively in accord with those found by Shorter in his study of 'senior staff from several SF colleges a few months after Incorporation' (Shorter 1994, p.461).

The origins of sixth form colleges and the sixth form college ethos

According to the Crowther Report (Central Advisory Council for Education [England] 1959) there were five distinguishing characteristics of school sixth forms. They had close links with the universities; they had a strong element of specialization; they favoured and fostered a spirit of working independently among the students; there was an intimate relationship between the tutors and the students; and they engendered a sense of social responsibility among the students. In these regards the state school sixth form strongly resembled and was closely related to the form and function of public school sixth forms. Taylor, Reid and Holley explored the closeness of these linkages, pointing to the importance of and the impact of Samuel Butler of Shrewsbury School who, in the period between 1798 and 1836, was instrumental in developing an atmosphere of 'intellectual discipleship' (1974, p.9; see also Reid and Filby 1982) (although it was much earlier at Harrow School where the term 'form' originated to refer to the benches on which the boys sat, the 'sixth form' being occupied by the oldest boys). To some extent this history and the desire to capture its spirit in state school sixth forms meant that as they developed there was a certain amount of reverence or awe involved – a reverence and an awe for the specialness of intellectual discipleship.

It was with this background and lineage in mind that various interested parties began to discuss the nature of sixth form education in the 1960s and 1970s and various concerns were identified. These included the relationship between the school sixth form and the external examinations structures (Reid 1972; Taylor *et al.* 1974), and the struggle between two competing curriculum ideologies involving on the one hand an 'alternative curriculum' concerning specialization, a limited range of subjects and a break with the 'classics' curriculum which was supported by the schools, and on the other hand an 'integrated curriculum' involving a mixture of science, mathematics, modern studies, Latin and Greek (Peterson 1960). The debate came to a head with the publication of the Schools Council Working Paper No. 16 which proposed that sixth form courses should be restructured in such a way that they reflect 'the teaching power available and the needs and interests of pupils in any particular school' (Schools Council 1967, p.5). Subsequently the Schools Council and the Standing Conference on University Entrance jointly proposed revisions to the sixth form curricular structure involving studying five subjects in Year 1 and three subjects in Year 2 (Schools Council and Standing Conference on University Entrance 1969). These proposals, however, did not find favour with many teachers and they foundered.

Against this backdrop concerning the nature of curriculum provision in the post-16 age group more radical debates were taking place. As early as 1943 Sheffield LEA had considered centralizing its sixth form provision, although it is claimed that it was at Mexborough in 1964 that the first genuine attempt at true innovation in sixth form provision in the sense of establishing an 'SF college' occurred. King (1976) disputes this claim, arguing that the Mexborough example was really a sixth form centre operating separately from the main school (of which there were many examples in, among others, Cambridge, Cardiff, Croydon, Lancashire, Northamptonshire, Norwich, Somerset and Warwickshire) (King 1976, pp.58, 67). It is generally acknowledged, however, that the first true SF colleges grew out of the experiences in Croydon (see King 1968, pp.124–128). King's vision of a sixth form or junior college was constructed within a wider view of radical changes of a comprehensive nature including the abolition of selection at eleven-plus. It is interesting to note, therefore, that Circular 10/65 is somewhat ambivalent in the way that it was permissive of SFCs which catered for the educational needs of the whole of the 16–19 age cohort and those which had entry criteria of an academic nature (MacFarlane 1978, p.39).

The emerging SFCs, then, had a history which was imbued with an élitism which was both academic and social in that mostly they emerged from already established schools rather than being newly born, and in general their parents were grammar schools (King 1976; Benn and Simon 1972; Monks 1968; Phillips 1972). It is in this parentage, to a large extent, that the root of the special ethos of SFCs can be found. Perhaps the crucial element of this lineage is the way in which the grammar school sixth form was modelled on the public school tradition. In emulating the public schools it was almost inevitable that as the sixth forms and sixth form centres transformed into SFCs these traditions and the ethos were also transferred. Furthermore, it was also inevitable that as they were being established the new colleges would initially be staffed by ex-grammar school teachers imbued with academic ideals (since sixth forms tended to be in grammar schools). Consequently, changes to the curriculum were received in some quarters reluctantly. New examinations, such as the Certificate of Extended Education (CEE) were viewed sceptically. Symbolic language was used to identify students enrolled on such courses. The 'new sixth' were apart, different, marginal to the 'traditional' sixth formers. Such marginalization was encapsulated in the euphemistic labels which were used to identify the new sixth formers. As one sixth form tutor interviewed noted, they were the 'leather jacketed brigade'.

That SFCs should have turned out like this, at least initially, was certainly not in the mind of Rupert Wearing King when he put forward his apologia for the establishment of SFCs based on the Croydon Plan. King noted that 'our educational progress has been inhibited too long by being designed to an unrealistic pattern. Arnold's public school should never have been used as the prototype for the national education system' (1968, p.120). King's vision was for a new type of educational establishment 'devised to give an entirely new look, and geared to the psychology of those in their later teens, who feel themselves emerging as young adults' (1968, p.119). However, it was into the ideological atmosphere described above that both the teaching staff and students entered as the new colleges developed. Just as it was the case for many of the teaching staff that their grammar schools had changed around them, so for the first cohorts of students, many of whom found themselves in the sixth forms of their own 11 to 18 schools (albeit refurbished and retitled), the difference being that they (staff and students) were now sharing space with some interlopers. Thus, early in the brief histories of the SFCs their ethos and their atmosphere were being set within an image created at a much earlier time, in a very different sort of institution and for a very different sort of student. This atmosphere and ideology has subsequently had a tendency to reinforce itself as new staff and students have been socialized into their roles. Clearly the professional socialization of the members of staff would turn out to be a potent force, particularly in relation to the balkanized nature of the curriculum organization of the colleges which meant that cross-college innovations would have a difficult passage since, as Hargreaves and Macmillan (1992) suggest, teachers tend not to have a capacity for empathizing with other colleagues, because this capacity is undermined by their within-subject mind-set. The inter-subjective agreements which develop in these within-subject subcultures provide the atmosphere for the socialization of newcomers who adopt the prevailing taken-for-granteds. Although it is clearly possible to overstate this case, the prevailing atmosphere in some SFCs immediately prior to Incorporation was not one that was conducive to the sorts of changes which were predictably to be the consequences (both intended and unintended) of the FHE Act (Robinson and Burke 1994).

Consequently, as Incorporation approached the SFCs tended to be characterized by a mission which was largely academic and (in a non-pejorative sense) élitist. Those curriculum innovations which had been taken on board in the intervening years, like CEE, were to some extent developed as lower level academic qualifications which, although they did have some regard for the target student population, remained within an academic framework. The cultural legacy of the origins of the SFC ethos and the newly emerging ideological atmosphere which was the consequence of the 1988 Education Reform Act and the 1992 FHE Act tended to make unhappy bedfellows. Incorporation impacted on the curriculum, teaching and learning strategies, inter-institutional relationships, working conditions, employment patterns, working hours and student mix (Robinson and Burke 1994). Furthermore, Robinson and Burke (1994) reported that SFC tutors appeared to be less than prepared for some of the consequences of these changes. Consequently, in what follows I explore how some SFC principals responded to the issues raised by the earlier research (Robinson and Burke 1994) and how some students have experienced one SFC before going on to explore some of the wider implications of these changes. In exploring these issues I will examine the possibility of protecting the 'specialness' of SFCs within the market place of post-16 education, as much of New Labour's strategy for sixth form education seems to depend upon the success (in academic terms) of the SFCs (Kingston 1999, p.13).

Elements of the ethos

Organizational structures and management styles

The management styles and organizational structures of the SFCs grew out of the sorts of traditions which have been described above. They were predicated upon academic criteria rather than the functional approach which the FEFC promotes. Some of the interviewees reported that they had responded to some of the perceived changes in the ideological climate within which they were now operating by maintaining the original, academic, emphasis of management with new functions 'added on'. These were usually identified as Finance, Estates and Personnel and the most commonly reported non-academic appointment related to Finance. Overwhelmingly principals maintained a responsibility for personnel issues, perhaps reinforcing the academic rather than 'functional' mission of the colleges. As a consequence of the responses SFC management teams, in relation to overall staff size, tended to be large, involving the principal, heads of Finance, Administration, Estates and Faculties. Clearly the level of control which principals wished to maintain over staffing is important. Some saw themselves as acting as a buffer between the staff and the demands of the FEFC. Managing the curriculum, the staff and the students was seen by several as the crucial task for the principal and, given the threat to the predominant human relations management approach, it was also the greatest challenge.

As if to underscore this challenge it was reported that principals felt that the vice- or associate-principals were being drawn too far away from the classroom by the needs of bureaucracy which involved them in a greater number of operational and strategic tasks. It is both interesting and paradoxical that principals used their vice- or associate-principals to manage 'FEFC-type' functions whilst seeking to maintain their 'specialness' based on academic principles (as will be discussed later).

There was some evidence of changes in managerial cultures. Although strategic planning had initially been undertaken by principals advised by a very small group (usually vice- or associate-principals), there were more attempts to involve more staff through changing structures and responsibilities and the data reveal signs of developing a 'moving mosaic' (Toffler 1990) approach to management. There is, however, a clear tension between the management and organizational needs of the post-Incorporation SFC as an FEFC-funded institution and the SFCs' mission founded in their histories and traditions.

What follows, as is the case for each of the following sections, are examples of principals' views. For reasons of space these are highly selective but are illustrative of the data collected. (For further details see Robinson and Burke 1995.)

> Initially we had three faculties but as numbers grew the structure was creaking and so increased it to six. This allowed us to keep able staff by promoting them. Faculty Heads became managers ... The Management Team is now eleven ... It is very principal-dominated ... In the future the VP in charge of Personnel will be chosen from the academic staff because they know the teachers and teaching ... There is enough money in the budget to appoint non-academic Finance and Estates managers – but the staff do not want this ... Another dampener is that VPs are getting too far away from the classroom and teaching.

> At Incorporation we kept a lean management structure to see what sort of system would be best. The Senior Management team

includes three non-academic members of staff with responsibility for Finance, Administration and Premises. We have restructured on the basis of strategic planning and management.

We have tried to maintain our original emphasis but to add on the 'new functions' which are required. For example finance, estates, personnel. Most of these roles can be staffed from within the college by using the strengths of the existing team. The one we had the greatest difficulty is with finance. There we have had to make an outside appointment.

Staffing, curriculum and pedagogy

Principals came across as being very protective of their staff, who needed to be sheltered from 'the harsher realities imposed by Incorporation and FEFC'. This approach mirrors that identified by Robinson and Burke (1994) prior to Incorporation. It was clear from the interviewees that the colleges had rather unresponsive cultures. Staff were felt to be largely unaware of the need for change in the curriculum, in markets, and in ethos. Although it is interesting to speculate cause and effect here this, once again, mirrors the perceptions elicited from a sample of SFC tutors prior to Incorporation (Robinson and Burke 1994).

There was little evidence of changing staff profiles as a consequence of Incorporation. Part-time staffing was a little-used option because it was felt that the difficulties of managing and deploying part-time staff might impact on quality in a deleterious way. There was also a reluctance (see below) to deploy full-time staff on developments outside what might be described as the 'normal day'. Some principals were categorically against full-time staff teaching in the evenings. There was also a concern that staff were ill-prepared for or ill-suited to the new tasks of post-Incorporation SFC life and potential curriculum, teaching and learning developments.

However, it could be argued that this ill-preparedness was a minor impediment. It was quite clear that GCE Advanced Level work would remain at the core of SFC teaching, and it would need to in order to achieve the present government's intentions for SFCs as providers of academic success. Few reported prioritizing GNVQs 'at the moment'. They did not want to be pioneers. If change to the curriculum was forced on the SFCs, the principals would prefer it to be driven by the imperatives of the Higginson Report (DES 1988) or for it to reflect International Baccalaureate principles. Whilst GCE A-level was seen as the 'gold standard' and worries were expressed about parity of esteem between GNVQ and GCE A-level, there were some positive responses to GNVQ. Some principals reported the intention to phase out GCSE work in favour of GNVQ, which was recognized as exemplifying some of the best teaching styles and it was felt that GNVQ motivated students much more than GCSE did. It would appear, from my analysis, though, that the principals who were interviewed were on the whole less positive about GNVQ than the picture portrayed by the Further Education Unit/The Institute of Education/The Nuffield Foundation (FEU/IoE/TNF 1994).

In some colleges there was a clear commitment to some form of 'entitlement curriculum' but this was oriented around GCE A-level provision with add-ons such as Study Skills or Health Education. It was felt, however, that such moves should not 'force' students into breadth. There was little or no evidence of NVQ developments.

Once again there is evidence here of the way in which the ethos of the SFCs, as described above, has impacted possibly to slow down the pace of change in this area. The academic origins of the colleges and the profiles of the staff give rise to a climate of unresponsiveness which is exacerbated by a strong sense of belief in the core purpose of the SFCs being related to GCE A-level teaching. As such, changes in curriculum and pedagogy were slow, both acting as a cause for and an effect of slowly changing staff profiles.

> Whatever developments take place in the future [they] must fit in with our ethos ... Our strategy is to play to the strengths of the staff and offer things like evening work where we are strong and staff are enthusiastic, and so it will remain voluntary.

> We want to stand back from GNVQ developments. We don't want to be pioneers – we have got enough work with A-level. We intend, over the next five years, to develop a GNVQ package of five subjects, but we will restrict the development.

> We do see GNVQ as an important development and our experience with BTEC has been an important preparation for GNVQ. In fact it is often that some of the best teaching and student motivation is to be found in the GNVQ areas.

The student mix

As might be expected from the foregoing, the student profiles in the SFCs were showing few signs of changes post-Incorporation. The principals interviewed were largely committed to full-time 16–19-aged students as their core populations. There were few or no part-time students. There was hardly any evidence of evening work, although there was some (limited) use of college facilities by adults during the weekends. Student profiles which were exclusive full-time, 16–19 with 80 per cent plus being GCE A-level students were not untypical. It was felt by the principals that this is what 'parents want'. It was also reported that parents wanted the colleges to be a 'reasonable size – not much bigger than at present'. Those changes in the student mix that were planned, it was reported, must not interfere with the quality of the core students' experience. It was reported by one principal that 'a substantial move into the adult market will change the ethos of the college'. It was also felt that the sorts of students who may be recruited as a consequence of any change in direction in relation to marketing strategies were largely the prerogative of the FE colleges. Changes planned were to be structured in such a way that they would involve discrete programmes, probably with different staff being involved. Changes in the post-16 student profile were seen as impacting on the FE college sector, not the SFCs.

There were, however, signs of changes in responsiveness in relation to the education of special needs students. Colleges were identifying the need to develop special needs policies and cooperation with other colleges and special needs schools was seen as important. In contradiction to the proposal earlier of an élitist origin of the SFCs, there were few signs of an 'élitist' approach in relation to admitting special needs students. Although one college principal did remark that 'we don't receive many applications from special needs students.'

It is very clear that we will remain a 16–19 full-time institution during the day with an emphasis on GCE A-level work. We are going for a niche marketing strategy with a predominance on Level 3 (GNVQ). But the core business will be A-level, it's what we are successful at. Although we will have to look at vocational qualifications, especially as they begin to affect the local rather than the 'outer zone' market. If we move substantially into an adult market it will change the ethos of the college and move us into (the FE) college's market where there is not enough room for both of us. We are not open to change in the 'evening' market.

This always was a comprehensive SFC. It was the first college to run vocational courses for students with moderate learning difficulties and Special Needs. One of the first to run BTEC Nationals. We have built on this experience. But 16–19 FT students will remain our core business with some diversification into things like twilight courses for Adult Returners and Access programmes during the day for adults.

Students at Stokingham Sixth Form College[1]

I have identified above the elements and origins which interrelate and give rise to the delicate ecology of the SFC ethos. The data reported on above give an indication of the tensions within and between these elements. These elements are symbiotically related. Change within one will impact on the nature of the other elements. In order to illustrate this, in this section I want to report on a series of interviews with a sample of students from one of the SFCs reported on above. As has been indicated above, SFCs are very different from most FE Colleges and Stokingham exemplifies some of these differences. It is a single-site college with a North West of England industrial town centre location. It shares post-16 education with an FE college, five 11–18 state schools and two independent schools. There are 1600 16–19-year-old full-time students and 300 part-time evening students. The vast majority of the full-time students follow an A-level diet (41 subjects being available) whilst the number of GNVQ students has steadily increased. The college community is relatively tightly defined, with 82 per cent being 16–19-year-olds.

Unlike some studies of FE colleges (e.g. Page 1996) show, most of the students at Stokingham wanted to study. Charlotte said, 'I do find myself studying in my free periods, I don't mess about.' The FEFC inspection report indicates high attendance levels, and a purposeful working atmosphere. Several of the sample students talked enthusiastically of their learning. In the early days, many described the value of doing private study in the library. As Charlotte describes, this happened because she saw that other students were working there:

> No one has sat me down and said anything to me, it just tends to grow on you and you just tend to follow the older students and what they do. I would never have thought of going to the library and working, I would have expected to be doing it at home, but you see everybody else going to the library and it just comes natural and you go in there and work. It's quiet in there and if you need any information it's just there for you, and the computers are there. I hated computers before I came ... but now I use them all the time.

---

1   This section is based on data provided by Phil Hodkinson and Martin Bloomer from interviews with fifty Stokingham College Students.

As Charlotte indicates, intellectual discipleship is as much to do with copying others as being inculcated into the ethos, but as Scott suggests, not all are smitten: 'I don't stay in college a lot and I work at home. I just prefer home.'

Many of the students interviewed did value being asked to take more responsibility for their own learning. As Simon said, 'there is much more emphasis placed on us taking the initiative to learn, rather than being spoon-fed and told what to do.' Allison agreed:

> You have to be more independent because we chose to come to college and so you are expected to come to the lessons ... The teachers are there to help you but not constantly watching over you. It works because we aren't being told what to do and so you take it in ... They trust us more, which is a good thing. If you feel trusted you work.

Arissa, unlike Charlotte, Simon and Allison, seemed to have not developed yet the sort of discipleship which Samuel Butler wished to promote:

> The friends I've made are a good laugh and if we have free periods together we might just sit and talk. I won't do any work or they won't, because if we have done our work then we just have a laugh together in the common room or sometimes I'll go and sit in the art room and just talk to the teacher because he is really nice.

Within this generally positive learning culture, whilst a range of teaching and learning styles was encountered, most of the teaching appeared to be fairly conventional. Allison described her GNVQ class as follows:

> The classes are just class work, you never split up into groups or anything ... They [the teachers] do spend the whole class talking to you and using the blackboard and we copy it down and have discussions, and everybody contributes.

Little evidence here of GNVQ teaching being at the forefront of innovations in teaching and learning as suggested earlier by one of the principals. This, however, was not Waqas' experience in a GNVQ Intermediate course. Waqas does exemplify the enthusiasm for learning in GNVQ classes:

> Here they make you use your head properly. We design the charts but we often work in pairs or groups and then you have other people's ideas plus your own, so it's quite easy. Groupwork means you can share the work ... Groupwork gets me going because if you start off with it individually you are really nervous and you don't

know what you are going to do. But if you are in a group you have more courage to do it.

The students interviewed, however, were well aware of the differential status attached to A-levels and GNVQs. For example Waqas went to Stokingham College to study for a GNVQ Intermediate in Business:

It's [GNVQ Intermediate] not what I expected because I expected it would be lower than this, but by coming here it's more like upper class to me. Compared with school it's upper class.

When probed, Waqas praised the quality of the college resources. One possible explanation of what Waqas meant is that the SFC was a high status institution, providing 'upper class' resources. Although GNVQ was of lower status, high status was attached to the students because they were attending the SFC rather than the FE college. In the same interview Waqas went on to say:

[the teachers] need to help the students get the results, because they've got to keep up the reputation of the college. I saw some notices last year that said that Stokingham came top, and they want to keep that record.

Other students also referred to the relative status difference between the FE college and the SFC as a significant factor in their choice of place to study. Fazarna, for example, preferred to study at Stokingham, even though it meant that she could not follow the A-level course she really wanted because of her GCSE grades whereas at the FE college she could have studied her preferred choice:

Well I had a problem when I first came here because I didn't get the grades I wanted. So they said try [the] FE college because they will put you onto the A-levels there with the grades you got. So I went there and they put me onto an A-level course, but I didn't like it there. It's not as good as at this college. I only stayed there one day. I took an exam. [there] because I only got three grade Cs, and I took an exam. for two hours, and passed that and they said I could do A-levels. So I went in for a day but I didn't like it at all, not as good as here ... It wasn't the sort of working environment I wanted to be in. The teachers were OK, but I just walked out. The only course I could do here was this one [GNVQ Intermediate, Information Technology]. I asked if I could do GCSE retake, but it was full. The only one [I could choose] ... is what I am doing now. It's not what I expected, but it's all right.

Attending the high status SFC was more important to Fazarna than following the A-level course she really wanted.

As I suggested earlier, the ecology of SFC ethos is in very delicate symbiotic balance. Evidence from the students at Stokingham Sixth Form College suggests that they will be a potent catalyst for changing the ethos. They do recognize the importance of status, but for them the status does not simply come from their course of study, as the principals seem to suggest. It is the place itself which is important. The students' notions of status is apparently more subtle than that of some of the principals interviewed. However, the problem arises that the principals' understanding of status is more synergistic with the present government's aspirations than is the students'. For some the intellectual discipleship which is the public school legacy passed on to the SFCs is welcome. For others it is more hard won. Whilst Stokingham exhibits many of the characteristics of SFCs identified above, a subtle form of élitism operates which illustrates a disjunction between the non-pejorative academic élitism which is at the root of the SFC ethos and the sort of cooling out which Fazarna experienced. Principals are, it seems, engaged in a precarious balancing act of managing change without too many undesired or unintended consequences. So far, however, I have been concerned with the internal elements of that dynamic. What I want to do now is to set that debate within a wider, external context.

External relationships: competition, cooperation and change

In the introduction to this chapter I referred to the different origins of FE and SF colleges. These differing origins have given rise to institutions which are very different in character and ethos. It has been the differences in provision in the post-16 sector which has been one of the causes of the tensions between the institutions and which Robinson and Burke (1994) noted as having a negative impact on quality of provision. Furthermore, as LEAs have lost control of the post-16 colleges there has been little to prevent them to allow 11–16 schools from developing post-16 provision, thus further complicating the topography of post-16 education, a complication exacerbated by FE colleges seeking to recruit 14–16-year-old students. These recent changes have combined to transform the context of post-16 provision. The scene is set for further changes with the publication in June 1999 of the White Paper *Learning to Succeed* (DfEE 1999). SFCs were developed at a time when staying-on rates post-16 were little more than 50 per cent, and A-level dominated the post-16 curriculum. Now staying-on rates are about 75 per cent nationally.

For the first time in British history we have a mass post-16 full-time education 'system'. This change is linked to new curriculum developments, particularly the rapid growth of GNVQ, which, at Advanced level, is supposed to have parity of esteem with A-levels. Post-16 colleges have an independence from the LEAs within a wider context of open enrolment for schools within LEA control. In the future the post-16 provision will also be influenced by the establishment of Local Learning and Skills Councils, Local Learning Partnerships and the increasing influence of Regional Development Agencies (RDAs) (DfEE 1999, pp.34–42).

The changes which have taken place and those to come mean that post-16 provision is problematic everywhere. However, there has been a particular problem for those areas where provision is 'mixed' (i.e. SF and FE college provision side by side). In theory, the whole of post-16 education in those areas has been removed from LEA control, yet it remains divided between SF and FE colleges, who are in direct competition with each other (although, as we have seen, students themselves can subvert this competition by operating the 'market' in a rather subtle way). In practice, where 11–16 schools begin to develop their own sixth forms this competition will be intensified. Such school-based developments may be attractive for funding and status reasons. LEAs have little reason to resist such pressures (especially when, in the past, this was combined with the threat to 'opt out'). In addition, open enrolment means that increasing numbers of people are crossing catchment area boundaries, widening the competitive market.

These changes in government educational policy raise serious questions about the effectiveness and appropriateness of post-16 education in the locality and also have major implications for democratic control. To oversimplify, the old LEA approach was based on notions of local planning and control. Planning mechanisms were ultimately controlled through democratically elected bodies, both locally and nationally. These approaches brought advantages and problems, and the balance of advantage depended partly on how a particular LEA worked. On the positive side, planned provision could cater for a wide spectrum of needs, carefully balanced, with a strong view of community. On the negative side, some LEAs were perceived of as overly bureaucratic and prone to interfere in even the most trivial details of provision. Also, the decision to set up an SFC, separate from the FE college, risked divisive post-16 provision.

These potential deleterious changes to local democratic provision with potential wider impact on issues of social justice are clearly not confined to the particular case under consideration here, nor are they related solely to England and Wales (see Walford 1994). Ball (1991) has demonstrated the 'marketizing' consequences of various Education Acts in the 1980s. Whitty (1991) has demonstrated similar developments in Japan, as has Grace (1994) in New Zealand, and Kenway, Bigum and Fitzclarence (1993) argue that these changes are part of a global adjustment of the market which subordinates social justice as an aspect of the agenda.

Thus paternalistic planning has been deliberately replaced by competition and market forces, driven by funding mechanisms related to recruitment and performance, within tight national controls and systems. At the root of these changes is a 'New Right' vision of individual empowerment, through a metaphor of the pupil (or parent) as a paying customer. Control, especially funding, is in the hands of unelected quangos. Nationally, colleges are funded by the FEFC, which is not itself elected but is answerable to the Secretary of State. Locally, a significant proportion of FE and SF college funding comes from the TECs, which are self-appointed groups of local industrialists, who won contracts with the, then, Department of Employment. Though locally based, the TECs have no democratic links with the communities in which they are located. Rather they have a commercial brief to administer an increasingly large range of Department for Education and Employment contracts. In the future some planning will return through the establishment of the Learning and Skills Council for England which will assume responsibility for post-16 funding from the FEFC. Local authority and community representation on the Local Learning and Skills Councils will afford some return of local democratic influence, and may well reintroduce elements of the LEA social justice agenda, but this will, in all likelihood, be heavily circumscribed by the financial agenda which will dominate. What approaches based on an ideology of individual empowerment, customer choice and rational decision making ignore is that issues like education (and other social policy arenas) have probably less to do with financial concerns than moral and ethical concerns. As the young people of Stokingham Sixth Form College demonstrate, the customer makes his or her decision according to their own criteria.

For some, for example Tooley (1993), the market will be the saviour of education. For others, such as Vincent, such an approach is an exploitation of the paternalism which is inherent in some professional practices like education (1993, p.371). A market-led post-16 education system, which is the consequence of the FHE Act (1992), is in harmony with the 1992 White Paper *Choice and Diversity* which, according to Cordingley and Kogan (1993), deliberately set out to undermine LEAs and LEA provision. This point is strongly reinforced by Gleeson (1993), in his analysis of the FHE Act (1992), which, he noted, had explicit political objectives of breaking the public service element of post-16 education. As Epstein (1993) noted, the period since the passing of the 1988 Education Reform act, with which the FHE Act (1992) is congruent in this regard, has been characterized by a deepening of a market forces ideology which, because of its inhumane consequences such as competition rather than cooperation, is the antithesis of achieving any social justice agenda and is also antithetical to quality provision. With colleges set against colleges and colleges set against schools what chance is there that the goals for post-16 education set out by the National Commission on Education (1993, pp.43–46) can be achieved? These goals resonate strongly with New Labour's intentions for post-16 education. It is clear that in the future a considerable agenda lies at the door of the Learning and Skills Council for England to undo much of what has been the consequences of the FHE Act (1992).

The principals who were interviewed identified several concerns which impacted on the external relationships of the colleges. These included funding, marketing, income generation, cooperation, the role of the LEAs and FEFC, and the relationships with the TECs and with governors.

The principals questioned whether SFCs were different from FE colleges and whether, therefore, funding arrangements should reflect these differences. It was felt by some that funding arrangements penalized SFCs because of their size. The culture of SFCs was identified as a factor which increased costs to the organizations, especially in relation to curriculum entitlement, pastoral arrangements and a collegiate approach. Funding arrangements, it was argued, did not fully recognize these costs. Although the interviewees felt that FEFC funding arrangements were fairly evenly handled there was an element of increased central control behind the arrangements. It was also felt that in having to consider the funding of the colleges so carefully the principals were being drawn into addressing much bigger issues, particularly the nature of the curriculum.

On marketing there was a general sense of a task needing to be tackled. There was a clear recognition of the size of the task on the part of some interviewees who noted that it was not possible, given the new competitive environment, to assume that the future would involve an unchanging post-16 provision and a static post-16 curriculum. New markets would have to be identified and tapped. Although, as some reported, demand had exceeded supply up to the time of the interviews, the future could not be considered to be so comfortable. However, several interviewees reported that the needs of the local community had not been researched and that expertise would have to be bought in to undertake this task. Others reported that their colleges sold themselves on the 'back of achievement', with an emphasis on maintaining quality and reputation rather than active marketing. Niche marketing was seen as being at the heart of the strategy. Others adopted a mid-range position noting that new markets would have to be developed but that the reputation of the college would rest on the A-level results. One factor which was constantly referred to as holding back a more active marketing policy was financial constraint with limited marketing budgets and no room for specialist appointments. Marketing was a low priority.

It was felt that extra income would be needed in the future to protect the SFC ethos, which was the basis of the marketability of the colleges. Paradoxically, though, it was also felt that income generation would distort the niche market. Income generation was seen as being very difficult given the backgrounds of the SFCs. As one principal said:

> I don't want to think about it. It doesn't fit in with the culture and strategy.

However, some institutions had approached income generation more positively with the appointment, in one case, of a leisure manager with clearly set targets and the setting up, in another case, of a Commercial Services Unit. There were clear signs that the ethos of the SFCs which gave rise, as identified earlier, to a particular professional atmosphere within which staff expectations developed was a significant factor in the restriction of income generation. Principals wanted to play to their strengths, which involved a strategy of keeping full-time staff with a strong 16–19 full-time (academic) student cohort and only deploying the staff on new markets or income generation on a voluntary basis. Income generation was not seen as an integrated strategy with funding. There was a clear impression given of an 'arms' length' approach. Earlier research by Robinson and Burke (1994) identified clear differences between the approaches of FE lecturers and SFC tutors in their considerations of the new competitive market. When interviewed, SFC principals manifested a belief that FE college principals were a 'buccaneering lot', but there was a consistent attitude of a positive approach to cooperation in the post-16 sector. Some expressed the view that cooperation was growing, but in reality the topography of college cooperation was patchy. The general sense of commitment was towards a 'loose' form of cooperation in areas such as staff development and curriculum development and the management of information systems, but not on issues like marketing. This, it was felt, would enable the colleges to share economies of scale without the consequences of a merger. There was strong support for some sort of 'pairing' with FE colleges which would allow the SFCs to remain roughly the same size and also avoid, therefore, the dilution of what they do best, although at the time of the interviews there was little evidence of networking and the overriding sense of maintaining SFC niche markets meant that concepts such as networking were seen as being different from those in an FE college context. Two interesting issues grow out of this data. One relates to the contradiction between the ideas expressed by the SFC principals and the ideology which underpins the competition and choice principles of the market-led approach to post-16 educational change. The other relates to the positive approach to curriculum development cooperation as demonstrated by the SFC principals and the overwhelmingly negative response to such cooperation as perceived by the FE college lecturers prior to Incorporation (see Robinson and Burke 1994, pp.7–8).

When talking about relationships with the LEAs the principals reported very mixed relationships from authorities which had been very supportive prior to Incorporation to those which were described as poor (but perhaps soured by a previous attempt to seek Grant Maintained School status). There was evidence of the colleges still working with the LEAs, particularly in relation to Special Needs Education provision (which was also a positive element in inter-college cooperation) and others reported the close involvement of the LEA in developing a common strategy for post-16 curriculum provision with other colleges. Some felt that the LEAs and the SFCs shared the same values and aspirations. If that view has been held onto then there may be some already existing good relationships at the setting up of the Local Learning and Skills Councils. This is unlikely to be universal, however, as some felt that LEA processes slowed things down. The FEFC was seen as a very distant and formal organization. Face-to-face relationships were rare and phone-call relationships were not viewed positively. It was felt that the FEFC was becoming more prescriptive and rule-oriented.

Although some interviewees reported that initial relationships with the TECs had been less than positive (indeed, especially prior to Incorporation, some SFC principals felt 'frozen out' of relationships by the FE colleges and the TECs), more recently treatment by the TECs was viewed as more even-handed. However, this was not seen as progress by all the interviewees. Some felt that to work more closely with the TECs would necessitate altering their college mission. So although relationships with the TECs were viewed warily there were examples of positive working relationships through things like Work Related Further Education (WRFE) flexibility monies and the support of the TECs for the colleges moving towards Investors in People (IIP) status. Some colleges reported the active involvement of TEC representatives on governing bodies. The membership of governing bodies had been heavily influenced by the principals. There was a caution to representatives from industry, unlike the experiences of many FE colleges. The SFC principals did not want 'hard nosed business types', although the expertise of such governors was seen as vital on finance subcommittees. As if to reinforce the points made earlier concerning the continued positive working relationships between SFCs and LEAs, and to underscore the wariness with which the principals approached representatives from local businesses, there was a very warmly reported continuing valued presence on governing bodies of local authority (LA) representation. One college reported having the LA Chief Executive and Director of Education on the governing body:

> Relationships with the TEC and the LEA are good – but then they need to be because they are important for the college. The way they behave to each other is important. They need to recognise that there is a revolution in education and Local Government going on and recognise that the old ways are gone. LEAs need to understand that the TEC and the SFC are both major players.

This exploration of the issues relating to the external forces which operate on the dynamic of SFC culture and ethos reveals a mixed landscape. There is a clear recognition of the forces operating on SFCs but a wariness about grasping hold of these forces too quickly or too positively for fear of upsetting the delicate ecology of the SFC ethos. What is clear, however, is that since Incorporation the colleges have developed a significant amount of knowledge and expertise with which to face the changes foreshadowed by the White Paper (DfEE 1999). What is unclear, though, is how willing the principals will be to let go of the freedoms they have won.

Conclusion: the future for sixth form colleges

The specialness of the ethos of SFCs within the post-16 sector seems to be holding on some years after Incorporation. This specialness is rooted in Samuel Butler's concept of intellectual discipleship. However, it would seem that the data reported above point to a considerable agenda for the SFCs in the period leading up to and beyond the implementation of the White Paper (DfEE 1999). Colleges need to address themselves to the issues surrounding changes in managerialism and leadership, the empowerment of tutors, particularly part-time tutors (who, as Robinson and Burke (1994) show, were often left in the dark by their principals), the academic ethos which sees students as learners rather than clients, the curriculum including GNVQ and the International Baccalaureate, changes in teaching and learning strategies including distance learning, relationships with funding bodies including the proposed Learning and Skills Council for England and the RDAs, the changing nature of the student body including more part-timers, more adults and students from the 14-plus age range and marketing. All these issues will affect tutors, students and colleges in the years to come. The dynamics of the delicate ecology of the SFC ethos are finely balanced and principals undertake a delicate balancing act with skill. The academic success of the SFCs is both a strength and a weakness and can be easily undermined by any significant change in any one of the elements which underpin the ethos of the colleges. This agenda will involve further delicate manoevrings by the principals as they steer a course through the ideological landscape of a Thatcherite inspired FHE Act (1992) and a more Blairite New Labour White Paper future. Some of the principles of the old order are certain to be retained. In facing this future the colleges seem to have few options.

One option is to expand in order to survive. This is going to be difficult because SFCs are probably achieving near to maximum intakes as far as their 'core purpose' (GCE A-level work) is concerned. Expansion will have to be at the margins involving increasing part-time students, evening work and vocationally oriented work. This will bring them into sharper competition with the FE colleges. We have seen how these changes impact on the student body at Stokingham Sixth Form College. Expansion will involve buying in managerial expertise from industry, commerce and the FE sector. The consequences will upset the fine balance which underpins the SFC ethos and might involve them transmuting into small (unviable) FE colleges.

A second scenario is to contract in order to survive. This will involve retreating to the core purpose (A-level teaching) exclusively. This is probably only a possibility for a few larger institutions who would be able to maintain a critical mass of students. Smaller colleges could combine this option with merging in order to protect their niche market, as has begun to happen. (This may be a strong attraction for colleges with particular ethnic, cultural or denominational mix of students.) It is probable that the option of merger will only be available in urban areas where transport facilities allow. However, this move would protect the ethos of the SFCs but it might involve the SFC sector as a whole contracting to below a viable, influential size.

A third scenario is to merge with FE colleges. This would clearly mean the disappearance of the SFC ethos as they became, possibly, the A-level faculties in tertiary colleges. There may well be changes beyond the control of the SFCs themselves, such as the future of A-levels and funding arrangements which makes this scenario no longer a choice but a necessity.

A fourth option is to pair with an FE college. This allows SFCs to gain advantages of economies of scale where they do not have negative, unintended consequences. These will include issues like staff development. In the short term this may appear to be an attractive option, but in the longer term it is easy to see it as the precursor for a full merger.

No matter what happens, particularly after the implementation of the White Paper, and the outcomes will be different for each college, several questions are raised by the data reported above. One of the central questions relates to the impact of any changes on the quality of teaching and learning and the student experience. Another concerns the future roles of the differing institutions now that the binary divide between FE and SF colleges is well and truly removed. Perhaps two quotations from two of the principals will serve to illustrate these stresses:

> There is a need to bring together the two culture – the Sixth Form/Post-16 and Adult Education cultures. Teachers will have the opportunity to teach across this divide. Although this will be

voluntary, if they don't many will face redundancy ... If the college is to expand or even remain viable it will need to exploit new markets like adults, but not necessarily as part-time day students or mixing with the 16–19 students ... In five years there will probably be only one college [in this town]. Rationalisation through market forces will bring about different annexes or centres offering different specialist sets of programmes all managed through one college.

There will be a need for change in order to grow but the problem will be whether to emphasise broadening the curriculum base beyond A-level or extending the student profile beyond 16–19 full-time. It is too easy to say we can do both and that it is only resources that are the problem.

Although the predictions of the first principal about merger have not come true, yet, SFCs do face an uncertain future. That they are successful and special is beyond doubt. It is certain that this is necessary for their survival, but whether this specialness is a sufficient condition for survival is more open to question. Their distinctiveness at the moment rests on a unique combination of staffing, attitude, management style, student mix, image and curriculum. All these elements are finely balanced. Changes beyond the control of the colleges may bring wholesale changes to the ethos and culture of the SFCs which the principals are keen to protect. Indeed, as Gleeson (1993) noted such changes are underpinned by the ideological and administrative objectives of the FHE Act (1992). Change seems to be inevitable. In managing that change so far the principals have been very energetic in privileging the specialness which characterizes the SFC ethos. Given the positive way in which the new Labour government views the SFCs their future looks bright for some time to come.

References

Ball, S. (1991) *Politics and Policy Making in England*. London: Routledge.

Benn, C. and Simon, B. (1972) *Half Way There*. Harmondsworth: Penguin.

Bloomer, M. and Hodkinson, P. (1997) *Moving into FE: The Voice of the Learner*. London: FEDA.

Burgess, T. and Pratt, J. (1970) *Policy and Practice: The Colleges of Advanced Technology*. London: Allen Lane.

Central Advisory Council for Education [England] (1959) *15 to 18: The Report of the Crowther Commission*. (The Crowther Report). London: HMSO.

Cordingley, P. and Cogan, M. (1993) *In Support of Education: The Functioning of Local Government.* London: Jessica Kingsley for the Joseph Rowntree Foundation.

DES (1988) *Advancing A Levels* (The Higginson report). London: HMSO.

DfEE (1999) *Learning to Succeed: A New Framework for Post-16 Learning.* White Paper, Cm. 4392. London: DfEE.

Epstein, D. (1993) *Changing Classroom Culture: Anti-racism, Politics and Schools.* Stoke-on-Trent: Trentham Books.

FEU/IoE/TNF (1994) *GNVQs 1993–94: A National Survey.* London: FEU/IoE/TNF.

Gleeson, D. (1993) 'Legislating for change: Missed opportunities in the Further and Higher Education Act.' *British Journal of Education and Work* 6 (2), 29–40.

Grace, G. (1994) 'Education as Scholarship: On the Need to Resist Policy Science.' Paper presented to the Standing Conference in Studies in Education: The Role of Theory in Education Studies, London.

Hargreaves, D. and Macmillan, R. (1992) 'Balkanized Secondary Schools and the Malaise of Modernity.' Paper presented to the Annual Meeting of the American Educational Research Association, San Francisco, California.

Kenway, J. with Bigum, C. and Fitzclarence, L. (1993) 'Marketing education in the post-modern age.' *Journal of Education Policy 8* (2), 105–122.

King, R. (1976) *School and College: Studies in Post-Sixteen Education.* London: Routledge & Kegan Paul.

King, R.W. (1968) *The English Sixth Form College: An Exceptional Concept.* London: Pergamon.

Kingston, P. (1999) 'Sixth sense at No. 10.' *Guardian Education,* Tuesday 1 June, 13.

MacFarlane, E. (1978) *Sixth-Form Colleges.* London: Heinemann.

Monks, T.G. (1968) *Comprehensive Education in England and Wales.* Slough: NFER.

National Commission on Education (1993) *Learning to Succeed.* Report of The Paul Hamlyn Foundation National Commission on Education. London: Heinemann.

Page, M.G. (1996) 'A Framework for Understanding Student Drop-Out in the Further Education Context.' Unpublished Ph.D. Thesis. Southampton: Southampton University.

Peterson, A.D.C. (1960) *Arts and Science Sides in the Sixth Form.* Mimeo. Oxford: Oxford University Department of Education.

Phillips, C. (1972) 'The sixth form colleges: a survey.' *Secondary Education,* No. 3.

Pratt, J. and Burgess, T. (1974) *Polytechnics: A Report.* London: Pitman.

Reid, W.A. (1972) *The Universities and the Sixth Form Curriculum.* Basingstoke: Macmillan for the Schools Council.

Reid, W.A. and Filby, J. (1982) *The Sixth: An Essay in Democracy.* Lewes, Sussex: Falmer Press.

Robinson, J. and Burke, C. (1994) *Competition, Cooperation and the Colleges: The Perceptions of Tutors Concerning the Act of Incorporation.* Post-16 Research and Development Centre Occasional Paper No. 1. Crewe: Manchester Metropolitan University.

Robinson, J. and Burke, C. (1995) *Tradition, Culture and Ethos in Sixth Form Colleges.* Post-16 Research and Development Centre Occasional Paper No. 2. Crewe: Manchester Metropolitan University.

Robinson, J. and Burke, C. (1996) 'Tradition, culture and ethos: the impact of the Further and Higher Education Act (1992) on sixth form colleges and their futures.' *Evaluation and Research in Education 10* (1), 3–21.

Schools Council (1967) *Some Further Proposals for Sixth Form Work.* Working Paper No. 16. London: HMSO.

Schools Council and the Standing Conference on University Entrance (1969) *Proposals for the Curriculum and Examinations in the Sixth Form: A Joint Statement.* London: Schools Council.

Shorter, P. (1994) 'Sixth-form colleges and Incorporation: some evidence from case studies in the north of England.' *Oxford Review of Education 20* (4), 461–473.

Smithers, A. and Robinson, P. (1993) *Changing Colleges: Further Education in the Market Place.* London: The Council for Industry and Higher Education.

Taylor, P.H., Reid, W.A. and Holley, B.J. (1974) *The English Sixth Form: A Case Study in Curriculum Reform.* London: Routledge & Kegan Paul.

Toffler, A. (1990) *Powershift.* New York: Bantam Books.

Tooley, J. (1993) *A Market-Led Alternative for the Curriculum: Breaking the Code.* London: The Institute of Education/The Tufnell Press.

Vincent, C. (1993) 'Education for the community.' *British Journal of Educational Studies 41* (4), 366–380.

Walford, G. (1994) *Choice and Equity in Education.* London: Cassell.

Whitty, G. (1991) 'Recent Education Reform: Is it a Post-modern Phenomenon?' Paper presented to a conference on Reproduction, Social Inequality and Resistance: New Directions in the Theory of Education. Bielefeld, Germany: University of Bielefeld.

Chapter 11

Mass Market Higher Education

Gareth Williams

Introduction

From 1979 till 1997 British higher education was the subject of rigorous scrutiny and radical reform by a right wing Conservative government. Since 1997 the centrist New Labour government has continued in broadly the same market oriented direction, with the added refinement of reintroducing fees for undergraduate students, the last vestiges of which had earlier been abolished by the previous Labour administration in the mid-1970s.

Since the 1960s many economists have been uneasy about equity and efficiency implications of the public finance of education and training for all above the age of eighteen. Few now deny that throughout the forty years after the end of the Second World War, the production, allocation and distribution of higher education tilted the balance of power and benefit in favour of universities and colleges and their more advantaged consumers. This became associated with management inefficiencies and levels of public expenditure that the political process showed to be unsustainable.

In the early years of Margaret Thatcher's government the main concern was with overall levels of public expenditure. In higher education one of its first actions was to remove all public subsidy for students whose home residence was outside the European Community. This was followed a year later in 1981 by a reduction of 15 per cent in the general funds for higher education.

Both these measures were taken with the sole objective of contributing to the reductions in public expenditure, which the new government believed to be too high to support an efficient economy. However, in retrospect, their main long-term significance lies in what they revealed about universities and polytechnics as economically motivated organizations. The reactions to 'the cuts' clearly influenced what followed in the later 1980s. In the case of foreign students the universities, which, unlike the polytechnics and colleges at that time, were autonomous institutions, soon realized that foreign students now brought with them significant income that was free of government constraints. Many universities abandoned their previous passive attitude to foreign student recruitment and undertook vigorous recruitment drives. The dip in recruitment of overseas students in 1982 and 1983, immediately following the fee increase, was soon recouped, and by 1987 there were more foreign students in British universities than in 1979. The polytechnics, which were not autonomous and were required to remit most of any fee income to the local authorities which owned them, did not undertake aggressive marketing strategies until much later, and their foreign student recruitment remained low for much longer.

The reaction to the 1981 15 per cent reduction in general income was almost the exact opposite of this. The universities, which were able to act like a cartel under the leadership of the University Grants Committee (UGC), responded by reducing student enrolments in order, they claimed, to maintain the traditional high quality of British university education. Individual polytechnics, which competed for resources from a fixed 'advanced further education pool', largely on the basis of the number of (UK) students they recruited, realized that the only way they could maintain their income from a pool whose overall size was diminishing was to recruit more students. There began a frenzied scramble for students, regardless of the fact that the overall effect was to reduce the income received for each student. This came to an end only when the government itself called a halt in 1983 by establishing the National Advisory Body for Public Sector Higher Education (NAB) which had, in broad terms, a similar coordinating function for the non-university sector as the UGC had for the universities.

The university increase in foreign students and the polytechnic expansion of home student enrolments were both essentially market responses, determined by the mechanisms by which the two groups of institutions were funded, and the regulations which governed them. They showed that higher education institutions would respond, like any other organization, to market and quasi-market incentives. The achievement of mass higher education at relatively low cost to the taxpayer owed much to these almost accidental early lessons.

Market concepts in higher education

The marketization of British higher education is not unique. It has been part of a worldwide, trans-sector trend of which the most dramatic manifestation was the downfall of the centrally planned economies of Eastern Europe. In higher education, governments in New Zealand and Australia have pursued similar policies, and there have been many moves in this direction in most OECD countries, although usually not so radical as in the UK.

This movement towards market approaches to the funding of post-compulsory education has taken several forms. It is possible to discern a common trend towards increased use of funding formulae, greater financial autonomy for institutions, growing reliance on fees from students and on commercial income from activities that are only indirectly related to the core higher education business. These have been accompanied by increased competition between providers of core educational services.

Ideology provided the main driver for these changes. This is demonstrated by the varying speed at which they occurred in different countries. However, underpinning them were the dramatic changes brought about by the rapid developments of information technology. These had, and are still having, three effects in particular which help to explain the current ascendancy of market ideology.

The first is simply that centralized bureaucratic control is too rigid to keep pace with rapid technological change of any kind. Long-term plans are out of date before the planners have finished formulating them. The Soviet economy in the 1970s and 1980s fell back further and further in comparison with those that were able to respond quickly to technological change. This is particularly relevant to higher education with its long production period and long-term effects. Inflexible universities can continue to do damage for many decades.

The second feature of the technological changes of the past two decades, a powerful acceleration of changes that have been happening for the past three hundred years, is the speeding up of global communications. Information about successful (and unsuccessful) innovations can be round the world in a matter of minutes. Evaluations of the causes of success or failure are usually not far behind. This is especially relevant to higher education, which is one of the leading information industries.

Third, and in practice almost certainly the most important as a proximate cause of developments in British higher education, is the implications of technology for management information systems.

The development of high-powered systems for the creation, transmission, storage and retrieval of management information has meant that governments have been able to loosen detailed administrative controls, while at the same time increasing their capacity to steer systems and institutions in directions indicated by their own policy priorities. The concept of steering a system or organization by the manipulation of management information is the main way in which complex systems like higher education can be 'steered from a distance'. It is closely related to what Neave has described as the 'evaluative state' (Neave 1987).

Nearly all the British government reforms of the 1980s and 1990s can be seen in terms of movement towards marketization. Essentially there have been two forms: harnessing private funds and the creation of quasi-markets for the allocation of public funds. There have been few examples of wholesale privatization in British higher education, though some of the outsourcing of non-core activities by many universities comes close. It is worth noting that commercialization of any public service is inevitably accompanied by the establishment of regulatory machinery to ensure that suppliers do not use their intrinsic monopoly power excessively to the detriment of consumers. 'Service level agreements' are widespread. The commercial organization undertakes to provide a certain level of service, often specified in considerable detail.

In what are seen as welfare services, such as education, health and other social services, for which full privatization is not deemed to be appropriate, the concept of quasi-markets has been introduced. In essence this means a government agency performing the role of surrogate customer, and purchasing services on behalf of the ultimate consumers, from service suppliers such as hospitals, schools and universities. This is what both the Higher Education and the Further Education Funding Councils are required to do by the 1988 and 1992 Education Acts.

In many ways higher education was a soft target. The funding of universities was already partly quasi-market in form, in that financially autonomous universities received public funds and spent them in accordance with their own priorities. The problem, at least in the eyes of the government of the 1980s, was that these priorities often did not always coincide with those that the government considered to be the interests of the community as a whole. It was a problem that higher education shared with many other public sector activities and gave rise to a growing interest amongst economists in what has come to be called the 'the principal–agent problem'.

The problem can be expressed very simply. How does the 'principal' ensure that the 'agent' acts in a way that the principal requires? At this level the issue merges with wider management and leadership theories. How do managers or leaders ensure that the individuals and organizations for which they are responsible behave in ways which the managers require? The answer is in one of five ways: coercion through physical force, bureaucratic or legal authority, charismatic persuasion, professional expertise or the provision of incentives. For a wide variety of technical, economic and ideological reasons, related to organizational size, the tendency of middle level bureaucrats and professionals to act in their own self-interests (which include inefficiency that results from bureaucrats acting in ways that make life easier for them at the expense of their clients), and the growing belief in individualistic democracy as the ultimate source of authority in any society, there has been a growing tendency to treat the last of these, the provision of incentives, as the most efficient and acceptable way for principals to 'persuade' agents to achieve outcomes desired by the principals.

Nowhere in the Western world was this new ideology taken up more enthusiastically than in the United Kingdom where the Conservative government viewed all public provision of services as undesirable, on grounds of both efficiency and democratic principle. Where, as in much of education, public provision was inescapable, they substituted quasi-markets for real markets. The principal–agent problem was 'solved' through a double-pronged approach: financial incentives to encourage agents to act in desired ways and market monitoring to ensure that they do so effectively. In higher education this has meant zero based formula funding and ongoing quality assessment of teaching and research.

The road to marketization

The 1988 Education Reform Act, the 1992 Further and Higher Education Act and the 1998 Teaching and Higher Education Act are the key milestones marking a complete transformation of the funding of higher education in the United Kingdom.

The key features, for higher education, of the 1988 Act were: the abolition of local education authority control of polytechnics, giving them an autonomous legal status and control of their own funding equivalent to the universities; the creation of a Universities Funding

Council (UFC) and a Polytechnics and Colleges Funding Council (PCFC) to replace the UGC and NAB; and the abolition of lifetime tenure for university staff. With these changes the polytechnics and colleges became free to act in their own best interests; academic domination of resource allocation decisions was brought to an end and the labour market for academic staff was freed of one dominant rigidity.

Whether the creation of what were in effect a majority of lay directors of the funding councils was an effective curb on academic influence on resource allocation decisions is an open question. An authoritative account of the consequences of the change has yet to be written. What is known is that there was considerable tension between the first chairman and the first chief executive of the Universities Funding Council over whether market or planning principles should govern its resource allocation procedures.

The issue of academic versus market values did not arise, at least it did not come into public view, in the case of the PCFC where both chairman and chief executive were new appointments from outside the sector. It was, therefore, not surprising that the PCFC led the way in creating mechanisms of formula funding which brought about the explosive expansion of student numbers between 1989 and 1994.

More important than the membership of the Councils, however, was a clause in the Act that provided for any financial allocations to individual universities to be accompanied by 'Financial Memoranda' that specified within closely defined limits what was expected in return for these financial allocations. On the day they were set up the two Councils received a letter from the Secretary of State setting out the government's interpretation of how the Councils should carry out their responsibilities. The key phrase was: 'I shall look to the Council to develop funding arrangements which recognise the general principle that the public funds allocated to universities are in exchange for the provision of teaching and research and are conditional on their delivery' (DES 1988). It was quite explicit that higher education institutions were henceforward to be seen as selling teaching (and, in the case of the universities only, research) services to the government which was the near monopsonistic purchaser of these services. This transfer of financial power from the suppliers of academic services to a proxy consumer has been extremely far-reaching. Henceforward, the only way universities could make effective use of their cloak of legal autonomy was by diversifying their funding sources.

The PCFC established a 'core plus margin' model for allocating funds to polytechnics and colleges. The essence of this model was that the institutions received their 'core income' (between 90% and 95% of their previous year's total income from the PCFC) plus a 'margin' which depended on how many additional students they agreed to recruit at a lower price. Thus the more off-quota students they recruited the greater their total income, but the lower their income per student. In effect a distinction was made between average cost and marginal costs of additional students. So long as marginal costs were below average costs the average was driven down year by year. Despite this, the number of students in polytechnics and colleges grew rapidly as each individual institution tried to increase its total income. The process was analogous to a street market in which competing traders bid down prices as each tries to increase its sales.

At first these new allocation mechanisms did not directly affect the universities whose funding council continued to allocate funds on an average historic cost basis. However, the government had by now espoused a policy of encouraging enrolment expansion to bring UK enrolment levels up to the levels of most other OECD countries and it aimed to do this as inexpensively as possible through the use of market mechanisms. In 1989 a package of measures was agreed with the Treasury whereby the fairly generous maintenance grants received by all full-time undergraduate students were to be progressively replaced by repayable loans and in return the Treasury agreed to pay fees up to about 30 per cent of teaching costs of an unlimited number of students.

The consequence was that many institutions increased their enrolments spectacularly, by as much as 25 per cent per year for two or three years in some cases. This reduced considerably their average income per student but, because of the open-ended nature of the Treasury commitment to support additional students at marginal costs, did bring rapidly increasing aggregate income to the sector.

An incidental feature of the policy was that the universities also received lower levels of government subsidy in respect of those part-time and postgraduate students who paid their own fees. Most universities, therefore, raised the fees of these categories of students proportionately to the government fees. Surprisingly this did not result in a decline in the numbers of self-funding students so another effect of the government strategy was to increase the amount of private income received by the universities. This also may have been taken as an indicator for subsequent policy making. Rises in fees did not necessarily choke off demand.

By 1994 the government was becoming worried about the effects of the policy on two counts. One was that the universities were showing insufficient regard for quality as student numbers exploded at ever-decreasing costs. (By this time, following the passage of the 1992 Higher and Further Education Act, the great majority of students were in institutions called universities.) The other, and from the government point of view more important, was that, despite the fact that each additional student was costing the government only one-third of the previous average cost, the expansion was so rapid that total government expenditure commitments were growing at an unacceptable rate.

It is hardly surprising that concomitant with these financial changes there were developments designed to ensure that the quality of teaching was maintained. The establishment of quality assurance procedures was typical of regulated markets in which commercial suppliers, while competing fiercely with each other, collaborate to meet an external threat to their collective well-being. In this case the threat perceived by the universities in the late 1980s was government infringement of their autonomy by setting up an agency to monitor and regulate the quality of their teaching. They set up the Quality Audit Unit, which had the mission of ensuring that suitable quality assurance mechanisms were in place in every university, and operating effectively. However, the government was not convinced that this offered adequate safeguards for students or taxpayers and, in 1992, established Quality Assessment Committees within the Funding Councils that allocated public funds to universities and colleges. In 1997 both agencies were combined into the Quality Assurance Agency, performing a function not entirely dissimilar from the regulatory agencies of the privatized public utilities. Acceptable standards of teaching, externally assessed, are now a condition of the receipt of government grant. The parallel intention to reward universities and colleges adjudged to have particularly good teaching has proved more difficult to implement. Why should extra taxpayers' money be given to institutions that are providing high quality teaching with the resources that they have already?

This contrasts with research, which has led to another market response. Universities have been encouraged to shift resources out of teaching, for which beyond the minimum threshold there are very few additional rewards, and into research for which the extra rewards of a high research assessment score are very considerable.

The Teaching and Higher Education Act 1998

The 1998 Act has taken the market approach one step further by shifting about a quarter of the cost of teaching on to students and their families by charging of fees to undergraduate students. However, this may be better seen as a rather crude attempt at finding a 'third way' rather than a further act of marketization. Universities are not permitted to decide the fees they charge. Fees are not related to the cost of courses nor to the anticipated financial benefits of studying different subjects or at different institutions. The aim is to transfer some of the burden of further expansion on to households, without further increasing inequality in higher education provision.

The Act is the government's response to the Dearing Report, which accepted that the only realistic way of obtaining significant additional income for basic undergraduate teaching is from the students. This is not unfair. Most graduates earn much more during their working lives than most non-graduates – some very much more. In 1996 the average employee with a university degree earned 85 per cent more than someone with only an NVQ level 3 equivalent qualification.

However, questions may be asked about whether the policy is really likely to achieve the aim of increasing the funds available for high level teaching in the most effective and the most equitable way. Despite a slight improvement in the past two years universities and colleges remain chronically short of cash in relation to the tasks they are expected to perform.

The present scheme may be necessary as a means of making fee-paying politically acceptable, but as a mechanism for bringing additional income into university teaching it is too modest. All undergraduate students pay the same fees, whatever and wherever they are studying. Universities are not allowed to charge higher fees, even if students are willing or able to pay them. Yet it is obvious to anyone who looks around the job market that some subjects and some universities bring much greater financial benefits than others. I am not aware of any research that has compared the incomes of the average Oxbridge graduate with the average Thames Valley University graduate. The research has probably not been done because the answer is so obvious. Yet the Thames Valley student pays the same fees as the Oxford student. There can be no doubt that many people would be willing to pay much more for an Oxbridge or an Imperial College education if they were permitted to.

The rationale for the government's position is that premium fees would benefit the university that received them but would do nothing for the system as a whole. The privileged universities and departments would become ever more privileged. Social class divisions between high-fee institutions and the rest, it is argued, would become as acute in higher education as in secondary education.

This need not be. Premium fees could benefit everybody with no adverse equity effects with a few, easily administered, modifications to the present scheme. The first is that universities should be allowed to charge a premium only in terms of a *percentage* of the standard national fee. Thus the *relative* effects on all students would be the same. Second, universities should be required to pay a fixed percentage of any premium they charge into the central pool of money distributed to all universities. Obviously the level of this levy would need to be a subject for negotiation. Too low and it would bring in little extra money for anyone other than the university charging the fee. Too high and it would not be worth the university's while incurring the hassle and the initial wrath of their students for introducing it. It would, of course, be essential to have a cast-iron undertaking from government that the Treasury would not purloin any extra income generated in this way and turn it, in effect into a tax on higher education. One way of achieving this might be to pay it into a separate teaching quality improvement fund.

Let us suppose that the University of Camford was able to charge double its existing fee for economists and still obtain an adequate number of applications from students of the ability levels it expects to recruit. The fees paid by all its students would rise proportionally to the fees they already pay. If they pay low fees because of low family income they would rise by only a few pounds. If their family income were so low that they pay no fees, they would still pay no fees after the change. In the unlikely event that even this proportionate rise meant that a few students who would study economics at Camford now, were unable to so, it could be argued that overall equity would increase if a few of the more able students were dispersed to other universities and subjects.

Of the income this generated a proportion, say 25 per cent, could be remitted to the common pool for all universities. Everyone who works in university departments is used to paying a levy on externally generated income to help pay the central costs of the institution and to subsidize worthy departments that are not in a position to earn a large amount of outside income. The principle here is no different.

Students who pay premium fees should be eligible for loans to cover the cost. There need be no cost to the taxpayer because the privatization of the student loans scheme means that the banks would be lending the money for any additional borrowing.

Of course some universities would continue to be more privileged than others. Some graduates would have a better start in life than others. But no more so than at present. With differential fees those who had obtained the head start would have a larger debt to repay to the rest of society.

Concluding comments

This chapter has examined the nature of markets and quasi-markets in British higher education, including the use of funding formulae and other systems of financial incentives. In this concluding section these developments are evaluated from an economic and a more general point of view.

Six different categories of market behaviour can be observed in universities and colleges in Britain.

- Allocation by government of resources to higher education in relation to anticipated economic benefits. (Although economic rates of return are not used explicitly the idea of value for money and public and private economic returns clearly underlie much of the public policy rhetoric.)

- Formula-based allocation of finance by government funding councils to individual universities and colleges using formulae as the 'price' the government is willing to pay for different categories of student place.

- Allocation of funds *within* universities and colleges to faculties and departments on a formula basis. (Usually this too is done largely on the basis of student numbers but a variety of other criteria such as incentives to recruit foreign students – who bring in more income – or to attract well funded research grants are also used.)

- The employment of rapidly growing numbers of staff on a part-time, casual, piecework basis to do specific teaching and research but who are otherwise not part of the university.

- Out-sourcing of many subsidiary activities such as student accommodation and eating facilities, cleaning services and maintenance of buildings.

- Setting up of subsidiary businesses, often linked to the provision of consultancy services, but including marketing of the physical plant for outside use (e.g. student accommodation for conference participants) and selling library, laboratory and computing services.

The first question is whether the conditions are met for the socially efficient functioning of competitive markets. These include issues of information, transaction costs and uncertainty and also questions of efficiency and equity.

An important condition for markets and quasi-markets to operate efficiently is that both sides of the market have access to accurate information. In education it is important for providers to know the costs of the services they supply and for purchasers to have good information about the quality of the services they are buying, in order to limit the opportunity for suppliers to reduce prices by lowering the quality of their services. These conditions are even more important in quasi-markets where a monopsonistic buyer purchases services on behalf of consumers.

The quality of higher education services can be assured through the professional integrity of providers; consumers' ability to judge the quality of the services they are buying; collective monitoring of the activities of individual providers to ensure that some are not surreptitiously lowering quality while trading on the good name of the sector as a whole.

In the traditional provision of élite higher education in Britain professional integrity was the paramount guarantor of quality. Universities appointed the most able people that could find and, after a long apprenticeship, they were given almost complete autonomy in their teaching and research. Reputation was the currency of this system. It was hard won and easily lost. Institutions and individuals guarded their reputation jealously and did not engage in activities that jeopardized it. In marketing terms this may be seen as a long-term marketing strategy. Universities were more concerned to optimize their long-term reputation rather than their short-term income. This is not an option in a fiercely competitive market. Long-term reputation depends on short-term survival. It is not surprising, therefore, that marketization has been accompanied by the development of collective and government imposed quality assurance mechanisms. The cost of these quality controls needs to be taken into account in any evaluation of the efficiency of market approaches to the provision of higher education. When all the preparation time within institutions is included they are certainly considerable.

Higher education is an extreme example of a service that produces many different outputs. Different consumers prefer different combinations of outputs. It is possible to distinguish several levels of satisfaction according to the preferences of the state, the universities or students. This confuses the analysis of principal–agent problems. Who in higher education are the principals and who the agents? In practice the quasi-market approach makes government the principal and academic staff the agents. Implicitly it assumes that majority preferences are the only form of legitimate authority in a democracy. The authority given by expertise is subordinated to the authority of the state.

The creation of market mechanisms is not the same as the establishment of a free market. There is not a free market in British higher education: in some ways it has become less free as a result of the changes outlined in this chapter. Universities are less free now to take many of their own academic and financial decisions than they were at the beginning of the 1980s. Some market features are combined with increased bureaucratic controls. The controls are concerned primarily with increased accountability for the use of public funds and liability to external quality monitoring.

What, then, is the balance sheet? The costs of higher education have fallen dramatically. Taxpayers are almost certainly getting better value for their money. Expenditure per student place is now some 40 per cent lower in real terms than it was at the beginning of the 1980s. An interesting exception to this is the full-cost fees paid by students from outside the European Community. These have risen by about 20 per cent on average since full-cost fees were first introduced in the early 1980s. It is widely recognized that in most universities foreign students are now providing a surplus over the costs of teaching them that helps subsidize other university activities such as teaching British students.

Second there is quantitative evidence to suggest that the outputs of both teaching and research have risen. Research performance as measured in the number of articles published has been rising sharply since the introduction of research assessment in the mid-1980s. Undoubtedly the rapid changes in information technology have been partly responsible for this increase in productivity.

In teaching, the existence of an implicit contract between students and their teaching institutions is now widely recognized and course aims, assessment criteria and teaching processes are now made much more explicit. The quality of qualifications awarded as measured by the percentage of graduates with good class honours degrees has been rising, though there is not universal agreement that the standards represented by degree class are constant between universities or through time.

Finally, the funding changes and the shift towards output-based budgeting and market-oriented income generation have made universities much more flexible institutions, able to respond to the growing demands of lifelong learning. Most universities and colleges now recognize that individuals of all ages have a right to have appropriate education and training for them on terms that are appropriate for them. The main danger is that the market pressures, which have on the whole made higher education a more attractive service for vastly more consumers, are making it correspondingly less attractive for the academic staff who are the ultimate providers of these services. The challenge for the early years of the new century will be to manage the market-oriented system in ways that maintain quality at acceptable costs without making teaching in higher education an unattractive occupation for an appropriate proportion of the nation's most able people.

Note

This chapter is partly based on a revised and updated version of Williams (1997b).

References

Ball. S.J. (1993) 'Education markets, choice and social class: the market as a class strategy in the UK and USA.' *British Journal of the Sociology of Education 4*, (1), 3–19.

DES (1988) *Letter from the Secretary of State to the Chairmen of the New Funding Councils* (31/10/1988). London: DES.

Glennerster, H. (1991) 'Quasi-markets for education?' *Economic Journal 101*, 1268–1276.

Jarratt, A. (1985) *Report of the Steering Committee on Efficiency Studies in Universities*. London: Committee of Vice Chancellors and Principals.

Le Grand, J. (1991) 'Quasi-markets and social policy.' *Economic Journal 101*, 1256–1267.

Moore, P.G. (1989) 'Marketing higher education.' *Higher Education Quarterly 43*, 2.

Neave, G. (1987) 'The all-seeing eye of the Prince in Western Europe.' In G. Moodie (ed) *Standards and Criteria in Higher Education*. Guildford: SRHE and NFER Nelson.

Teichler, U. (1996) 'Recent research in higher education policy in Europe.' *Higher Education Policy 9*, 2, July 1996.

Williams, G., Blackstone, T. and Metcalfe, D. (1974) *The Academic Labour Market*. Oxford and Amsterdam: Elsevier.

Williams, G. (1992) 'An evaluation of new funding mechanisms in British higher education: some micro-economic and institutional management issues.' *Higher Education in Europe 11*, 65–85.

Williams, G. (1997a) 'Principals, agents, producers and consumers in higher education.' In K. Watson, C. Modgil and S. Mogdil (eds) *Reforms in Higher Education*. Volume 2 of *Education Dilemmas: Debate and Diversity*. London: Cassell.

Williams, G. (1997b) 'The market route to mass higher education: British experience 1979–1996.' *Higher Education Policy 10*, 3/4.

PART IV

Initial Teacher Education

Chapter 12

Accrediting Lecturers Using Competence-based Approaches

A Cautionary Tale

Geoffrey Elliott

Overview

Learning, as lecturers know, is a complex process involving a multi-faceted interrelationship between the learner, what is learnt and, often, what is taught. Learning involves sets of beliefs, attitudes and values, it takes place in a situated environment, and is frequently described as life-changing. The concept of lifelong learning, with its emphasis upon learning from cradle to grave, begins to recognize the potential for a new settlement around this broad and comprehensive view of learning. However, the development of competence-based models of assessment, with their preoccupation with observable phenomena, has led to narrow, restricted and mechanistic models of learning, and they have been judged to be ineffective at assessing any but the most basic skills. Pre-ordained performance criteria have been found wanting as benchmarks for high-order skills within management and teaching which require judgement, intuition, behaviour under stress and the ability to weigh up ethical issues. A significant danger is that if the competency movement is successful, it may wittingly or unwittingly lead to the replacement of trained lecturers by part-time agency lecturers or technician-demonstrators.

Introduction

Vocational education and training in the UK has a chequered history. There have evolved some 600 accrediting and awarding bodies which award about 6000 different qualifications to students on vocational courses. The big three boards are City and Guilds, Royal Society of Arts (RSA), and Business and Technology Education Council

(BTEC), whose qualifications are differently structured to each other, and non-interlocking. The system is described in the further education staff college report on NCVQ as 'a jungle of qualifications' (Hall 1987). The diversity of provision, the generally regarded inferior status of vocational qualifications compared with A-levels, and the low proportion of qualified people in the workforce compared with our economic competitors, combined to prompt government to act.

In April 1985, the government decided to set up a working group, the Review of Vocational Qualifications (RVQ) to review the whole range of vocational qualifications in England and Wales, and 'to recommend a structure which was relevant, comprehensive and accessible, which recognised competence and was cost effective' (Deville 1987, p.10). The key outcomes of the working group were the setting up of the National Council for Vocational Qualifications (NCVQ) to address the lack of coherence which was widely felt to characterize vocational education and training, and the recommendation of the development of a National Vocational Qualification (NVQ) framework, designed and implemented by the NCVQ. Existing vocational qualifications offered by BTEC etc. would, if satisfactory to NCVQ, be brought under the umbrella of the new national framework. The working group went further, and specified the character of the new qualifications:

> ... the review group felt strongly that vocational qualifications had to be first and foremost statements of competence which took account not only of skills and knowledge but of the ability to apply these in a working situation. The group therefore recommended that the new National Council should provide for the specification of standards of competence which would be reflected in vocational qualifications brought within the NVQ framework. (Deville 1987, p.11)

Two key principles of the NVQ framework are made clear, then, from the outset. The qualification is to be competence-based, and competences are to be demonstrated in the workplace. These two principles hold for the full range of qualifications which fall within the NVQ framework. The requirement that the framework is a comprehensive one means that it is intended eventually to encompass all occupations at all levels from school-leaver trainee to manager. NVQs currently cover some 80 per cent of the working population, and extend across all major sectors of employment.

In taking on board the principle that vocational qualifications are to be consequent upon assessment in the workplace, NCVQ was drawing upon the framework already in use by the Training Agency (TA), which adopted a competence-based assessment model established in Youth Training Scheme training, aimed at low-level occupations. The model has, however, also been widely used for management training and development, and adopted by the industry lead body, the Management Charter Initiative (MCI) and the National Forum for Management Education and Development (NFMED). NCVQ levels now range from 1 (basic/unskilled/trainee) to 5 (advanced/professional/managerial).

Problems with competence–based assessment

A general criticism of criterion-referenced assessment approaches *per se*, of which competence-based assessment is one example, is a direct consequence of their ancestry which is rooted in philosophical positivism and psychological behaviourism:

> In behaviourism, learning is studied only at its observable level and all other terminology or interpretation in terms of hidden entities or mental processes is denied. Early behaviourism was influenced by a philosophical movement known as positivism which dismissed as meaningless all statements which were not empirically verifiable. Accordingly the cardinal educational principle derived from this set of beliefs was that the only meaningful goals of learning and teaching were those which are objectively measurable as observable outcomes. Other aims are dismissed as little more than pious hopes. (Satterley 1989, p.44)

However, it can be argued that there are many aspects of learning which are not directly observable. A preoccupation with observable phenomena leads to a narrow, restricted and mechanistic model of learning and teaching which excludes the higher order domains of beliefs, attitudes and values.

The logic of the NCVQ approach, acknowledged by NCVQ itself, is that the breadth and scope of a course or learning programme is determined by the requirement to demonstrate the competencies to which it leads:

> The focus and starting point of this new system is different from the one many of us have been used to. It is the competence, the performance which is required, which establishes the baseline and which is specified. Once this has been established, enabling objectives (many of them possibly knowledge-based) can be identified

and appropriate learning experiences leading to the competence can be designed. (Ellis and Gorringe 1989, p.10)

Pring brings out the difference in emphasis between vocational and academic standards which competence-based approaches foster:

> Unlike academic standards, vocational ones are not mysterious entities slowly internalised, requiring a gradual apprenticeship, possessed 'more or less' and in varying degrees. Rather, one either is or is not competent. One can either do the job that is analysed in terms of a range of performances or (as performance indicators show) one cannot ... Courses might or might not be necessary for the achievement of competence – the end is logically disconnected from the means. And therefore courses (where they exist) are assessment led. They are but a means to an end. They, unlike the context of academic standards, do not require, as intrinsically necessary, the apprenticeship, the participation in the very activities through which the standards come to be recognised. (Pring 1992, p.14)

He also points out that the quest for 'absolute standards' within the core GCSE subjects, the development of attainment targets at ten different levels in the National Curriculum, and the attempts to equate levels of achievement at GCSE and A-level with levels of NVQs, are all manifestations of the same desire to equate standards with competence criteria or 'fitness for purpose'. Quite simply, the competency model is inadequate to the task of assessing any but the most basic skill or task whose complete performance can be described in terms of observable, empirically verifiable outcomes. That is, the standard to be specified is absolute. However, it is arguable that even some basic skills cannot be so reduced and assessed in terms of an 'absolute' standard. Within the NCVQ framework, for example:

> ... either you can or you cannot turn a piece of wood at level 2. You either are or are not competent. There is no room for shades of competence – or at least, where there are such shades they are thought to be a defect in the analysis, not a reflection of things as they are. And yet quality is often reflected in such adverbial qualifications of competence (or 'can do's') as 'elegantly', 'gracefully', 'imaginatively', 'intelligently', 'creatively'. Such adverbs imply judgement which is irreducible to the application of pre-conceived performance indicators. (Pring 1992, pp.15–16)

A further difficulty is that the assessment of competence is no straightforward matter:

> Assessment of competence by anyone is fraught with difficulties. Competence is hard to define and is open to interpretation. What, for example, degree of infallibility is required before we accept that someone is really competent? Does the ability to type a letter with acceptable accuracy today mean that the operator concerned will be capable of doing so again tomorrow or next year? (Needham 1988, p.46)

NCVQ, in describing competence in terms of performance, subsumes competence within performance. The NCVQ model blurs a crucial distinction between competence and performance. The *locus classicus* of the competence/performance dichotomy is in Chomskian linguistics (Chomsky 1971). Linguistic competence is that part of a speaker's knowledge of the language system ('langue' in Saussure's terms) which enables the production of language. Performance, on the other hand, refers to actual language behaviour, and this is influenced by contextual factors such as social conventions, emotion, social and situational context, and beliefs. The distinction which Chomsky draws between competence and performance is similar to Saussure's distinction between 'langue' and 'parole'. Both Chomsky's and Saussure's distinctions have been heavily criticized, which itself serves to underline the complexity of the relationship between competence and performance. Certainly any conflation of the two is theoretically unsound.

The rationale for competence-based approaches to assessing performance in the workplace is that there are generic competences underlying all jobs. Boyatzis, one of the founding fathers of the management competence movement in the USA, justified the development of a competence-based model of effective management by defining competence as an underlying characteristic which may be apparent in a wide variety of different observable actions and forms of behaviour. The emphasis here is upon the capability which is causally related to effective and/or superior performance:

> A person's set of competencies reflect his or her capability. They are describing what he or she can do, not necessarily what he or she does, nor does all the time regardless of the situation and setting. (Boyatzis 1982, p.23)

NCVQ, building on the TA approach, adopted a definition of competence which focused more centrally upon observable actions and behaviours:

> The ability to perform work activities to the standards required in employment. (NCVQ 1988)

Problems with a lead body for FE

Garland (1994) has suggested that the problems of applying lead body standards to the teaching role in further and higher education (FHE) can be ameliorated through the involvement of practitioners in setting the standards, and more painstaking attention to the real complexities and dilemmas of teaching. However, we are left with the criticism of competence-based education (CBE), which Moss (1981) first exposed, that the observable parts of tasks describe neither their complete nor even their most significant elements in most cases. The key point is that the TA/NCVQ definitions of competence, by embracing skills and abilities, are limited by their own terms of reference to actions and behaviours which can be observed and empirically verified. Hyland (1992), in examining the implications of such a competency model for adult education, legitimately questions its epistemological basis:

> Clearly, there is something unsatisfactory about a theoretical perspective which apparently recognises knowledge and understanding only to the extent that these are revealed in the performance of occupational tasks. (Hyland 1992, p.9)

The competency movement, then, has profound implications for the nature of education and training; the consequences for educational institutions are similarly devastating. One nightmare vision is that of a 'cafeteria' model of educational institutions, where customers pick and mix from budget-priced units, and quantify their experience and prior learning in training credits. However, it is to the implications for practitioners that I now turn.

The assessment and certification of managers using competence-based approaches has drawn a fair amount of critical attention. This is briefly reviewed below in order to provide a context for a critique of the use of such approaches, and associated procedures, for the assessment and certification of teachers, lecturers, advisers, consultants, assessors, external examiners, and others, whose professional duties, like those of managers, require a mixture of creativity, intuition, intellectual skill and contingent behaviours.

MCI/NFMED, the lead body for management, arrived at a list of management competencies by using a functional analysis approach, which separates out specific skills and abilities which are described in terms of a range of specific competencies. This represents, according to Everard (1990):

> ... a disaggregation process that reduces management to an amorphous bundle of elements each with their own performance

criteria. This is like using a quantity surveyor rather than an artist to capture the grandeur of St Paul's Cathedral. (Everard 1990, p.15)

This graphically makes the fundamental point which underlines many specific criticisms of competence-based approaches in management, that management is a 'higher order' activity. Ironically, this point is recognized by NCVQ in its specification of level 5, the highest level in the NVQ framework:

> ... competence which involves the application of a significant range of fundamental principles and complex techniques across a wide and often unpredictable range of contexts. Very substantial personal autonomy and often significant responsibility for the work of others and for the allocation of substantial resources feature strongly, as do personal accountabilities for analysis and diagnosis, design, planning, execution and evaluation. (NCVQ 1991)

By its nature, management defines its own task – particularly at the most senior levels, or in teaching and other circumstances where the agenda is not straightforward or pre-defined, and where problems need defining, and solutions need operationalizing, in context, by the manager, teacher or other professional. In such situations, pre-ordained performance criteria are clearly not appropriate as the reference point for the assessment of managerial and professional ability. A final irony, of course, is that if you ask most managers to describe their daily activity, for the most part you will be given a list of the most routine, fragmented and trivial tasks! This applies both to business and education management (Mintzberg 1973; Hall, Mackay and Morgan 1986).

A related point, and another difficulty which arises from the exclusive use of observable criteria, is that competence-based approaches are inappropriate for assessing so-called 'soft' management skills, such as the exercise of judgement, intuition, weighing up ethical issues, behaviour under stress, intellectual ability, and balancing competing demands. Such skills are extremely difficult to reproduce – for example by role-play or simulation – outside of the work context; they are extremely difficult to infer from observable behaviour; and there is the practical problem of how in practice an assessor might observe performance which may occur spontaneously, infrequently, or worse, only in one-to-one contacts between managers and subordinates!

A further problem for competence-based assessment of managers arises where, as is frequently the case, management teams exist. It can be impossible to separate out an individual manager's contribution to team success. And, as Belbin (1981) has pointed out, successful management teams are often comprised of individuals with very different skills and abilities, who complement each other's strengths. Individual competence is not the same as team or overall competence in this context, and the search for individual competencies as a measure of managerial effectiveness is both misdirected and iniquitous.

These are some of the major criticisms which can be levelled at the use of competence-based approaches to the assessment of managers. In focusing down to the context of education, the above criticisms remain, and can be supplemented by others which are mostly predicated on what is argued to be the inappropriate transfer of a model devised for and by management in business and industry to management in education.

The attempt has been to provide a generic model of management competence which covers the skills and abilities of all managers across all job sectors. The Confederation of British Industry (CBI) has commented upon the limited notions of occupational standards developed by industry lead bodies:

> ... the emphasis on standards setting by separate industry bodies has not naturally led to the development of cross sectoral 'generic' competences (which) ... should be concerned with adaptability, management of roles, responsibility for standards, creativity and flexibility to changing demands. Task competence is not enough to meet this need although some employers concentrating on their own short-term needs may believe it is. (CBI 1989)

This begs the question as to how similar management jobs are, and in particular, how similar managers in business and industry are to managers in education. Many would claim that there are many significant differences, attributable to fundamental differences in goals of service institutions and businesses (Drucker 1989). In developing a competence model for school management development, Earley (1992) identified over 40 elements, only 'half of which have been adapted from the MCI generic management competencies' (1992, p.2). Everard (1990) cites evidence to show 'that only 7/16 of the competences of secondary school heads are "universal", the rest being education-specific' (1990, p.15).

Despite these difficulties of differences between education management and business management, the MCI/NCVQ generic management qualification is being taken by a growing number of senior staff in education. Additionally, many professions have submitted, or are expected to submit, their own qualifications for NCVQ accreditation, including training and development, counselling, personnel management, journalism, administration, management services and accountancy (NCVQ 1992). Qualifications for lecturers in adult education, and some teacher training qualifications, are also being redesigned to bring them within a competence-based framework.

Government proposals (strongly supported by college employers) to carry out a functional and occupational mapping exercise of FE occupations (teaching and support staff) have led to the setting up of a Further Education National Training Organization (FENTO). The functional map that has been produced by this exercise does not, *de facto*, view teaching and lecturing as a co-intentional, transactional process, in which both student and teacher engage as equal participants (Freire 1972).

It appears likely that government has in mind the eventual establishment of an education lead body, that would specify common competence-based occupational standards for all educational practitioners, and that the FE sector has been chosen as a soft target for a pilot exercise, since a number of occupational roles carried out within the sector, such as Customer Service, Training and Development, already fall within the NVQ framework. It is evident that the performance criteria which are determined by FENTO are no less narrow and prescriptive than those produced so far for other occupations, in that they fail to extend beyond a technicist summary of the most instrumental and directly observable competences associated with the lecturer role. The danger of this, of course, is that once teaching is defined in such terms, the status and esteem of the lecturer as a reflective practitioner is in question. College managers may well be tempted to replace highly trained and experienced lecturing staff by part-time agency lecturers or technician-demonstrators who can carry out effective performance of a limited range of so-called 'lecturer competencies', who do not belong to teaching unions which are organized in colleges, who can be easily hired and fired, and whose contribution will include reducing the organization's expenditure on human resources (Elliott and Hall 1994).

Conclusion: some benefits of an alternative model of teaching

There is insufficient space here to do other than suggest an outline of an alternative model of teaching which avoids the pitfalls noted above. One way forward would be to forgo reductionist notions of teaching which disaggregate the lecturer role, thereby reducing it to a simplistic collection of discrete competencies, in favour of a strategy which recognizes the diversity and complexity of the role, and the sensitivity and reflectiveness required of those who effectively carry it out. A good place to start would be to look at the language of the tributes paid to effective teaching and lecturing by pupils and students, and to note the frequency with which such perceptions are described in whole person attributes. The centrality of biography, personality and identity to the teaching role has only recently been fully recognized (see e.g. Huberman 1993; Goodson 1994; Hargreaves 1994). The model of teaching which underpins such work is one which fully recognizes the importance of the notion of empowerment of teaching staff. Fundamental to this is a view of staff which is diametrically opposed to the hard HRM theories which inform the description and analysis of teaching as an occupation characterized simply by the performance of competences.

The view presented by Garland (1994), that competence-based approaches to teacher education 'enable a basis from which to develop learner-centred approaches and to allow greater learner autonomy' (1994, pp.17–18), is disingenuous. Competence-based education in the UK has not so far realized these advantages, but as Garland himself acknowledges, has brought about 'over-prescription in the assessment specification and unnecessary bureaucracy' (1994, p.19). The consistent focus upon learning outcomes, rather than learning processes, has led to the situation where professional development is undervalued, and uncoupled from accreditation. Regardless of how much teacher educators may encourage participation in group-based, open-ended learning experiences, it is improbable that lecturers as 'resourceful humans' (Bottery 1992), rather than 'people', in the incorporated FE sector, will either be empowered or funded by their managers to participate in such professional development.

There is no sense in which the reorganization of the NCVQ within the new Qualifications and Curriculum Authority (QCA) has brought about a re-examination of the model of competence that originated within the old Training Agency. There has also been a major review of NVQs (Beaumont 1996) which pointed out fundamental weaknesses of the system, yet there has been no serious or systematic attempt to implement changes that would improve the framework for vocational qualifications. As things stand, the development of NVQs in lecturing, tutoring, learning support and so on would bring about a radical overhaul of the initial teacher training (ITT) and in-service training (INSET) curriculum, bringing both ITT and INSET within the NCVQ (QCA) framework. The deskilling of teachers and lecturers, and the dominance of a rationalist curriculum, will have been confirmed and consolidated. The implications of such developments for policy and practice in schools, colleges and universities, suggest an agenda for educational policy studies and research, and highlight the importance, for all educational practitioners, of addressing as a matter of urgency the issues raised by this chapter.

References

Beaumont, G. (1996) *Review of 100 NVQs/SVQs*. London: NCVQ.

Belbin, R. (1981) *Management Teams: Why They Succeed or Fail*. London: Heinemann.

Bottery, M. (1992) *The Ethics of Educational Management: Personal, Social and Political Perspectives on School Organisation*. London: Cassell.

Boyatzis, R. (1982) *The Competent Manager*. New York: John Wiley.

Chomsky, N. (1971) *Chomsky: Selected Readings* (edited by J. Allen and P. Van Buren). Oxford: Oxford University Press.

Confederation of British Industry (1989) *Towards a Skills Revolution – A Youth Charter*. London: CBI.

Deville, H. (1987) 'Vocational Qualifications.' *Education Today 37*, 4, 9–13.

Drucker, P. (1989) 'Why service institutions do not perform.' In C. Riches and C. Morgan (eds) *Human Resource Management in Education*. Milton Keynes: Open University Press.

Earley, P. (1992) 'Using Competences for School Management Development.' Unpublished paper, BEMAS Fourth Research Conference, University of Nottingham.

Elliott, G. and Hall, V. (1994) 'FE Inc. – business orientation in further education and the introduction of human resource management.' *School Organisation 14*, 1, 3–10.

Ellis, P. and Gorringe, R. (1989) 'Continuing education and training through competence-based vocational qualifications.' *Educational and Training Technology International 26*, 1, 7–13.

Everard, B. (1990) 'A Critique of the MCI/TA/NCVQ Competency Approach to Education Management.' *Educational Change and Development 11*, 1, 15–16.

Freire, P. (1972) *Pedagogy of the Oppressed* (translated from the Portuguese by Myra Bergman Rumos). Harmondsworth: Penguin.

Garland, P. (1994) 'Using competence-based assessment positively on certificate in education programmes.' *Journal of Further and Higher Education 18*, 2, 16–22.

Goodson, I. (1994) 'Studying the teacher's life and work.' *Teaching and Teacher Education 10*, 1, 29–37.

Hall, V. (1987) 'NCVQ and Further Education.' *Coombe Lodge Report 20*, 5, 292.

Hall, V., Mackay, H. and Morgan, C. (1986) *Headteachers at Work*. Milton Keynes: Open University Press.

Hargreaves, A. (1994) *Changing Teachers, Changing Times: Teachers' Work and Culture in the Postmodern Age*. London: Cassell.

Huberman, M. (1993) *The Lives of Teachers*. London: Cassell.

Hyland, T. (1992) 'The vicissitudes of adult education: competence, epistemology and reflective practice.' *Education Today 42*, 2, 7–12.

Mintzberg, H. (1973) *The Nature of Managerial Work*. New York: Harper and Row.

Moss, J. (1981) 'Limiting competency based education.' *Studies in Curriculum Research 19*, 1, 14–18.

National Council for Vocational Qualifications/Employment Department (1988) *The NVQ Criteria and Related Guidance*. London: NCVQ.

National Council for Vocational Qualifications/Employment Department (1991) *Guide to National Vocational Qualifications*. London: NCVQ.

National Council for Vocational Qualifications/Employment Department (1992) *The NVQ Framework*. London: NCVQ.

Needham, R. (1988) 'Work-based learning and assessment.' *Forum 30*, 2, 46–48.

Pring, R. (1992) 'Standards and quality in education.' *British Journal of Educational Studies 40*, 1, 4–22.

Satterley, D. (1989) *Assessment in Schools* (second edition). Oxford: Basil Blackwell.

Chapter 13

Towards Professionalism
Teaching in Further Education

Norman Lucas

Introduction

This chapter is based upon the view that the quality of teaching staff and their professional development is central to meeting present and future demands made upon the FE sector in the twenty-first century. It will start with a short history, showing that initial teacher education and professional development reflects the historic neglect of the FE sector in general and of vocational education in particular. I will show that within this context the professionalism of FE teachers has been marginalized and fragmented, often reinforced by FE teachers who regard themselves more as subject/vocational experts rather than professional teachers.

The next section will examine what has happened to FE staff since Incorporation, discussing the narrow competence approach taken towards initial teacher education (ITE) and staff development exemplified by the TDLB assessor awards. I shall show that teaching in FE is demanding broader skills, requiring the teacher to work in new ways, to be innovative and to move towards a wider professionalism not fully reflected in the majority of ITE and staff development programmes.

I will then critically examine recent developments and government policies, with a focus on the development of 'standards' and the strategy of setting up a National Training Organization for FE (FENTO). Whilst welcoming recent improvements in the government's approach to teacher education in FE, I will propose a series of measures, including the establishment of a professional body for FE which can develop a coherent professional development framework where initial teacher education is treated as only a first stage of professional development. In an analysis of the professional pressures on FE teachers I put forward the view that a reconcept-ualization of professionalism is required moving beyond the concept of 'reflective practitioner' towards a concept of the 'learning professional'. The chapter concludes by suggesting a number of short- and long-term policies that could be pursued in order to raise the standards of teaching, learning and professionalism in the FE sector.

The historic legacy

Until quite recently the history of FE and its staff has been one of benign neglect, reflecting the low status given to vocational education by successive governments and society as a whole (McGinty and Fish 1993). In the 1970s some prominence was given to schemes for pre-service and in-service teacher education (James Report 1972); however these were never made mandatory.

Until Incorporation in 1993, the governance and management of the FE sector lay in the hands of LEAs; no strategic leadership was provided by government departments or their national agencies. Although ITE in FE was accepted as desirable by colleges and LEAs during the 1980s and 1990s, arrangements for ITE and professional development varied enormously throughout the sector and were rarely subject to any systematic monitoring. During this period some colleges continued with, and expanded, their existing ITE arrangements, some in partnership with universities and others embracing the National Council for Vocational Qualifications (NCVQ) competence-based approaches. This reinforced the 'mixed history' of staff development and initial training in the FE sector (Hudlestone and Unwin 1997). With no national quality assurance body for FE teacher education a multiplicity of arrangements for accreditation towards the Certificate of Education and PGCE exists, raising fears about the comparability, quality and value of many ITE courses and staff development qualifications (Young *et al.* 1995).

This situation of fragmentation, voluntarism and benign neglect of FE was reinforced by FE teachers themselves who often perceived themselves as specialist practitioners who happened to teach rather than professional teachers (Guile and Lucas 1999). There is a strong tradition in FE that subject or vocational expertise and experience alone is adequate for teaching. Research based in a technical college in the 1970s showed how the diversity of staff and the competitive nature of departments conspired against collegial identity; in fact departmentalism was the focus of allegiance (Tipton 1973). Staff interviews showed little interest or vocation towards teaching, very few were qualified and the teaching observed was mechanical and repetitive. Teaching was the transmission of applied skills and occupational culture with no tolerance on the part of the FE teacher towards questioning or non-conformity (Gleeson and Mardle 1980). The whole history of FE plays down the need to address discussions about teaching and learning. Consequently FE has failed to address the pedagogic implications of the growing diversity of the FE learner or the particular contexts that FE finds itself in. Unlike schools and universities, which have relatively clear roles, FE has a broader set of roles reflecting its unique interface acting as a bridge between school, university and employment.

FE is a sector where a spectrum of fragmented and largely isolated traditions of pedagogy confront each other. This includes the 'school tradition' of subject-based teaching, the more recent pre-vocational tradition currently expressed as GNVQs, the experiential tradition associated with the teaching of adults, flexible learning and the training and instruction tradition linked with apprenticeships and NVQs, (Young and Lucas 1999). There have been few serious attempts to see how these traditions might relate to one another. ITE and professional development programmes have not really addressed the implications of these disparate teaching traditions, particularly important in the light of the growing diversity of FE learners. On the contrary most staff development money in the post-incorporation era has been spent ensuring that staff became accredited assessors (Guile and Lucas 1996). As the FEFC inspectorate stated in a recent report, very few CPD programmes 'give priority to the development of teaching skills even when lesson inspection grades revealed pedagogic weakness' (FEFC 1999, p.7).

Following Incorporation, the FEFC assumed that decisions about the level of investment in continuing professional development (CPD) were the responsibility of individual colleges and not a concern of theirs (Cantor, Roberts and Prately 1995). FE colleges, however, gave their priority to meeting FEFC funding criteria and efficiency targets. Colleges had to survive in the short term and change staff contracts rather than think about long-term human resource development strategies.

The latest information, produced from staff individualized data and case study visits of a selected number of colleges (FEFC 1999), confirm much of the analysis in this chapter. It shows not only the proportion of full-time to part-time staff being 38 per cent and 62 per cent respectively. It also shows that approximately 68 per cent of full-time staff have a QTS-type qualification with seven per cent having a City and Guilds 730. Part-time staff showed only 25 per cent with QTS and 9.5 per cent with a City and Guilds. Given that there is no QTS requirement, the report congratulates the sector on the proportion of staff with teaching qualifications. However, it would seem that Incorporation has reversed the trend of a steady increase in the proportion of teacher trained FE teachers of the previous two decades. Let me justify that assertion. In research that we carried out at the Institute of Education, Post-16 Centre (Young *et al.* 1995), it was estimated that at the time of Incorporation 60–70 per cent of full-time staff had recognized teaching qualifications. According to our estimates at the time, the figure had only slightly increased in the few years up to Incorporation but was boosted by sixth form colleges being incorporated into the sector, bringing with them their very high levels of QTS staff. It is hard to be accurate about these estimates, but when compared to the 1999 FEFC data it would seem that there has been no advance since Incorporation in 1993 and given the proportionate increase in part-time staff it has got worse. If we take the FEFC data (which is over-generous as BAs and BScs do not constitute teaching qualifications), only 68.4 per cent of full-time staff have DfEE-recognized ITE qualifications and only 24.9 per cent of part-time staff. Putting both full and part-time staff together, the total qualified is 41.3 per cent. Taking into account the increase in part-time staff, this represents a fall in those with DfEE-recognized ITE qualifications.

Furthermore, the FEFC inspectorate estimate that the allocation made to staff development ranged from 0.15 to over 2 per cent. There is no reliable way of comparing these figures as colleges calculate costs differently, sometimes based on a calculation of the staffing cost, or on a percentage of total income. However, our estimates, which had the same difficulties of accuracy explained in the FEFC report, estimated that between 1.5 and 4 per cent of the total budget was spent on staff development. This again indicates a significant decline in the amount spent on staff development since Incorporation in 1993.

The FEFC report discussed above concludes with a list of strengths and weaknesses. Some of the main weakness are: 'the shortage of adequate national data on the workforce and its training needs; the relatively low level of finance allocated to staff development, in a sector which should be convinced of the benefits of training; the low priority given to training in pedagogic skills; a general decline in opportunities for networking with colleagues in other colleges; inadequate arrangements for training part-time staff, who make up an increasing proportion of teachers; and insufficient opportunities to prepare thoroughly for curriculum change' (FEFC 1999, p.22).

The FEFC report praised some staff development schemes and systems with 92 per cent of those questioned stating that they used FEFC inspection reports to identify good practice. Whilst not questioning the FEFC findings, the nagging question is the extent to which staff development initiatives based upon FEFC inspection reports go down to, and influence, FE teachers and support staff.

Staffing issues since Incorporation

When colleges were Incorporated in 1993, the level of targeted funding for staff development was about one per cent of income. The FEFC makes no recommendation regarding expenditure on staff development and there is no targeted funding. The average is difficult to ascertain as data is unreliable. According to the FEFC (1999) it varies from 0.15 per cent to over two per cent. According to a NATFHE analysis of FEFC inspection reports the level of funding dedicated to staff development is declining (Lucas and Betts 1997) and most is spent on immediate needs and management training arising from the demands for data from the FEFC.

Since Incorporation FE has had to achieve considerable efficiency gains and although it is difficult to get an exact picture there is little doubt that the number of teaching hours for FE staff has increased. Even more significant has been the extra pressures outside of 'formal' teaching hours, regarding curriculum development, tutoring, and responding to the massive increase in information required by the FEFC funding regime such as Individual Student Records. Furthermore, recent studies (Leney, Lucas and Taubman 1998) have shown that A-level students on average receive only 15 teaching hours per week and GNVQs vary from 5 to 22 hours. According to the FEFC Chief Inspector (FEFC 1996) the 20 per cent efficiency gains achieved since Incorporation have been brought about by reducing taught hours rather than increasing class size, which remains at an average of 11. Cuts in course hours are quite dramatic and some of today's full-time FE students would have been considered part-time in the past.

Alongside cuts in course hours and the lack of investment in staff development by a 'sector that should be convinced of the benefits of training' (FEFC 1999, p.22) there has been a big increase in the amount of part-time teaching staff. A recent estimate of the effects of Incorporation showed that in the last five years 20,000 permanent jobs had been lost with an estimated increase of 33 per cent in student numbers between 1993 and 2000. Furthermore, levels of funding had declined in real terms by 29 per cent and there had been a shift between 1995/96 and 1998 from 52,000 to 48,000 full-time staff and an increase from 82,000 to 100,000 part-time posts (Williams 1998). Colleges are spending around 30 per cent of their staffing budgets on part-time staff. This statistic hides a huge variation in local practice. The range is from one (large) college which devotes just 5 per cent of its budget to part-timers, to another (small) college which is spending 64 per cent. It is true to say that the majority of colleges fall in the 20 per cent to 40 per cent category, but a significant minority lie on either side of the middle range. This increase in part-time posts signals the growing use of temporary staff in general, which, in turn, not only raises the levels of insecurity but also has implications for the quality of teaching and learning. The FEFC report *Quality and Standards in Further Education in England* (1996) confirms this trend, reporting that funding and financial considerations, not educational ones, are dominating the debate in FE, and fears of redundancy are sapping staff morale with the shift from full-time to agency part-time staff raising real concerns about quality which 'are not always in the best interest of students'. For many colleges human resource management has replaced human resource development (Guile and Lucas 1999) by attempting to achieve flexibility by increasing the division of labour rather than seeking to develop and empower the individual FE teacher to work in new and more flexible ways. FE has always had a 'core' and 'periphery', although since Incorporation the 'contractual fringe' or 'flexible labour force' has grown, often with staff provided by employment agencies such as Education Lecturing Services (ELS) whose promotional material (ELS 1996) spells out the virtues of a human resource strategy for colleges which is made up of a tight core of full-time staff and a large non-core, contract or part-time staff.

Many colleges simply do not provide staff development to part-time staff, who rarely engage in curriculum development, student support, guidance activities, extra curriculum provision, formal staff appraisal and in-service training (Williams 1998). Because quite a high proportion of full-time staff have initial teacher qualifications, covering new entrants is relatively simple; the more difficult challenge for FE is raising standards amongst transitory part-time staff and putting in place a first teaching qualification that will be more than a verification process and will be accredited towards further professional development. The implications of the growing number of part-time teachers in FE and recent strategies to raise standards in FE will be explored further in the next section.

Developments under New Labour

The new Labour government has reiterated its wish to ensure that all new FE staff are teacher qualified (DfEE 1998) and has accepted the need for a more strategic approach to ITE and CPD. It affirmed the importance of initial teacher education and the professional development of FE staff and managers (Blackstone 1998), deciding to waive the payment of fees for those undergoing initial teacher education for the FE sector alongside primary and secondary ITE.

Labour has stayed within the paradigm created by the previous Conservative administration of creating employer lead bodies. These are National Training Organizations (NTOs) established to encourage employers to express a greater interest in and commitment to the training and development of their staff, thus de-emphasizing the government's own role in promoting training and development within UK industry (Cantor *et al.* 1995). NTOs are, principally, employer-led bodies which represent employers' interests in relation to the national skills agenda (DfEE 1998).

The Secretary of State for Education and Employment approved the establishment of FENTO in late 1998. The details of its composition, budget and role is not yet known although there is agreement that it must be representative of the whole UK and be employer led. The standards adopted by FENTO were officially launched in January 1999. These have been broadly welcomed by those concerned about the sector not only because of the move away from the narrow competence-based approaches such as those being used in Scotland (SOEID 1997), but also because it is the first historic attempt to arrive at national standards for FE teachers (Nash 1999).

Whilst any development towards more coherence is welcome, what is of concern is that government is treating FE differently from the other sectors. Primary and secondary teachers are to be represented by a General Teaching Council (GTC); teachers in higher education will in due course be represented by an Institute of Teaching and Learning. Both of these stress the professional nature of teaching. However, FE has only an employer-led body, FENTO. This blurs the important distinction between professional concerns and employer concerns (Hoyle and John 1995) which is recognized in most other professions.

A further concern is that at present there is a proposal to create a separate NTO for Adult and Community Education alongside FENTO, while other NTOs such as Local Government, Science, Technology and Mathematics, an all-sector employment NTO, Higher Education and Training and others have already been established. This proliferation of NTOs could result in FE teachers working to different standards set by different NTOs. Whilst FENTO itself seems committed to working in an inclusive manner the government strategy of setting up many NTOs is likely to perpetuate the fragmentation of post-16 education and training and not reinforce the need for a more strategic approach to these issues.

Another concern is that FENTO is working to standards different to those of the FEFC inspectorate and there seems as yet no attempt to match them across the two organizations. Whether the FEFC adapt the FENTO standards when inspecting teaching and learning and staff development in colleges remains to be seen. Furthermore, not only are there many NTOs but they have to be UK-wide, spanning, in the case of FE, quite different traditions and standards. How NTOs fit into plans for devolution and regional planning is difficult to see; how FENTO will deal with national dimensions remains to be seen.

Despite reservations, the establishment of FENTO could represent a first important stage in establishing a professional development framework for FE teachers. At the recent launch of the standards, establishing a professional body for FE teachers was seen as one aim of FENTO (Melia 1999). I would not claim that it is easy to bring about coherence into the diverse and fragmented sector that is called FE – but the haphazard way in which NTOs are being established indicates that the government is not thinking in the strategic manner which is so important if it is to implement effective lifelong learning (Green and Lucas 1999).

De-professionalization and re-professionalization

According to my analysis the professionalism of FE teachers has never been homogeneous or particularly well formed in the FE sector, lacking the professional culture that can be found in the school sector. There has been no 'golden age' in the past of FE professionalism that is now eroded. Rather, there have been fragmented practices that have changed (or not) in the face of pressures that have swept over FE over in the past decade or so. Just as there are tendencies towards de-professionalization and fragmentation so there is a reconstruction of professionalism (Gleeson and Shain 1999). This professional reconstruction is complex and multidimensional. When 'professional' is used in FE it refers more to competence in a technical, compliant sense, with discussions about pedagogy and wider professionalism marginalized. Below I will take my analyses further by examining FE teacher qualifications and the pressures for change. This will allow me to develop my argument for a reconceptualization of the professional role of the FE teacher.

Estimates vary concerning the type of teaching qualifications that are currently held by FE lecturers. From the fragmented information in the inspection reports, it would appear that 85 per cent of lecturers have at least one teaching qualification but it is not possible to differentiate between initial teacher training (QTS-type) qualifications and others such as qualifications ranging from the City and Guilds 7306/7 variety to assessor awards such as TDLB units, which are technically not teaching qualifications and are by themselves quite inadequate for the complex demands of a teacher's role in further and adult education (Elliott 1996; Hyland 1992).

Furthermore, the assessor qualification has led to a more fragmented workforce, typically reflecting the division between the academic and vocational curriculum. Teachers in FE need to be multi-skilled, making holistic judgements according to the needs of learners, particularly with the growth of independent learning and guidance practices in the FE sector. Alongside the growing numbers of part-time staff already mentioned above, there is a blurring between teaching and non-teaching staff with the introduction of instructor or assessor grades into FE. This development has been matched by a shift in salary bands ranging not from £12–24,000 as was the case but divided into new categories such as £12–15,000, £15–18,000, £13–21,000 and £21–24,000 (Williams 1998). Each category has its own job description, and the implications of this are quite complex. It could be argued that this is an appropriate response to a more flexible curriculum and changing teaching and learning patterns in FE which do not require full initial teacher training or a full repertoire of pedagogic skills. However, individuals need learning support, counselling and guidance, and setting of individual learning goals, all of which an instructor or untrained person is unlikely to be equipped to do. The problem, as I see it, is not the employment of instructors or technicians, but the replacement of qualified teaching staff by instructors with D32/33 assessor awards who are often part-time as well. This concern is reflected by some in government who are worried about its effect on quality, arguing for a proper career structure for FE teachers in the future (Nash 1999).

Within the general context of technological developments and the changing nature of work, new demands are emerging on FE teachers, such as promoting the acquisition of skills and knowledge by students, trainees and employees with a very wide diversity of learning needs and attitudes (Hudlestone and Unwin 1997). This requires lecturers to broaden their forms of expertise to include resource-based learning, modular curriculum design, offering advice and guidance to individual students, maximizing the potential of Information and Learning Technology (ILT) as a resource for learning. This is important because of the role of IT and communication technology in the workplace and the potential of ILT for transforming the location and process of education and training (Hayton and Guile 1999). Up to now, despite some progress from the government and FEDA on this issue, the main emphasis towards ILT has been as though it is a 'key skill' or technical competence which teachers need to acquire rather then focusing on the pedagogic implications of ILT. In addition teachers need to keep up-to-date in their own academic/vocational specialisms as well as understanding how their specialism relates to the curriculum as a whole. Taken in combination, therefore, these pressures point to a very different concept of the professional role of teaching staff within FE and a proper framework for professional development, quite opposite to those of fragmentation and technical competence.

Furthermore, a related demand upon FE teachers is the requirement to support their students/trainees in developing 'key skills'; these are generic skills which are generally assumed to underpin a student's ability to transfer their knowledge from one context to another (CBI 1991), and to operate effectively within different educational or workplace contexts. At present government policy for post-compulsory education and training mainly emphasizes the key skills, i.e. literacy, numeracy and IT, which are mandatory for GNVQ students and those on Modern Apprenticeships. Recent research (Bailey 1991; Guile and Fonda 1998) has argued that in future the emphasis will need to be more upon broad work roles rather than occupationally specific jobs. There is a clear implication that the challenge for FE will be to produce students with more than functional literacy, numeracy or specific technical skills.

There will be new demands impacting upon the FE sector to develop more broad-based forms of 'employability' skills and knowledge. Examples include those associated with 'boundary crossing' and teamwork, which enable students and trainees to take responsibility for their own learning, all very important factors for lifelong learning (DfEE 1998). Therefore, teachers have had to embrace developments around more flexible approaches to learning, modularization, setting learning targets and facilitating more independent learning. This has led to what has been described as a 'pedagogy of guidance' (Lucas 1997).

The growing demand in the UK for work-based and community-based learning programmes, particularly in realizing the aims of the New Deal and Welfare to Work programmes, means that new sites for learning are emerging as well as new client groups. Consequently, yet again, FE teachers are taking on more diverse roles acting as project managers, course tutors and course designers for the delivery of both on and off-site courses, work which involves much higher levels of knowledge and skill than has previously been recognized (Ollin 1996). In response to the growing demand and greater diversity of learners, FE teachers are having to develop what Engestrom has referred to as 'poly-contextual skills' (Engestrom, Engestrom and Karkkainen 1995), moving across boundaries that have traditionally divided different kinds of specialists, programme areas and sectors. I wish to develop some of the conceptual implications of this below.

Beyond the reflective practitioner

Many of the changes described above have been occurring in FE for some time with a gradual change in emphasis from FE teachers adopting a curriculum-led to a more learner-led perspective (Shackleton 1988). Building upon previous work (Guile and Lucas 1999), I wish to outline a new concept of professionalism for FE teachers which would reflect the developments described above. Little research has been undertaken on teaching in FE and there has been a very limited discussion of the question of professionalism (Elliott 1998) for FE teachers. Teacher educators have in the absence of an FE model tended to rely upon either technical competences as professional or conceptions of professionalism derived from primary or secondary education. Deriving a conception of professionalism from such sources, however, is unlikely to provide an adequate basis for understanding the diversity and complexity of the current situation. For example, the FE teachers' union NATFHE has traditionally addressed contractual duties (i.e. class contact hours), reflecting an out-moded model of practice. Recent research suggests that FE teachers themselves no longer see class contact as adequately describing their professional practice and some colleges are working on new contracts based upon the concept of 'case loading' (Lucas and Betts 1997).

Because no strategic forum or body exists for FE, ITE programmes for the sector have mainly followed research in schools which has emphasized Schon's (1978) concept of the 'reflective practitioner' to provide the basis of a model of FE professionalism (Curzon 1995). The reflective practitioner model does emphasize the importance of practice-based tacit knowledge, defined as knowing-in-action. This implies that professionals will develop their knowing-in-action through the complementary processes of 'reflection-in-action' and 'reflection-on-action'. 'Action', however, primarily refers to the action of a teacher in the classroom with their students, rather than the extensive range of their other professional activities and responsibilities. This rather narrow interpretation of 'action', i.e. delivering subject knowledge in classrooms (the National Curriculum), can marginalize FE teachers' new broader cross-college roles, thereby implying that classroom teaching is the end of their professional responsibility.

It is not at all clear whether Schon's theory of the reflective practitioner is urging professionals to discard completely the relevance of research-based knowledge or simply challenging the inflated views of its significance (Eraut 1995). It has been suggested that the concept of the 'reflective practitioner' actually serves to separate theory from practice (Usher, Bryant and Johnston 1998) because the self-referential nature of 'theories in use' and 'knowledge-in-action' is highly situated. Furthermore the concept is dependent upon interpretations made in particular contexts and in relation to specific cultural conventions and contexts; it does not therefore readily provide concepts or criteria that allow professionals to assess and relate different 'theories-in-use' to one another or to research-based knowledge.

In the context of more flexible and independent learning strategies raised by the policy of lifelong learning, this is a rather restricted view of the role of the FE professional and has led some teacher educators to justify on ethical or educational grounds the continuing relevance of traditional occupational cultures and fragmented professional identities in FE (Elliott 1996). Although I am not disputing that the classroom dimension is absolutely critical, I am arguing that it has to be balanced by what has been referred to as a broader, extended or 'connective' perspective on professional practice (Guile and Lucas 1996).

The concept of the reflective practitioner was certainly an advance on previous conceptions of professional work and celebrated the professional artistry of practitioners (Eraut 1995). It was also an advance on the apprenticeship model of training historically prevalent in FE. Many FE teacher educators use the concept of the reflective practitioner to ground ideas about professional practice in FE teachers' own understanding and experience of their working practices (Hudlestone and Unwin 1997) and it has assisted FE teachers to develop a critical approach to their professional practice (Elliott 1998). Without going into a long exposition and critique of the 'reflective practitioner' I would like to highlight some concerns about the limitations of using it as a model of professionalism applied to FE teachers.

Based upon research undertaken by myself and colleagues at the Post-16 Education Centre, an alternative conceptualization of the FE teachers' professional role has been developing (Young *et al.* 1995; Young and Guile 1997; Guile and Lucas 1999). The research identified the changes in the FE teacher's knowledge base, summarized as a series of shifts away from traditional notions of professionalism, arguing that the 'insular' knowledge base that has characterized the work of professions in the past was changing towards a more 'connective' one. The changes were identified as shifts from subject to curriculum knowledge, intra-professional to inter-professional knowledge, a shift towards organizational knowledge yet at the same time taking a more learner-centred approach to teaching and learning. These developments reflect broader trends that were increasingly occurring in many professions as the context and nature of professional work changed (Young and Lucas 1999).

These shifts suggest that existing ideas about the FE teacher's professional knowledge base and the conception of professional practice which underpins it will need to be rethought. This has led to the concept of the 'learning professional' being put forward as a means of rethinking the concept of reflective practitioner and for describing the FE teacher in the twenty-first century (Guile and Lucas 1999).

The concept of the 'learning professional' highlights the growing trend in FE for teachers to take more managerial responsibilities and highlights the need for FE teachers to think about the relationship between their particular form of expertise and the process of learning. It implies relating their own discipline-based or vocational specialism to other specialisms as well as supporting the development of students' more generic (or 'key') skills, including offering guidance and counselling. This indicates a professional domain that moves beyond the classroom to more generic capabilities needed in responding to the demands of their ever-evolving work contexts and the new lifelong learning agenda.

The model of the FE teacher as a 'learning professional', described above, stresses the need for an active engagement with those economic, educational and technological changes which have brought about new professional responsibilities and have profoundly altered the context of professional activity. The concept suggests that colleges and FE teachers need to develop a more holistic perspective, embracing lifelong learning (DfEE 1998), and widening participation (Kennedy 1997). This requires a significant rethink of current assumptions about teaching and learning, and FE teachers will need to find ways of relating the knowledge gained outside of colleges to more formal qualifications enabling learners to progress. Furthermore, it requires FE teachers to innovate and try to change, from below, the rigid delivery of present qualifications (Young 1999). Consequently, further thought will have to be given to how ITE and CPD programmes can prepare FE teachers to address these new professional challenges as the FE curriculum moves from course-based learning to credit-based learning, embracing varied sites of learning within a framework of lifelong learning.

Conclusion: toward the learning professional

In the light of the argument outlined above I would suggest that there is a need for the government to formulate a clear strategy to professionalize the FE sector. This requires a renewal of professionalism in the FE sector as the quality of the teaching staff in FE is central to the quality of the service, particularly in the light of the government's ambitious agenda of widening participation, lifelong learning and welfare-to-work policies. There are a number of short-term and long-term dimensions that could be taken. I argue that what is not needed is more qualifications and more bodies existing alongside existing ones, and that the tendency of FE to proliferate and duplicate qualifications and structures needs to be resisted.

In the short term the government could implement its policy so that all new FE teachers be teacher educated (DfEE 1998). This is relatively straightforward under the present system of in-service Certificates of Education and Post-Graduate Certificates of Education (FE) provision. There would be some cost involved but it would only apply to new FE teachers. If cost were a factor it is not unreasonable in the present context that full-time staff should pay some contribution or that a generous loan system be made available. A basic teaching qualification should also be compulsory for certain categories of part-time staff. Rather than create a new qualification, a revised and thoroughly moderated City and Guilds 730 Further Education Teacher's Certificate Stage One could be used. This has the advantage of using an established basic teaching qualification. Certain categories of part-time staff could be targeted, such as those above certain teaching hours or those teaching 16–19-year-olds. Targets could be set for colleges, inspected by the FEFC as part of its business of raising standards. If all colleges were obliged to raise standards amongst part-time and full-time staff the fear of losing qualified staff to others would be overcome. The City and Guilds 730 series already attracts FEFC funding, thus the reluctance of FE colleges to spend money on part-time staff could also be overcome, although the FEFC would have to accept the extra cost. The FEFC could also insist on, and fund, a mentor scheme for new staff that could be set up in every college. Universities and other providers could agree to accredit the basic teaching qualification towards existing Cert. Eds and PGCEs. A framework to include part-time staff has broad support and could be achieved quite easily if FENTO and other bodies acted in concert.

In the medium term, the government should ensure that the FEFC give more emphasis in its inspections to ITE and CPD. This would be particularly timely since FEFC reports (e.g. 1996) have already expressed concern about the growing number of part-time staff and its effects on quality. Moreover, the FEFC could be asked to investigate how guidance could be given to colleges and other organizations on the long-term quality implications of the drift towards FE being staffed by a small core of full-time with a large periphery of part-time staff as outlined above. Furthermore, new priorities need to be agreed between the DfEE and the FEFC to ensure that the FEFC identify targeted funding for staff development instead of giving just 'one line' budgets.

If the traditionally fragmented and voluntary nature of professionalism is to be overcome in the FE sector in the longer term, a strategic move to establish a General Teaching Council (GTC) for FE is required. The GTC could provide a forum to help to realize the aim of developing FE teachers as 'learning professionals' by bringing about a more coordinated approach to ITE and CPD, creating a professional development framework which could include qualifications for managers and principals. This could include the difficult question concerning the core skills of FE teachers, such as Maths, English and Information Technology. This would not only represent a profound shift in the historic neglect of FE staff but would also allow for the first time a strategic approach to be taken towards human resource development, placing ITE within a coherent programme of continuous development, including part-time staff.

Important areas for discussion by the GTC might be the implications of the new knowledge base discussed above and a coordinated approach to targeting certain categories of staff, both full-time and part-time. The GTC could, for example, coordinate a review of the content of ITE programmes to identify what aspects of the FE teachers' new knowledge base should be learnt during professional practice in the college and how it relates to learning in higher education. Another area for discussion might be to take a dispassionate look at the long-term human resource development of the FE sector, bringing about a more unified perspective on all strands of post-16 education and training, including those provided by employers, based upon progression routes and regional partnerships between colleges, universities and work-based training. The development of FE teachers as 'learning professionals' could ensure that all staff feel valued and capable of assisting students to respond to the challenges of the next century.

References

Bailey, T. (1991) 'Jobs of the future and the education they will require.' *Educational Researcher 20*, 2, 11–20.

Blackstone, T. (1998) 'Go boldly into new age of learning.' *FE Focus. Times Educational Supplement.* 27 March.

Cantor, L., Roberts, I. and Prately, B. (1995) *A Guide to Further Education in England and Wales.* London: Cassell.

CBI (1991) *Towards a Skills Revolution.* London: CBI.

Curzon, R. (1994) *Teaching in Further Education* (Fourth Edition). London: Cassell.

DfEE (1998) *National Training Organisations. 1999/2000 Prospectus*. Sudbury: DfEE.

DfEE (1998) *The Learning Age: A Renaissance for a New Britain*. London: The Stationery Office.

Elliott, G. (1996) 'The assessment and accreditation of lecturers in post compulsory education: a critique of the use of competence based approaches.' *British Journal of In-service Teacher Education 22*, 1, 19–30.

Elliott, G. (1998) 'Lecturing in post-compulsory education: profession, occupation or reflective practice?' *Teachers and Teaching: Theory and Practice 4*, 1, 161–174.

ELS (1996) *Education Lecturing Resource Pack*. Leeds: Education Lecturing Service.

Engestrom, Y., Engestrom, R. and Karkkainen, M. (1995) 'Polycontextuality and boundary crossing in expert cognition.' *Learning and Instruction 5*, 1, 319–336.

Eraut, M. (1995) 'Schön Shock: A Case for Reframing Reflection-in-Action Teachers and Teaching.' *Theory and Practice 1*, 1, 9–22.

FEFC (1996) *Quality and Standards in Further Education in England*. Chief Inspectors' Annual Report 1995/96. Coventry: The Further Education Funding Council.

FEFC (1999) *Professional Development in Further Education*. National Report FEFC Inspectorate. Coventry: The Further Education Funding Council.

Gleeson, D. and Mardle, G. (1980) *Further Education or Training?* London: Routledge and Kegan Paul.

Gleeson, D. and Shain, F. (1999) 'Managing ambiguity: between markets and managerialism – a case study of middle managers in further education.' *The Sociological Review* (forthcoming).

Green, A. and Lucas, N. (eds) (1999) *Further Education and Lifelong Learning: Realigning the Sector for the Twenty-first Century*. London: Bedford Way Publications.

Guile, D. and Fonda, N. (1998) *Performance Management Through Capability*. London: Institute of Personnel and Development.

Guile, D. and Lucas, N. (1996) 'Preparing for the future. The training and professional development of staff in the FE sector.' *Journal of Teacher Development 5*, 3, 47–55.

Guile, D. and Lucas, N. (1999) 'Rethinking initial teacher education and professional development in FE: towards the learning professional.' In A.

Green and N. Lucas (eds) *Further Education and Lifelong Learning: Realigning the Sector for the Twenty-first Century*. London: Bedford Way Publications.

Hayton, A. and Guile, G. (1999) 'Information and learning technology: implications for teaching and learning in FE.' In A. Green and N. Lucas (eds) *Further Education and Lifelong Learning: Realigning the Sector for the Twenty-first Century*. London: Bedford Way Publications.

Hoyle, E. and John, P. (1995) *Professional Knowledge and Professional Practice*. London: Cassell.

Hudlestone, P. and Unwin, L. (1997) *Teaching and Learning in Further Education: Diversity and Change*. London: Routledge.

Hyland, T. (1992) 'Expertise and competence in further and adult education.' *British Journal of In-Service Education 18*, 1, 23–28.

James Report (1972) *Teacher Education and Training*. London: HMSO.

Kennedy, H. (1997) *Learning Works: Widening Participation in Further Education*. Coventry: FEFC.

Leney, T., Lucas, N. and Taubman, D. (1998) *Learning Funding: The Impact of FEFC Funding, Evidence from Twelve FE Colleges*. London: NATFHE.

Lucas, N. (1997) 'The "applied route" at age 14 and beyond: implications for initial teacher education.' In A. Hudson and D. Lambert (eds) *Exploring Futures in Initial Teacher Education*. London: Bedford Way Publications.

Lucas, N. and Betts, D. (1997) 'The Incorporated college: human resource development and human resource management: contradictions and options.' *Research in Post-Compulsory Education 1*, 3, 329–343.

McGinty, J. and Fish, J. (1993) *Further Education in the Market Place: Equity, Opportunity and Individual Learning*. London: Routledge.

Melia, T. (1999) Speech given at FENTO Standards Launch, London, 25 January.

Nash, I (1999) 'Super-lecturer age dawns.' *Times Education Supplement. FE Focus*, 8 January, 31.

Ollin, R. (1996) 'Learning from industry: human resource development and the quality of lecturing staff in further education.' *Quality Assurance in Education 4*, 4, 29–36.

Schon, D. (1978) *The Reflective Practitioner: How Professionals Think in Action*. London: Avebury.

Shackleton, J. (1988) *The Professional Role of the Lecturer: Planning and Curriculum*. London: Further Education Unit.

SOEID, (1997) *Draft National Guidelines on Provision Leading to the Teaching Qualification (FE) and Related Professional Development*. Edinburgh: The Scottish Office and Industry Department.

Tipton, B. (1973) *Conflict and Change in a Technical College*. Brunel Further Education Monographs. London: Hutchinson Education.

Usher, R., Bryant, I. and Johnston, R. (1997) *Adult Education and the Post Modern Challenge*. London: Routledge.

Williams, E. (1998) 'Leaner and Fitter?' *FE Now*, Issue 50. December, 8–9.

Young, M. (1999) 'Reconstructing qualifications for further education: towards a system for the twenty-first century.' In A. Green and N. Lucas (eds) *Further Education and Lifelong Learning: Realigning the Sector for the Twenty-first Century*. London: Bedford Way Publications.

Young, M. and Guile, D. (1997) 'New possibilities for the professionalisation of UK VET professionals.' *Journal of European Industrial Training 21*, 6/7, 203–213.

Young, M. and Lucas, N. (1999) 'Pedagogy and learning in further education: new contexts, new theories and new possibilities.' In P. Mortimore (ed) *Pedagogy and its Impact on Learning*. London: Sage.

Young, M., Lucas, N., Sharp, G. and Cunningham, B. (1995) *Teacher Education for the Further Education Sector: Training the Lecturer of the Future*. Report produced for Association of Colleges by Post-16 Centre, University of London Institute of Education.

PART V

International Comparisons

Chapter 14

Finding New Ways to Work
Learning and Risk in Changing Labour Markets

Karen Evans, Martina Behrens and Jens Kaluza

Anglo-German comparisons of education and transitions to employment have taken on new significance in the 1990s. The European Union has focused its socio-economic policy debates on questions of the degrees of regulation which are necessary and desirable both for economic growth and for the protection of workers' and citizens' rights. As Roberts (1998) has argued, Britain and Germany (despite being untypical within the wider Union) have come to represent the main socio-economic alternatives 'on the agenda' for the current and prospective member states.

The contrasts between the regulated German and unregulated British approaches to young adult transitions have been the subject of the authors' previous Anglo-German Foundation Studies, published as *Youth and Work: Transitions to Employment* (1991) and *Becoming Adults in England and Germany* (1994). These contrasts have been maintained, and in some respects have become more sharply drawn through much of the 1990s. The 'reunification' of Germany from 1990 has involved economic and political transformations whose effects will shape the future development of Germany and its place in the European Union for years to come. This chapter is based on a recent study carried out in Eastern Germany. The study is closely linked with the earlier researches, which enables comparisons to be made with Western Germany and England. It has developed the approaches pioneered in the earlier work, in examining the relationships between policy-as-espoused, policy-as-enacted and policy-as-experienced in the labour markets of the 'new Länder'. The ways in which social and political changes have impacted on the lives of individuals are central to the rationale. The Eastern and Western parts of Germany shared common culture but operated totally different socio-economic systems during communism. West Germany and Britain had different versions of the same socio-economic system, but different cultural histories. Britain and Eastern Germany have experienced, from different starting points, strong effects of market forces and deregulation of previous systems. This chapter reviews insights gained from young adults' experiences of both smooth and broken transitions in the new Länder, together with continuities and discontinuities as seen through the eyes of key players, including vocational trainers, and as documented in structural data and reports.

Apprenticeship is highly developed in Germany. It covers all occupational sectors and is entered by the large majority of young people leaving school before the age of 18/19 years. Employer-sponsored apprenticeship is entered at the age of 16/17 years via the Realschule (intermediate school) or Hauptschule (general high school). Training is undertaken for three years involving 3 or 4 days per week in firm-based training and the remaining 1 or 2 days in the Berufsschule. Acquisition of skills is certified by the diploma, which qualifies young workers for entry to skilled worker grades through mutual recognition by the social partners. The involvement of the social partners in defining the contents of training and the weight given to firm-based training ensures a good match between certification and qualification to practise, in that the certificate is recognized as qualifying its holder to practise in the skilled occupation in question. More males than females enter employer-sponsored apprenticeships, with the training for female-typical occupations concentrated more in vocational schools.

The 'dual system' of apprenticeship in the West of Germany has historically been the dominant mode of vocational education and training, in relation to which all other forms of provision have been planned. The former East has provided the prime test-bed for extension of the German dual system. As Roberts (1999) has argued, the German dual system, although admired internationally, has never been successfully exported. Brown and Evans (1994) also argued that the dual system has worked well in Germany, not because of its inherent strengths but despite its weaknesses, because of a high degree of consensual support from both sides of industry and its embeddedness in Germanic culture and traditions. Roberts (1999) has proposed that if the dual system can be made to work *anywhere* other than West Germany, it should be able to work in the East of

Germany, with its common cultural foundations. Conversely, if it cannot be made to work in the East, it is unlikely to be successful in any other national context experiencing the economic transformations of the time. Furthermore, the strains in the system already showing in the West of Germany could mark the start of its decline in its place of origin. Great Britain, by contrast, exemplifies the alternative socio-economic model being proposed for European development, based on deregulation and opening of markets to globalizing trends. The associated education and training systems are market-led and weakly institutionalized, 'flexible' and 'responsive' to meet the demands of increasingly unregulated labour markets. This model was not only practised but also widely advocated, by the previous government, as the model for other European countries to follow. It is this model, not the dual system nor the extended comprehensive schooling model of Scandinavia, which has been most readily implemented by other post-communist societies, such as Poland. For the countries of the former Eastern-Bloc countries, Roberts argues that the unregulated approaches have had the apparent advantages of being a practical option because of cost and also because of the free market ideologies which surrounded the market 'reforms' at their outset.

What does the situation in training and employment in the new Länder show about the strengths and limitations of the dual system and the potential for emergence of new models? What is the wider significance of these findings for Europe?

Labour market structures and the processes of transition

Considering the structural changes in the economy and the implications for the labour market, this analysis of transitions will focus on the school-to-work transition as well as on the transition process into and out of employment. The previous Anglo-German studies concentrated on the school-to-training transitions, and showed how the training systems in Britain and West Germany have been contributing to labour market segmentation since those who receive training obtained qualifications for certain types of occupations. The entry level into the (western) training market therefore determines to a great extent which segment of the labour market a person will enter. According to Doeringer and Piore (1971) two segments can be distinguished: a primary and a secondary segment.

Primary segment jobs are characterized by high productivity, good working conditions, stable employment patterns, high wages and well-established systems of initial and continuing training. Implementation of new technologies through training is widespread practice in this segment. Firms are usually large, capital-intensive, highly unionized. Good working relationships are ensured by means of above-average wages, seniority rules and structured promotion ladders.

In contrast, in the secondary segment there is no stable employment, lower wages and few opportunities for initial and continuing training within or outside the company. The tasks to be performed are usually learned through a short training period and even when different tasks are performed the training is similarly minimal. Workers in this segment are recruited easily on the labour market so that the abundance of workers able to perform these repetitive tasks together with a low level of unionization in this segment keep wages low.

The types of qualification obtained led to a lack of mobility between labour market segments. A 'secondary worker' can usually only move into the primary segment through further education and/or courses providing more general training, so that these acquired characteristics can overcome characteristics ascribed by employers to secondary workers concerning skill levels and work attitudes. Undoubtedly, great flexibility and many individual decisions are required within both segments to ensure 'survival' in the labour market and the making of a career.

The school and vocational training system of the German Democratic Republic (GDR) served a hardly changing labour market. Because of the way industry was organized and the absence of unemployment, segmentation in this labour market context had a totally different meaning: rather than primary and secondary segments, a static part and a more mobile part made up the labour force. In 1985 only 15 per cent of the working population was unskilled, 64 per cent Meister or skilled worker, and 21 per cent graduates. Once young people had entered a profession through an apprenticeship they expected, in the majority of cases, to remain in it – very often with the same employer, or in the same area – for the rest of their working lives. The vast majority of people worked in this segment of the labour market. The entry level into the labour market was very likely to define the social position of the individual in society in a way which excluded risks but at the same time left the person without much opportunity to change his or her position through individual activities.

The number of people working in a more mobile labour market with access to higher earnings and privileges (e.g. travel, consumption) was much smaller. In many cases the allocation of privileges depended on Party membership and connections. The education and VET systems thus predominantly served the needs of the static (and secure) mass labour market while access to the professional and 'élite' careers came through the higher end of the education system and political structures which permeated all parts of the system.

The educational system of the GDR

Two aspects of education in the GDR had considerable importance for system maintenance and employment entry. All pupils attended the polytechnical high school where they acquired general knowledge and were introduced to practical skills important for a future working life (Figure 14.1). Another stronghold in the curriculum was political education. After 10 years school leavers had to decide on and apply for the route into work, on the basis of a 'diagnosis' of their capabilities. In general it was not a question of gaining access to the labour market, as every school leaver was guaranteed a training place. It was a case of where one would be accepted. The existing school–company ties (networks) ensured the school leavers' knowledge about local and regional in-company training opportunities. Selection strategies of companies and the allocation of school leavers did not depend on the standard of general school work alone but also on performance in political education and various other attitudinal and behavioural criteria.

Education to work – new transitions

Young people were socialized in the GDR for entry to the static and secure labour force and into the morality of collective endeavour. They were not socialized in ways that anticipated having to cope with Western forms of competition in school and labour markets. Once the entry level into the labour market was settled the transition to work and family life used to be much more continuous than in the West (Evans and Heinz 1995). When in 1989 the structural changes took place, however, individuals had to face tough competition from other workers and employees for a reducing number of jobs in a rapidly changing labour market. This does not affect individual transitions negatively in all respects. The research has found that those who managed a smooth transition into the new labour market – irrespective of whether this was

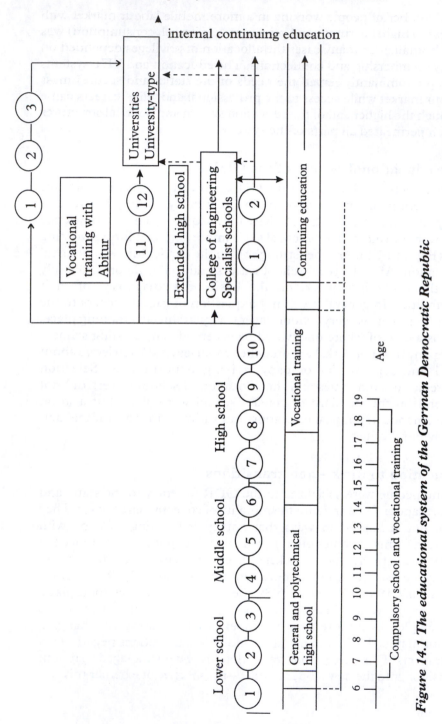

Figure 14.1 The educational system of the German Democratic Republic

due to individual activities or by pure chance – had to identify the 'new rules of the game' in a less transparent working environment. Those new rules were not necessarily the conveyed behaviour patterns and values from the West. The discovery of new routes into a new labour market has been essential for those young people whose transition has been broken. The vocational trainers who worked with young people under the GDR system, and who continued as trainers after the political changes, are uniquely placed to make comparisons according to their own experience.

Eighteen such trainers were interviewed about their experiences. The interviews were carried out by the East German interviewer and have been interpreted against a backcloth of survey data from more than 100 companies in the new Länder. This survey data has been provided by kind permission of the Bundesinstitut für Berufsbildung (BIBB) (Federal Institute of Vocational Training).

The interviews were analysed with the help of the software package TAKT.WIN, with reference to the three central questions:

- How do trainers consider vocational training has changed with regard to structure, curriculum and status after the political change?

- How do trainers perceive that young people have changed with regard to their abilities and behaviour?

- How do trainers see themselves professionally?

Perspectives of vocational trainers

Trainers' perspectives on content of the training vary widely. An emphasis on manual skills reflects the level of industrialization in the former East at the time of reunification – these were preoccupations of the 1950s and 1960s in West Germany and Britain. On the one hand a higher level training and more time for training in the corresponding skills is demanded. On the other hand there are statements which say that the curricula and the contents of the training have not changed much in comparison with former days, where there was a gap between the high level of the theoretical training and the low standard of work-based provision for the practical training. All trainers are satisfied with the improved teaching aids and the means for training. For the trainers the separation of institutional responsibility for theoretical and practical training seems to be a central problem. This often leads to coordination problems between the places of training and the vocational school:

When the apprentices start their training nowadays they are far less well prepared than formerly in the times of the GDR, because the polytechnic classes were abolished. The apprentices only have a short stay in a company when they are in class 9 and often these work experiences are badly chosen, so that they don't have much to do with the profession which they will choose one day. So we now have to start where formerly the polytechnic classes had started. Question: To what does that lead in the training? Answer: There is too much time lost in the beginning. (Trainer interview 6)

The different affiliations of vocational school (a matter for the Ministry of Education and the Arts) and the training within the company (assigned to different branches of industry) also causes problems. From the trainers' point of view the vocational schools often react with inflexibility to the necessities within the companies, so that some trainers see themselves as forced to teach certain theoretical skills in order to get certain jobs done.

In response to the question 'What could have been taken on from the old training system of the GDR?' the following statements typify the answers given:

What I don't like about the dual system is the separation of company and school. The training regulations and the curriculum of the schools don't add to each other any longer. I think we could take a leaf out of the book of the former GDR in this respect where curriculum and training regulations were coordinated. That means that what was trained in practice was at the same time looked into at school. Unfortunately, this is no longer the case to-day. (Trainer interview 18)

The dual system has strictly separated both and made both independent. In this way certain useful organizational things, which up to then were nicely settled, have been dissolved. (Trainer interview 5)

The dual system as it stands does not fit the situation in new Länder. Cities such as Leipzig do not have the stratum of flourishing middle-sized companies providing the optimum conditions for the dual system to operate effectively. In big companies it is better to have the integrated training school, but bigger enterprises in Leipzig are not, in practice, training large numbers, since labour market polarizations have reduced the demand for high-skill workers, and they train only to their needs. Small companies do not train, but take on casual labour from the large pool of 'job-seekers'. The Berufsschulen, finding themselves having to serve increasingly mixed populations of students, have increasing difficulty in linking theoretical training effectively with in-company training.

How trainers saw themselves professionally

The question of how instructors see themselves professionally and whether they felt differently after the political changes and unification was central to the survey. A few instructors stated that the way they saw themselves professionally had not changed. Most say it has changed, but maintain that the skill level of high-quality training has not changed. In high-quality training, the essential role of the trainer was, and still is, to set an example and at the same time to be the apprentices' partner.

But there are also various clues in the interview transcripts which do indicate significant changes. The trainers generally saw the ceasing of political training content as an increase in value of their work.

The release of the trainers from political training corresponds with a perceived *increase in the scope of action*, which was new for the trainers. (Here we talk about an increase in the scope of action for the head of the training department with regard to the management. We also talk about an increase in the scope of action concerning the training itself.) The trainers who, like the apprentices, worked to targets in 'socialist teams' in the GDR are now faced with new challenges. Apprentices were included in the production process to achieve the target output (quota number), especially in the consumer goods industry. (The consumer goods production originates in the planned economy of the SED. Bigger industrial companies, in particular, had to produce goods of all kinds even if these did not belong to the company's range of products.) For the apprentices this meant that they had to do a lot of repetitive work and thus did not learn as much as they could have done in training periods where creativity is asked for. This restricted the scope the trainer had in the work with apprentices. Lifting of these expectations and constraints meant that the trainers now experienced more scope for developing the learning programme and introducing new ideas and ways of doing things. Conversely, though, many trainers perceived losses in their status and power in management terms, seeing themselves as reduced to 'supplicant' status in the fight for declining training resources, and acting at all times under the 'Sword of Damocles'.

As the work of the trainer changes, with it emerges a new and changed professional self-image. The apprentice is no longer a passive recipient of professional contents imparted by an (often) authoritarian trainer. Rather, the apprentice is expected to get actively involved in the training. According to the trainers' statements this was already working, because of the changed basic conditions and environment. The trainers recognized the changed constellations in the training, in the planning and organization of the work, in the possibilities for individual debates with the apprentices and also in a stronger acceptance of their 'individual personalities'.

Some of the trainers do not deny that 'liberality' and 'strengthened rights of personality', especially regarding the ability to assert themselves in relation to the apprentices, were met with mixed feelings. They noticed that their power of assertion had grown less. They felt that there were limits when trying to push through decisions. One trainer said, 'those who use authoritarian means are faced with problems now.' Another trainer emphasized that apprentices nowadays could virtually 'play him up'. On the one hand they know there is no alternative to self-determination and personal freedom, which they do themselves welcome. On the other hand these new rights are in contradiction with the traditional and formerly successfully practised behaviour patterns. In order to cope with these conflicts the trainers have embarked on a long-term process of learning and experience, markedly different from their earlier socialization.

The emphasis on the self-learning process by the trainers is to be seen as another important factor in the description of professional self-image:

> As a trainer, as a Meister, I need to be on top of things – facing the apprentice who now comes. The training contents of the professions that we train here now are more varied and more modern compared to those professions we formerly trained – in the times of the GDR. So I had to go back to school myself. I was taught in computer training and in the CNC-training. That's the section I took over here. That also made it necessary to learn English at the Volkschochschule [adult education centre] for two years. (Trainer interview 11)

> First of all I need to further qualify myself and then run the training to a high standard. I need to start with myself and go to classes – that's what I'm still doing, learning the fundamental principles of legal protection and everything concerning jurisprudence, so that I first of all qualify myself to reach a new standard of the training. Of course we demand a lot more of these apprentices than we formerly did, but what I demand of myself has increased as well. (Trainer interview 3)

Motivation of the apprentices to achieve their qualified status is essential. The trainers find themselves faced with a dilemma here. They know that some of the young qualified workers will be faced with unemployment after their training; nevertheless, they need to get them to achieve a successful end to their training. In this respect trainers need support and instruction in how to cope with the difficulties of motivation:

> Well, nowadays you somehow have to motivate the young people – formerly it was easier to motivate them. I think that I'm responsible for the apprentices, that I have to prepare them for a working life. I found that easier formerly – there wasn't the problem of finding an adequate job afterwards. Today I need to make them see necessity ... no matter where they end up. And that is not easy nowadays. Everywhere training places are reduced. And sometimes you ask yourself – what for? But as a trainer I mustn't let the apprentices see that I ponder about it. (Trainer interview 15)

> To put in a certain optimism, never let them feel reluctance, but rather try to be optimistic ... There is more to a profession than the mere learning of skills. There has to be some praise as well, so that they recognize that there is more to it, that they have a profession that has perspective. To make the positive come across – that's something that I should know how to do. (Trainer interview 3)

Statements concerning doubts about their own position in the labour market also have to be taken into consideration in this context:

> It's nice to work together with people. That's really nice, that's what I like. The disadvantage maybe is that if one's own company closes down, well, that other companies then just think of me as a trainer, who can't do anything practical himself – but that's the only thing I can see. (Trainer interview 14)

Help with personal problems of the apprentices is another important factor which influences how these trainers see themselves professionally. All trainers with the exception of one reported positively that they are willing to help apprentices with personal problems. And this help is still given – but the atmosphere points at a decreasing readiness in this respect. This could be due to the fact that the apprentices increasingly name problems for which the trainer does not feel competent enough, or maybe the trainers shrink back from interfering because of increasing individualization processes. Also the legal conditions in training seem to cause trainers not to 'interfere' so much with the young people's problems.

The following thesis can be formulated: the social structure 'master–apprentice' which originates in traditional socialization processes changes, weakens. The Meister becomes 'trainer' and 'motivator' and – more often than in the GDR – has to undergo training for continuing qualifications. The trainer, who does not have any obligations other than the training, thereby takes on a changed position towards the apprentice, being paid for training the apprentice in an optimal way, not more and not less.

How typical are the experiences of these trainers?

The trainers' perceptions of young people, abilities and previous training can be tested against comparative data from East and West Germany Berufbildungstricht (1997) in the same (metal and electrical) industries. Qualification levels of entrants to the industry were comparable, with 82 per cent of apprentices from the East having Realschule leaving certificate or Abitur, compared with 72 per cent of apprentices from the West. Only one or two entered the industry without certificates. In 1996, 59 per cent of apprentices in the East reported participation in 'process skill' training such as problem solving compared with 44 per cent in the West; 70 per cent of East and 61 per cent of West considered that the quality of team work in training was 'rather good' or 'very good'. Differences in trainers' and apprentices' perceptions of optimum leadership styles were small between East and West.

In 1995, five years after reunification, the total numbers of people involved in training in the old and new Länder were as shown in Table 14.1. While 45 per cent of trainers in the new Länder are in the 'crafts', less than 40 per cent are in this sector in the old Länder.

Table 14.1 Numbers of trainers and Meisters (1995). (Total number of people involved in training in companies in FRG was 733,123)

	Old Länder	New Länder
Industry, trade, public service, agriculture, home economics, self-employed, maritime shipping	449,738	58,316
Crafts*	177,366	48,003
Total	627,104	106,319

* In crafts the Meister is responsible for training. The numbers given are those of the companies training young people. Therefore the numbers of persons involved and responsible for training could be higher.

Source: Berufsbildungstricht (1997)

According to a survey undertaken by BIBB in 1996, 'Die Wertschätzung der dualen Berufsausbildung und ihre Einflußfaktoren' companies in East and West Germany expressed the following priorities concerning training.

The vast majority of companies engaged in training stated that training for their own future staff recruitments is of great importance (33%) or importance (52%). The East–West comparison showed that training is of less importance for companies engaged in training in the East. The number of training companies stating that training is of great importance (23%) is 11 per cent below the number for the Western companies (34%). Those companies stating that their own training is of less importance or not important explain that plenty of well qualified persons are available in the labour market, or they qualify their own staff through in-company training.

The trainers whose experiences have been recorded here are the survivors of the reunification process. Other evidence (Diewald 1998) has shown that the survivors in the reunification process have been male, professionally well-qualified with ambitions and clear progressive career trajectories in clearly defined occupational sectors. The trainers interviewed will, to this extent, be typical of the survivors. In the other occupational fields covered by our study, there was less continuity between the old and the new, for trainers.

Smooth transitions: young people's experience of transition, VET and work entry

The views of trainers are grounded in their experiences of two systems and the personal comparisons of what the changes of 1989 meant for them, their lives and their ways of operating in the world. In Diewald's (1999) terms, they had to invent entirely new scripts and routines almost overnight. For younger adults, their early experiences in the socialist system appeared to have receded much more quickly as they struggled to make sense of the options available to them in the 'here and now' in very concrete ways.

For the majority of our young research participants in Leipzig the transition processes into the labour market took place under the exceptional circumstances of the political changes. The earlier Anglo-German studies showed how the socio-economic and cultural contexts affected the routes which are taken to 'adulthood' and the importance of the socialization processes underlying skill formation. Those of the sample who began their apprenticeships under the GDR system had to adapt to a new political, social, and economic situation while they were being trained or after they had finished their apprenticeship.

In the GDR choosing an occupation was a decision for a lifetime, in the majority of cases without great expectations for geographical or upward mobility. Once a decision for an occupation was taken, integration into the labour market was guaranteed. As in Britain and Western Germany, young people had aspirations and the decision making was subject to multiple influences:

> In the GDR the choice of career is free. Each skilled occupation is open to every young person as long as he (sic) achieves good results and is in good physical and psychological condition for the occupation chosen … Each year the number of training places equals the number of school leavers therefore each school leaver will find a training place. The number of training places in each occupation are a result of economic requirements (of the combines and nationalised concerns). (Akademie 1989, p.102)

Although young people applied for training places, de facto many of the vacancies were filled through a central agency in cooperation with the combines or other institutions. Keeping in mind that all school leavers had to be provided with a training place, the central agency had great influence.

Interviews were carried out with twenty-four young adults aged 20–25 years of age. Group A (12 interviews) had smooth transitions into the labour market; group B had broken transitions of some kind. The interviews demonstrate a range of individual behaviour and strategies within the bounds of the availability of training and social norms in the GDR. After reunification, transitions behaviour and career strategies had to be applied in the new labour market.

For example, young workers in smaller companies found it especially difficult to make career plans. The typical hierarchy in such a company is apprentice–skilled worker–Meister. Having reached the second level it depends very much on personal determinants how they envisage a further career under current labour market conditions.

Others consider becoming self-employed after they have gained the Meister status, but fear this will make them vulnerable to labour market changes. Nevertheless, for the time being they identify a number of problems going along this route:

> Well, I don't know how it will continue, but I hope I … I try to become self-employed. (Heating and ventilation technician)

Difficult question. Not a lot will change [over the next 5–10 years]. For example, I had the idea of going for a Meister, one can do that after three years work experience. Surely after three years one doesn't have the necessary wherewithal to finance the Meister. I think at the moment it was at the minimum 10,000 DM. And if one wants to become self-employed this isn't all one needs' (Electrician)

The young adults in group A who had experienced smooth transitions generally demonstrated, in their interviews, the dynamic interaction between labour market structures and individual action. It can be argued that all of them were actively engaged in the construction of their careers after they had finished their vocational training in ways which keep them on track for successful entry to primary segment occupational careers. In two cases active participation did not occur before the young persons had actually finished their training. Meanwhile individual activity was replaced by close networks consisting of family and friends. Others were active and experimental in seeking out training places as well as adjusting to the new labour market structures and conditions at a later stage, and there was evidence of ability to weigh advantages and disadvantages and to take decisions. The interplay of this ability and personal agency in an institutional structure offering further qualification helped to overcome professional disappointments and dissatisfaction and/or prepare for advancement.

Those whose labour market entry had been smooth and continuous considered formal vocational qualification as a necessary condition for labour market entry. Summarizing their experiences within the Eastern and Western versions of the dual system, most of the interviewees found the contents, structure and organization of training good. The duration of the transition from training to work was perceived differently and relied on the interplay of the person's expectation, training experiences and the acceptance of the newly skilled worker by his (sic) colleagues. In general the respondents found it easier to perform the new role in a different environment.

The necessity of competitive behaviour was recognized and performed in various ways in order to secure chances or to derive some advantage. To achieve this, access to further vocational training or continuous learning was of great importance for the young people. Depending on the entry level into the labour market and the size of the company, opportunities ranged from 'learning by doing' on the job to formal seminars. Those young people in small companies with fewer promotion prospects felt the need to 'continue learning' in order to stay in the labour market, whereas those in larger companies with a structured promotion ladder participated in education and training as part of their advancement strategies. The way respondents formulated their professional goals corresponded to the structural framework. Those working in stable employment patterns found it easy to describe their next career step and had a picture of long-term goals. In other cases the respondents formulated as their professional goal the avoidance of unemployment or, in the tradition of the dual system, to reach 'maturity' as a worker.

A smooth and continuous transition was possible for the respondents in group A despite the social, economical and political changes surrounding them. Although they shared some perceptions and experiences with those who had experienced broken transitions (group B) the careers of the latter were broken at this turning point for different reasons.

In our previous studies differences emerged between those who are actively engaged in the construction of their own occupational identities and pathways and those who remain much more passive. In Germany, as in England, a clear distinction emerged between those who are still looking for a career (through an apprenticeship) and those who will be happy just to find a job, even if it is unskilled work.

In the East, the differences are even more sharply drawn. The strong awareness of the value of qualifications and experience is shown by all respondents, as it was in comparable West German samples. This is highlighted even more strongly in the contracting labour market, with young people seeking new apprenticeships and retraining well into their 20s. Even those whose lack of qualifications means they will be excluded, and those who, despite qualifications, find it difficult to gain suitable positions, accept the need to become formally qualified to gain access to skilled, secure or well-paid employment.

We observed from our earlier West German interviews and from those in Leipzig 'group A' (smooth transition) that this was frequently coupled with another 'mature view', that one cannot be considered fully skilled until several years after completion of an apprenticeship. That is, an acceptance that sustained and successful experience of work is necessary for subsequent job moves.

There is another feature emerging from the interviews from group B (broken transitions) which is distinctive and significant in the Eastern German situation. While it is accepted that formal qualification is highly desirable and a *sine qua non* of higher level, skilled and secure work, there is also growing awareness that 'first steps' into the labour market may now more easily be found at the unqualified levels, given the shortages of training places. In the old Länder, this route is not officially recognized in that no formal agency would route young people in this direction. The state of the job market together with the fluidity created by the upheavals of the Eastern German situation have a profound effect on job-searching strategies employed by young people. More are using employment agencies and are inserting themselves into jobs through family and social networks. These young people are more likely to emphasize the importance of gaining some experience, as a basis on which they can subsequently build. Here, the similarities with our previous English samples emerge. While there was also universal agreement among our young English respondents that qualifications mattered in the job market, the importance of getting a job at the earliest possible opportunity (for the given career track), getting experience and learning what you needed to know thereafter was emphasized more strongly, and demonstrated in practice.

That local labour market characteristics should have a profound effect on the type of job-searching strategies employed is to be expected. There was another factor, however, which was significant in most contexts. Those who showed active transition behaviours were far more likely to find work than those who were passive. Not only do the 'active' have advantages in that their job-searching is likely to begin earlier, be more comprehensive, imaginative and purposive, but also their earlier foundation of career goals was likely to mean that their employment, work placements or other experience were likely to have greater coherence; as a result they found it easier to convince employers of their commitment to their chosen path.

A difference to emerge between our Eastern German cases and those from the West is the complex combination of transition behaviours employed by East German youth to meet the uncertain, unfamiliar circumstances with which they were faced. 'Taking a chance' was often part of a protracted transition process involving 'step-by-step' transition behaviour or 'wait and see' behaviour as new and unfamiliar situations were encountered. This reinforced our earlier assertion that these transition behaviours should not be equated with personal flexibility or rigidity but arise out of experiences in education, social life and the labour market. In the setting of the political and economic upheavals in the new Länder, the hypothesis that the chances and the risks perceived by young people will be greater, and personal agency can therefore be expected to play a very significant part in shaping life chances, tends to be borne out by these cases. 'Taking a chance' at some stage of the process was a feature of many of them. The underlying structural foundations for those life chances are in evidence, however, with advantages of parental background and circumstances and gender-based inequalities suggested by the interview analyses. Some of the sources of advantage and disadvantage are intact and unchanged (e.g. acquired characteristics such as Abitur qualifications have carried their currency through to the new situation). Other sources, such as gender, have changed. Diewald (1999) showed that mature women were losers in the changes, with loss of provision for childcare and employment options. The West German labour market is highly gendered, as our previous studies have shown. It is a feature of our small sample that those who had regained a place in the restructured Leipzig labour market at their originally intended skill level were all male, while those who dropped into 'unqualified' but stable employment below their original skill level were all female. Parental and social networks which may have worked to advantage previously (particularly around Party membership) are also displaced by parental and social networks built around other forms of cultural and material resource.

In both countries, for those who successfully enter the primary segment, progression to skilled and experienced worker status has to be supported by company training and updating. What of those who have entered, then become unemployed through closures and company restructurings? Programmes for those affected by unemployment have to enable them to 'keep pace' to get back into the labour market. In Britain, 'Individual Learning Accounts', invested in by both individuals and employers while in work, is the policy under development by the 'New Labour' government, in line with a manifesto commitment. While the intention to encourage and support adult learning taken on the individual's initiative must be welcomed, this policy has similarities to the previous Youth Credits and Nursery Vouchers schemes in that funding is attached to individuals rather than providers. This has the effect of making 'learning entitlements' the subject of transactions in markets in which the more powerful always dominate. The lessons of these market-led initiatives need to be taken into account. If the aim is to promote social inclusion through entitlements and incentives for those at the margins of the workforce and society, policies are required which reassert education as a collective good and provide for 'lifelong learning' as though it were a public responsibility as well as a private good.

Continuing education and training policy in Germany, particularly in the new Länder, has to take account of the decline of importance of the dual system, and will also have to assume a multiplicity of starting points, as in Britain, and find appropriate ways of establishing 'entitlement'. Glowka, writing in 1989, observed that the strong German beliefs in the regulation of educational systems for 'effectiveness and social balance' will ensure that any moves towards marketization of the education system will encounter considerable resistance. Similarly, Green (1997) argues that the trends we have seen in Britain, and which are beginning in the East of Germany, are likely to come up against 'bedrock opposition' in the FRG strongholds of state regulation. The traditional regulatory frameworks may be too much under pressure to continue in their present form; the construction of new forms of social partnership and new approaches to regulation are the most likely responses to globalizing influences.

Risk, social polarization and personal agency

... the German reunification process is far more problematic than is widely believed. The tensions between East and West are evident everywhere and while Berlin itself resembles the rebuilding and development of Docklands, there are vast tracts of former East Germany that are untouched – littered with decaying industries and very high levels of unemployment. The problems of the German economy are far more severe and structural than the financial pages of the UK press have led us to believe. When German politicians talk of the need for the EU to look to the east, a train journey from Potsdam to Dresden illustrates all. (Walters 1997)

Inequalities are not new in the former East. Social inequalities are now realigning with Western patterns while becoming greatly heightened under conditions of high unemployment, still running at twice the levels suffered by the Western Länder, although the rate of redundancies has reduced and some new jobs are now appearing.

Previously, trajectories were predictable in both East and West Germany, in different ways. In the East, the fixed tracking into the labour market was part of the system. It was argued earlier that how people fared was partly determined by achievement (academic and political) from an early age, as defined by the system and partly by social connection and Party membership. In the West, the structures are less transparent, but similarly powerful. The strongly institution-alized West German system sets young people at an early age on their trajectory into the primary or secondary labour markets, through tripartite schooling. In spite of many advantages identified with the German system, such as the development of strong work values, the drawbacks of the system cannot be overlooked. The apprenticeship system reinforces structural inequalities, a process started in the stratified schooling system. Gender-based inequalities are particularly marked, with males outnumbering females by significant margins in the more advantaged academic and vocational routes into the labour market (Bynner and Evans 1994). Apprenticeships for young women tend to be of poorer quality and prospects than those for boys, and many young women are channelled into vocational schools full-time with a domestic orientation. More and more young people now try first to complete the highest school track (*Abitur*) and then start an apprenticeship. This has resulted in major problems in recruitment to the traditional lower tracks of the German school system (*Hauptschule*), because of the reduced opportunities these now provide for an apprenticeship.

There is, therefore, some displacement of trajectories, one by another, in terms of outcomes in the labour market, but social stratifications remain intact. For those at the bottom of the heap, the labour market has been hostile to those without qualifications and there are few openings for flexible forms of work-based learning available in Britain. Special schemes may all too often serve to stigmatize and disadvantage further. The difference for young people is that opportunities to change their position now appear to be there, and failure to achieve change in their position is perceived and experienced as personal failure.

Young people in Germany are increasingly caught in a double bind: a hostile labour market which effectively excludes unqualified young people but which can no longer sustain the training routes and social support previously provided for the large majority. The striving for work identities, so strongly fostered by German culture and tradition, does not diminish, and there is evidence of growing frustration of marginalized and excluded youth. There is, at the same time, a growth in casualized work opportunities available for unqualified adults, producing a situation which begins to mirror the British. Ways into the labour market are becoming diversified, and more dependent on displaying the characteristics employers want, as well as qualifications. These trends are most marked in the former East, but signal wider trends throughout the FRG.

The evidence from our previous Anglo-German studies, extended by the present study, shows that active transition behaviours are important in overcoming setbacks for those already in precarious situations. The active transition behaviours most likely to overcome setbacks are those associated with taking chances in fluid market conditions and taking advantage of new openings in secondary labour markets. Structural factors, however, remain paramount, and we find with Diewald (1999), who reports findings of a study of three cohorts of mature adults from the former East Germany, that the transformations are not such that release of new forms of individual competence leads to major reallocations of social position. When they are unsuccessful, the outcomes of 'taking chances' are likely to be downward movements from already precarious situations. Young people take calculated risks (rational action). Policies which promote action competencies and proactive behaviours have to recognize the 'risk' side of the equation, and ensure adequate support if young people are not to be further disadvantaged by accepting the message that their own shortcomings are to blame for predicaments which are beyond their individual control.

The study has supported findings of studies conducted since 1989 which find that there are no dramatic differences between the two young generations in Eastern and Western Germany concerning life conceptions (e.g. Fischer and Zinnecker 1992). Values concerning autonomy, variety of life experiences and the importance of work and qualifications are shared. However, institutional and material resources to cope with everyday life and to prepare for the world of work are far less available for the young in Eastern Germany. The transition to work and family life used to be much more continuous than in the West. They took the normative steps faster than their contemporaries in the old federal states: VET, employment, marriage and parenthood were coordinated in such a way that adulthood was reached in the work-conscious German Democratic Republic several years earlier. Today the young generation, after socialism, has to shift to another transition rhythm. This requires many individual decisions in a much less transparent social environment. Moreover, the extension of the transition to adulthood has to be subsidized by the institutional help of the welfare state for quite a number of young people who are not yet in the employment system.

The features of a society undergoing structural transformations do not necessarily affect timing, duration and results of individual transitions negatively. They may also enhance the young person's capacities for exploration and self-direction. But the experiences with VET and the labour market, with parents' unemployment, and with welfare agencies will require the development of strategies which support transition by extending the period of education or generating and sustaining new training or work-creating programmes by the state. The latter, in turn, may lead to transitions with uncertain destinations and set people on life-course trajectories in which they are constantly threatened by unemployment and under-employment. Young people in the former GDR were not socialized to cope with individualized competition in school and market-based employment. They have to find out how to navigate the second and third decades of life under new social forces and their own direction. This creates the danger that some of them, those who have developed high hopes for a quick improvement of living standards, turn their frustrated expectations into aggression against others or into resignation and distance from the political system. There is some evidence of the latter in our findings, and of the former in studies of social trends in the East (e.g. Hormuth 1998) Citizenship education has been identified in Britain in 1998 as an area requiring new and stronger policy interventions in order to address issues of social cohesion.

Hormuth (1998) reports that, by 1995, survey findings were showing that 50 per cent of East Germans felt themselves to be excluded, demonstrated pessimism and felt that all the previously state controlled areas of life were worse than before. Yet, in the run-up to the German elections of 1998, the necessity of education for citizenship as part of the training for young people was being questioned. The situation in the East suggests that removal of this characteristic feature of the German system, at the moment when social cohesion is most threatened, would be difficult to justify.

Lessons for Germany, England and Europe

With constraints on public funding and diversified demands on the system, neither the stratified 'trajectories' of Germany nor flexible but confused (and often foreshortened) British 'pathways' are working well as routes into changing labour markets.

In Britain, student experiences reflect the considerable change and unrest in the FE sector. A related study (Rudd and Evans 1997) shows that group sizes increased as colleges strived to recruit the necessary target numbers of students and new funding arrangements meant that many colleges faced financial difficulties. Funding issues in FE were not a direct concern for the young people taking part in this research. They were largely positive about their teaching and learning experiences, though it has to be said that some did raise the topic and several showed at least an indirect awareness of how influences of 'the market' and 'competition' were having an effect on their college experiences. Additionally, the fact that a large proportion of the questionnaire sample had part-time jobs (over 60%) indicated that many felt that they needed to put in extra hours of paid work in order to fund their studies and their leisure activities. This seems to have become the norm for 16–19-year-old college students. The need to establish breadth and depth has been embraced in policy for post-compulsory education and the previous down-playing of knowledge in British vocational qualifications has now been recognized as a policy error. Allowing a work-based route to qualification recognizes its importance for a significant number of young adults, but better incentives and support are needed for provision of educational breadth in work-based programmes, as well as giving priority to training trainers and key workers. Finally, targeted financial support must be provided to enable people to participate and withstand the difficulties of combining study with working life and life transitions. The 'New Labour' moves to establish Lifelong Learning Partnerships at local level signals a move towards new approaches, designed to tackle underachievement and promote high quality post-learning opportunities through collaboration. These local partnerships are voluntary arrangements, with a minimum core membership from further education, local authorities and schools, careers services and Training and Enterprise Councils. The last of these, as the lynch-pin of employer-led quasi-markets in training provision, are unlikely to survive in the moves to establish an overarching funding and regulatory body for the full range of post-compulsory education provision, including work-based learning. Employer and Trades Union representation may be included in the partnerships, which will initially produce local learning plans tied to targets for qualification and widening participation. This ambiguously framed and weakly regulated approach to partnership is likely to be progressively strengthened in line with restructuring of the post-16 funding framework and with devolution of new powers to regional levels of government. However, as Green (1997) points out, high-achieving educational systems are generally those which place much more emphasis on strong forms of regulation and consistency of practice.

For Germany, the Berufsschule is proving increasingly inefficient and difficult to sustain in the polarized labour market situation, when operating in 'traditional' mode. It is hardly surprising that trainers have been very quick to point out the advantages which would have accrued from retention of some of the features of the 'old' unified polytechnic education of GDR, instead of wholesale introduction of the FRG model. The challenge for Germany is now to improve and re-orientate the Berufsschule, with more flexible partnerships between educational institutions and industry which enable the former to support those elements of VET which the latter are finding increasingly difficult to sustain within available resources. Probably for the first time, there are some signs that Germany is looking towards the flexibility of British further education as a model to be considered (Stach 1997).

The answer, in dual system critics' terms, which our research supports, is to break down the distinction between general and vocational education. This can be done by, for example, opening up access to higher education via the vocational education route and encouraging a much greater mixture of academic and vocational experience for all young people – a new version of polytechnical education, perhaps? The more conservative response in keeping with the 'trajectory' approach has been to call for two types of apprenticeships: the high-status academic entry type lasting three years, and the vocational type, lasting two years and not offering qualified entry.

Germany now shares with Britain the end aim of a flexible, future-oriented and inclusive provision, though the starting points and the structural and contextual factors are quite different (Koch and Reuling 1994). Germany already meets the criteria for work-based learning, but needs to make its predominantly firm-based route to skilled status more open. The challenge is to sustain strong work commitment but to be more able to deal with instabilities in labour markets and the demise of the expectation of stable and continuous upward careers which underlie having a 'Beruf' (long-term profession). The options of stratifying the system still further with 'two-tier' apprenticeships feeding into different levels of the labour market is in tune with the 'trajectory' approach but may present many of the same drawbacks of the present system over time as well as contributing to polarization. Moves towards a European model of VET suggest that both need, in differing ways, to achieve greater permeability of the systems and structures by which people can draw on (and gain recognition for) combinations of education-based and work-based learning. Germany has the advantage of having considerable continuities in VET and the 'anchors' in place enable continuous evolution of the dual system, with mechanisms for a new consensus to be constructed (Brown 1996). It has much to do, however, in providing support measures and guidance for young adults in the new Länder which enable and support them in negotiating more permeable and flexible structures. The withdrawal of its traditional commitment to citizenship education would be neither timely nor appropriate, given our findings and those of related research (Evans 1998). These are vulnerable groups with a high risk of social exclusion. These young people have been quick to respond to market 'signals' and have traditional German working values, ethics and identities. Evidence from the present study suggests that young adults in the new Länder are finding their way, but are also displaying considerable uncertainties about their futures, particularly where they have experience of broken transitions.

Many young people who have responded quickly to systemic and market changes have taken chances, in individualized ways. They need to have non-stigmatizing forms of material support readily available, to ensure that they are not stretched beyond their capacities to deal with difficult life situations unaided. In short, our findings show that an unreformed dual system cannot be made to work in labour market conditions such as those emerging in Eastern Germany. Stop-gap measures may fuel the polarization into primary and secondary segments, and heighten social inequalities.

References

Akademie (1989) Gemeinschaftsarbeit der Akademie der Pedagogischen Wissenschaften, des Zentralinstituts für Berufsbildung, des Instituts für Fachschulwesen, des Zentralinstituts für Hochschulbildung und der Humboldt-Universität das Bildungswesen der Deutshcen Demokratischen Republik. Berlin: Volk und Wissen.

Berufbildungstricht (1997) Bundesministerium für Berufsbildung (1997) *Analysis of Leadership Style and Training Methods in the new Länder*. Berlin: BIBB.

Bynner, J. and Evans, K. (1994) 'Building on cultural traditions.' In K. Evans and W. Heinz *Becoming Adults in England and Germany.* London: AGF.

Diewald, M. (1999) 'Processes of social exclusion and inclusion on the labour market in the transformation of East Germany: Continuities and discontinuities in the life course and development control.' In J. Bynner and R. Silbereisen *Adversity and Challenge in Life in the New Germany and England.* London: Macmillan.

Doeringer, P.B. and Piore, M.J. (1971) *Internal Labour Markets and Manpower Analysis.* Lexington, KY: M.A. Heath and Co.

Evans, K. (1998) *Shaping Futures. Learning for Competence and Citizenship.*

Evans, K. and Heinz, W.R. (1994) *Becoming Adults in England and Germany.* London and Bonn: Anglo-German Foundation.

Evans, K. and Heinz, W.R. (1995) 'Flexibility, learning and risk: Work, training and early careers in England and Germany.' *Education and Training 37*, 5, 3–11.

Fisher, A. and Zinnecker, J. (1992) *Jugend '92.* Opladen: Leske und Budrich.

Glowka (1989) 'Anglo-German perception of education.' *Comparative Education 25*, 3.

Green, A. (1997) *Education, Globalization and the Nation State.* Macmillan.

Hormuth, S. (1998) 'Individual coping with the transformation process in East Germany.' In J. Bynner and R. Silbereisen *Adversity and Challenge in Life in the New Germany and England.* London: Macmillan.

Evans, Behrens and Kaluza (2000) *Learning and Work in the Risk Society.* London; Macmillan.

Roberts, K. (1999) 'Europe's choice: Regulation or deregulation. Old alternatives and new test cases.' In J. Bynner and R. Silbereisen *Adversity and Challenge in Life in the New Germany and England.* Basingstoke: Macmillan.

Walters, N. (1997) *Beyond the Horizon: Spotlight on East Germany.* Report of EU Transitional Horizon Project on European Refugees and Migrants. Guildford: University of Surrey.

Bynner, J. and Evans, K. (1994) 'Building on cultural traditions.' In K. Evans and W. Heinz *Becoming Adults in England and Germany.* London: AGF.

Rudd, P. and Evans, K. (1998) 'Structure and agency in youth transitions: Students' perspectives on vocational further education.' *Journal of Youth Studies 1*, 39–62.

Stach, M. (1997) *The Crisis of the Dual System.* Paper presented at the International Conference sponsored by the *Journal fo Vocational Education and Training*, July.

Walters, N. (1997) *Beyond the Horizon: Spotlight on East Germany.* Report of EU Transitional Horizon Project on European Refugees and Migrants. Guildford: University of Surrey.

The Contributors

Patrick Ainley is Reader in Learning Policy at the School of Post-Compulsory Education and Training in the University of Greenwich. He has published widely in the generalist and specialist press on the basis of extensive experience of teaching and research at all levels in schools, further and higher education. Recent publications include *Learning Policy: Towards the Certified Society* and *Apprenticeship: Towards a New Paradigm for Learning*, both published in 1999, and *The Business of Learning: Staff and Student Experiences of Further Education in the 1990s*, published in 1997 with Bill Bailey.

Bill Bailey is Senior Academic in the School of Post Compulsory Education and Training at the University of Greenwich. In recent years he has researched and published on policy and curriculum developments in further and secondary education.

Martina Behrens studied continuing and higher education at the Universities of Hanover and London. She has worked as research fellow in several comparative international studies focusing on skill formation, social attitudes and transition behaviours at the University of Bielefeld and the University of Surrey.

Don Bradley is the Head of Faculty of Lifelong Learning at the Royal Forest of Dean College, Gloucestershire. He has worked extensively in the college and LEA sectors. He has undertaken and published research in relation to management in Further Education. His doctorate was concerned with the policy changes in relation to FE and in particular the disjunctions between the intentions of policy producers at a national level and policy implementers at a local level. He has a commitment to extending learning to those who for many reasons have not pursued learning beyond school.

Clyde Chitty is Goldsmiths Professor of Policy and Management in Education and Head of the Department of Educational Studies at Goldsmiths College, University of London. He has taught at the University of Birmingham and at the Institute of Education in London. Between 1977 and 1985, he was vice-principal and their acting principal of a community college in Leicestershire. He is the author, co-author or editor of over 20 books and reports on education, notably (with Caroline Benn) *Thirty Years On: Is Comprehensive Education Alive and Well or Struggling to Survive?* (1996), a major study of the British comprehensive school. He is co-editor of the journal Forum: for promoting 3–19 comprehensive education.

Martin Dyke is a Senior Lecturer in Education at Farnborough College of Technology. Research interests include the relationship between education, economy and late modernity and improving student learning through reflective practice.

Geoffrey Elliott has carried out teaching and research in all sectors of post-compulsory education. He is currently Director of External Affairs, University College Worcester and Chair of the Further Education Research Association.

Karen Evans is Professor of Educational Studies at the University of Surrey. She has directed numerous studies on aspects of learning and the world of work in Great Britain, the European Community and Canada. Interests in international and comparative studies are reflected in her recent books, which include *Shaping Futures: Learning for Competence and Citizenship* and *Learning and Work in the Risk Society*. She is currently research director of a major comparative study of the experiences of 18–25-year-olds in England and the new Germany, funded through the Economic and Social Research Council's Youth, Citizenship and Social Change Programme and a grant holder in the ESRC Teaching and Learning Programme. Correspondence: School of Educational Studies, University of Surrey, Guildford, Surrey GU2 5XH, UK. email: K.Evans@surrey.ac.uk

Denis Gleeson is Professor of Education in the Institute of Education at the University of Warwick and was previously Professor and Head of Department at the University of Keele.

David Gray is Director of Work-based Learning in the School of Educational Studies at the University of Surrey. He taught at the FE chalkface for thirteen years before spending three years involved in securities industry training at the Stock Exchange, London. During his eight years at Surrey he has managed and taught on the Postgraduate Certificate in the Education of Adults programme, a course designed specifically for those entering the post-16 sector as teachers. His current post involves the design and delivery of a variety of work-related programmes at degree and postgraduate level. His research interests include the uses of communications and information technology in learning, work-related learning and developments in post-16 education.

Colin Griffin is an Associate Lecturer in the School of Educational Studies at the University of Surrey and a member of the Centre for Research in Lifelong Learning. He formerly worked at the London School of Economics, Kingston University, the Open University and in adult and teacher education. He is the author of several books and papers on adults and lifelong education, particularly in relation to curriculum and policy analysis.

Phil Hodkinson is Professor of Lifelong Learning in the Department of Continuing Education at the University of Leeds and was previously Professor of Post-Compulsory Education at the Manchester Metropolitan University.

Barry Hutchinson is a senior lecturer in curriculum and management studies in the School of Education at the University of Ulster. Previously a secondary school teacher and head of department, his main interest lies in the area of professional development through educational action research. He has explored the possibilities of this personally empowering approach in a number of areas including education management, nurse tutoring and the teaching of many school subjects, besides vocational education. His research and publications have explored the limiting conditions of many of the recent education reforms in terms of their effects on teaching and education management practices. He has outlined some of the changes needed to be made to these reforms.

Peter Jarvis is Professor of Continuing Education, University of Surrey. He is the author/editor of over 20 books on adult, continuing and lifelong education and of many papers and book chapters. He is editor of the *International Journal of Lifelong Education*. He is a frequent consultant and lecturer on these issues in many parts of the world.

Jens Kaluza studied philosophy at the University of Leipzig where he gained additional postgraduate qualification in social psychology. He has worked as research fellow in several studies focusing on analysis of trainers in the new Länder, and on comparative studies of youth transitions and labour market entry for ZARDOF (independent Research Institute in Leipzig) and the University of Surrey.

Norman Lucas is a member of the Lifelong Learning Group at the Institute of Education, University of London. He was an elected member of the ILEA and a former FE teacher. Until recently he chaired the University Council for the Education of Teacher's Post-16 Committee (UCET). His research interests include initial teacher education and professional development, institutional management, FE incorporation and funding. He is co-editor of *Further Education and Lifelong Learning: Realigning the Sector for the 21st Century, Funding Issues and Social Exclusion: Reflection on the Marketisation of the Further Education Sector*, both published in 1999.

John Robinson is head of research at the Manchester Metropolitan Institute of Education (Crewe). He has taught in secondary schools in England and Scotland and was head of Social Sciences in a sixth form college in the North West of England for thirteen years. His main research interests lie in the area of Sustainability Education and the applicability of Postmodern thinking to the Environmental Crisis.

Gareth Williams is Professor of Education Administration and head of the Centre for Higher Education Studies at the Institute of Education, University of London. An economist of education, he has worked in recent years mainly on higher education policy and finance.

Subject index

Name index